The Lord Chamberlain Regrets…

The Lord Chamberlain Regrets ...

A History of British Theatre Censorship

Dominic Shellard and Steve Nicholson

with Miriam Handley

THE BRITISH LIBRARY

First published 2004 by
The British Library
96 Euston Road
London NW1 2DB

ISBN 0 7123 4865 4

British Library Cataloguing-in-Publication Data
A catalogue record for this book is available from The British Library

Designed by Bob Elliott
Typeset by Hope Services (Abingdon) Ltd
Printed in England by Cromwell Press, Wiltshire

Errata Slip: *The Lord Chamberlain Regrets*, 2004

The publisher would like to apologise for the following errors:

Page and line number	*for*	*read*
p. 120, line 14	(see Plate 2)	(see Plate 12)
p. 150, line 22	(see Plate 18)	(see Plate 14)
p. 154, line 11	(see Plate 20)	(see Plate 16)
p. 155, line 8	(see Plate 21)	(see Plate 17)
p. 159, line 13	(see Plate 22)	(see Plate 18)
p. 160, line 16	(see Plate 23)	(see Plate 19)
p. 168, line 37	(see Plate 24)	(see Plate 20)

071006-3162 TDI

Contents

Acknowledgements

THE editors would like to record our thanks to the following:

The Arts and Humanities Research Board for awarding a Research Grant to Dominic Shellard and periods of Research Leave to Miriam Handley and Steve Nicholson; the British Academy for awarding a Small Research Grant to Miriam Handley to complete her chapter; the Universities of Sheffield and Huddersfield for granting invaluable periods of study leave; the staff at the Windsor Archive and the Royal Archives; Her Majesty the Queen; and Kathryn Johnson, Curator of Drama at the British Library, for her support and advice for this project.

List of Illustrations

LIST OF ILLUSTRATIONS

(Between pages 118 and 119)

Preface

T HE evolution of British theatre from the early nineteenth century until 1968 was
shaped in no small degree by the Office of the Lord Chamberlain. By exercising,
at times quite arbitrarily, the power to censor theatre, his office influenced the type of
drama that the British public was permitted to see and that writers were able to write.
The story of censorship has been told with varying degrees of success by a journalist
(Richard Findlater's *Banned!*), a theatre critic (Nicholas de Jongh's *Politics, Prudery and
Perversions*) and a member of the Lord Chamberlain's staff (John Johnston's *The Lord
Chamberlain's Blue Pencil*), and the purpose of this book is neither to attempt a
recapitulation of these books nor to correct their more questionable conclusions.
That has been achieved by Steve Nicholson in *The Censorship of British Drama:
1900–1968*, who alone has consulted the entire collection of Lord Chamberlain's
papers and correspondence at the British Library. This book aims to offer a detailed
focus on how censorship treated some of the key plays produced in Britain between
1824 and 1968, ranging from *Charles the First* to *Mrs Warren's Profession*, *Six Characters
in Search of an Author* to *Our Betters*, *Waiting for Godot* to *Look Back in Anger* and *The
Birthday Party* to *Saved*.

Among the most common questions asked by students of twentieth-century
theatre are 'How did *A Taste of Honey* escape being censored?' and 'Were people really
shocked by *Miss Julie*?' and 'What was so terrible about *Saved* that resulted in it being
banned?' (it wasn't). The answers are to be found in this book, in which the brush
with the censor of playwright, producer and, occasionally, audience member are all
set out for examination. To have access to the detail of some of the discussions, the
arguments and the negotiations which occurred in relation to these texts offers the
possibility of insights not only into the history of theatre censorship, or even of
theatre itself, but also into the social and political fabrics of the times which produced
them, and the attitudes and ideological assumptions not just of individual Lords
Chamberlain or their Readers of Plays, but of the class which believed it was born to
rule and to control. And one of the insights most obviously revealed on every page of
this book is the absolute certainty that if you wanted to keep control of society, then
you needed to control the medium of theatre. It is not, perhaps, for nothing that the
Lord Chamberlain's Office habitually began the nouns 'Play' and 'Licence' with
capital letters. This is not to say, however, that the book resorts to tiresome Lord
Chamberlain bashing. Faced with the task today of providing a 300-word synopsis of
some of the key plays between 1911 (when Readers' Reports were first introduced)

and 1968 (when the third Theatres Act removed the Lord Chamberlain's power to censor), few of us would be able to match the focus and clarity of many of the summaries produced by Readers such as Charles Heriot, St. Vincent Troubridge and Henry Game.

This book is unique in that it is the first publication to transcribe in full significant Readers' Reports and correspondence (with addresses, handwritten comments and uncorrected mistakes); to include photographic plates of actual Readers' Reports (eg. *Miss Julie, Our Betters, Waiting for Godot, The Birthday Party, Cat on a Hot Tin Roof, Look Back in Anger* and *Saved*); and to reproduce selected unpublished documents from the Lord Chamberlain's papers, such as the petition submitted to the Lord Chamberlain in September 1917 supporting the licensing of *Mrs Warren's Profession*, the 'Secret Memorandum' clarifying the regulations on homosexuality in 1958 and the 'Spy's' report on a performance of *Saved* that was used to launch a prosecution against the Royal Court. It is our intention that the material is presented for present-day readers to examine against the context of contemporaneous theatrical activity so that individual, original connections can be made and conclusions drawn.

Thus, Miriam Handley explains how censorship operated between 1824 and 1901 in an era before Readers' Reports were produced. Steve Nicholson concentrates on the period between 1902 and 1944, when the individual précis of a play (begun in 1911) was generally the starting point of the possible process of censorship, and Dominic Shellard examines the disintegration of the Lord Chamberlain's power from 1945 to 1968.

There are, then, three ways in which we suggest that this book can be read: (1) it can be dipped into for information on key plays; (2) a particular period of theatre history can be examined for its relationship with the censor; or (3) the whole book can be considered to gain an overview of how the major works were treated from age to age. As Steve Nicholson points out in his chapter, though, the key casualties of censorship were not necessarily limited to the *Peer Gynts, Waiting for Godots* or *A Patriot for Mes*, but also the plays that were conceived but never written by playwrights constrained by the all too real restrictions of theatre censorship. In partial recognition of this, some attention is given to little remembered works, such as *Alone* and *Surface*, which were banned and never saw the light of day. Many of these still languish in the archives of the British Library, yearning for an enterprising company to dust them down and stand them up. Perhaps this book might encourage somebody to undertake this task in the not too distant future . . .[1]

DOMINIC SHELLARD

Maltby,
February 2004

---

[1] Stimulated by the research that was undertaken for this book, Dominic Shellard directed a production of *Sex for Sale* by Ernie Kaplan (banned in 1950) at the University of Sheffield in May 2004. A one-day festival, sponsored by the AHRB British Library/University of Sheffield Theatre Archives Project, investigated the themes of production, reception and censorship that were generated by this performance. Further details about this project can be found at both www.theatrearchive.org and http://www.shef.ac.uk/english/literature/staff/ds.html.

PART I

Eternal Interference: 1824–1901

CHAPTER I

The Foundations of Censorship

SHORTLY after Henry Brooke's *Gustavus Vasa* earned the dubious honour of being the first British play to be banned after the formalization of theatrical censorship in 1737, Samuel Johnson produced a highly satirical 'vindication' of censors. Having expressed concern that the task of censorship might place too onerous a burden on government officials already hard pressed with the work of bribery and corruption, Johnson proposed that the government should abandon half measures and institute a method to prevent the British people from voicing any opinion whatsoever. Perhaps, suggested Johnson helpfully, the government should consider simply closing schools and banning the teaching of reading and writing.[1]

Anxieties that theatrical censorship was an attack on fundamental liberties, that it degraded the theatre and represented audiences as too witless to protect themselves, lie at the heart of most critical works on the subject. Critics writing at key moments in the history of theatrical censorship, such as 1909 when a cadre of playwrights agitated for its abolition and 1967 when this abolition was achieved, are particularly virulent in their expressions of outrage.[2] More recently, however, critics have tempered indignation with a more reasonable approach. As John Russell Stephens has admitted, censor baiting may be an easy sport but there should be more to the study of censorship than simply the administration of jibes.[3] This book's reproduction of the reports written by examiners in response to the plays they read is intended neither as an attack on nor a defence of censorship. Its interest centres instead in recreating and critiquing the acts of interpretation that took place when a play was sent to the Lord Chamberlain's office for licensing. Opportunities for dwelling on the absurdity of certain decisions may be frequent but this introduction to pre-twentieth-century censorship intends only to set out responses to examiners and reactions to the mechanisms under which they worked. Only by looking at the development of censorship over time can the sharpest criticisms and the most generous praise be contextualised.

This introduction charts the development of theatre censorship to 1900 focusing primarily on the period between 1824, when the British Library's collection of licensed plays begins, to the death of Queen Victoria in 1901. It looks at the ways in which particular censors were characterized, sets out how censorship worked, and considers the pre-1900 debates over whether it should be abolished. It also resists the temptation to see the period before the *fin de siècle* attacks on censorship by William Archer and George Bernard Shaw as a dark age of drama, when playwrights were too talentless, drama too puerile and audiences too prim to engage in arguments with the censor.[4] Such a reading of pre-twentieth-century censorship is provided by Richard Findlater, who asserted that after the initial furore over the 1737 Licensing Act had died down, 'the censorship took care not to blow too hard. For the next century and a half it provoked no major riots or scandals. No outstanding dramatists were openly martyred, and no great plays were overtly suppressed. Few were written, although for that sterility the Lord Chamberlain cannot take all the blame.'[5]

This book challenges Findlater's representation of a century-long ellipsis in the narrative of censorship and counters his claim that censorship is only of significance if it affects 'great plays'. It does not deal solely with great plays or with notorious acts of suppression. Nor does its interest in examining the written record of censorship blind it to the fact that much of an examiner's work went unrecorded. It is aware that, behind the readers' reports, diary entries and private correspondence of examiners, lie untranscribed conversations in which a play's fate was negotiated. Like Shaw who, in 1895, reviewed not the play he had seen but the 'better play' that had been 'strangled at its birth' by the existence of the censor, this book makes its arguments based on the understanding that extant sources present only a partial history of nineteenth- and twentieth-century censorship.[6]

Findlater's perception that there was an absence of 'major riots and scandals' overlooks the real impact of the Lord Chamberlain on the theatre. In the nineteenth century, the examiner relied on censorship, pre-censorship (where managers checked scripts before sending them for licensing), and even pre-pre-censorship, where playwrights checked the suitability of their play's subjects before embarking on writing. In 1866 Spencer Ponsonby-Fane, the long-serving comptroller of the Lord Chamberlain's Office, explicitly commended examiners for operating this 'indirect system of censorship' because it enabled the Office to keep the number of prohibited plays to a minimum and forestall concerns about repression.[7] The examiners were equally forthcoming at parliamentary inquiries and admitted that they would relax the rule that excluded playwrights from their discussions if it meant avoiding the prohibition of a manuscript.[8] William Bodham Donne, who served officially and unofficially as examiner between 1849 and 1874, explained the usefulness of this approach:

> I have been asked the question beforehand, 'Will you admit so and so,' and I have said, 'Certainly not;' and if I have come to any knowledge beforehand of a piece not likely to be passed, I have, when possible, said to the author, 'Do not send it to me since you must in that case pay me for the trouble of reading it.'[9]

Although some playwrights obligingly cut their plays according to the examiner's dictation, others objected to such behind-the-scenes negotiations. Martin Shee, who was asked to make substantial changes to his first play *Alasco* (1824), wrote:

> Imagine the mortification of genius preparing for such a review! – cooking his conceptions to the taste of authority; – anxiously picking out, as poisonous, every

ingredient of good feeling and seasoning his production, not to his own liking, . . . but according to the official relish of distempered court zeal.[10]

Shee abandoned theatre altogether after his brush with the censor, but those who continued to write after having a play prohibited displayed new levels of caution. After Mary Russell Mitford's *Charles the First* was banned in 1825, for example, the playwright commented that, 'not licensing that play will do great harm to my next by making me timid and over careful'.[11] This was certainly the case, for Mitford wrote a letter to the examiner two months after this prohibition to check whether a new, as yet unwritten, project would be likely to meet the same fate. Having heard that it would not be licensed, she replied:

> Sir, I trouble you only to thank you for your kind attention to my request and the implied warning. I shall not now meddle with Henry the Second – especially as I believe that I perceive the reason which induced you to think the subject a bad one.[12]

Nineteenth-century dramatic censorship cannot boast numerous prohibitions or 'major riots', but, as one MP put it, it achieved its effect through a system of 'eternal interference'.[13]

Attitudes to censorship in the nineteenth century

The extent of the censors' interference may not have been widely appreciated in the nineteenth century, but the ideology that supported its protection of unwary audiences was clear to all. Perhaps the most enthusiastic in defending its aims were the examiners themselves. George Colman, play examiner between 1824 and 1836, compared his work to that of a benevolent woodsman, willing to 'lop off a few excrescent boughs' for the good of the tree.[14] Subsequent examiners abandoned this pastoral simile, but they each asserted that they took up their pens only out of a desire to safeguard British drama. The examiners' characterization of themselves as guardians of dramatic good health and as protectors of audiences remained fixed even if the diseases they fought changed during the period.

The most extensive official account of the censors' role is provided in an 1883 memorandum by examiner Edward F. Smyth Pigott. This text sought to prepare anyone likely to be questioned on the subject of censorship with stock answers to familiar criticisms. In this memorandum Pigott, who was examiner between 1874 and 1895, argued that historically censorship defended drama against its own helpless predilection for the scurrilous and licentious. 'No one acquainted with ancient or modern history of dramatic art', he wrote, 'will deny that it has always been prone to excesses from which it could only be preserved by an independent and disinterested authority.'[15] Censorship, according to Pigott, protected the theatre from playwrights who wished to enjoy 'an unrestricted license in their importations of obscenity', and from 'needy and unscrupulous managers and against those theatrical speculators and parasites who would willingly degrade the one and the other by turning theatres into disorderly houses if not into houses of ill fame'.[16]

Pigott's representation of a profession and art form predisposed to unruliness extended to its audiences. He argued that:

> to talk of the public protecting themselves and being their own censors, is to forget that everybody's business is nobody's business, and that they do not even protect themselves, their health, their safety, their comfort and convenience, their lives and property against street nuisances, . . . against a thousand injuries and scandals promoted by human craft and knavery and supported by human inertness and credulity.[17]

Pigott's picture of hapless audiences was not shared universally. Some declared that the skill of audiences in detecting political nuance and immorality had become so highly tuned that it rendered censors redundant.[18] Others, gripped with rage at the lack of protest against censorship, grimly agreed that audiences must be witless if they allowed the continuation of such an outrage.[19] According to Pigott however, members of the theatrical profession and theatregoers alike needed to be protected from themselves, preferably by one whose 'liberal spirit' and 'discernment and discrimination that belong to a wide knowledge of the world' are on hand to protect the 'noble art'.

In his role as an indulgent and fatherly censor Pigott boasted that there had not been 'so much as an audible murmur of dissatisfaction from any authorised representative'.[20] In spite of this, he equivocated about the language used to describe the act of play licensing. As Pigott put it in 1883: 'what is sometimes rather invidiously called "censorship" is nothing, in effect, but the friendly and perfectly disinterested action of an adviser who has the permanent interests of the stage at heart'.[21] Official distaste for the word 'censorship' became marked during the nineteenth century. By 1892 Ponsonby was correcting a member of the Select Committee for describing the work of the examiner as censorship:

> Then as to the censorship of plays?
> – We do not like it to be called 'censorship'.
> What do you call it?
> – The examination of plays.

As Pigott later explained, the word 'censorship' had 'an invidious sound, and may be used in an invidious sense, and to many minds it represents the Star Chamber and the Inquisition, and all manner of ancient institutions'.[22]

Concerns about the association of play 'examination' with acts of state-sponsored repression suggest that, despite Pigott's claims, the Lord Chamberlain's office knew there were negative reactions to their work. Despite this, nineteenth-century examiners continued a tradition of dismissing complaints against their work as insignificant. Just as, in 1737, Lord Chesterfield's speech against the formalization of censorship was described as a unique protest,[23] criticisms levelled against nineteenth-century censors were characterized as isolated, uttered out of pique rather than principle. The censors' campaign against their critics, particularly against playwrights who protested against the treatment of their plays, was surprisingly successful. As Shaw pointed out after George Redford banned *Mrs Warren's Profession* (1894), the fact that he had written something worthy of the examiner's prohibition was enough to convince many that he was a blackguard whose protests were unworthy of attention.[24]

Pigott's depiction of the lack of sustained opposition to censorship represents a highly partisan response to the complaints voiced in the nineteenth century. When he denied even murmurs of discord he meant, presumably, that since Chesterfield's speech he could find no evidence of an attack on the principles of censorship which did not derive from the treatment of a particular play. In fact the concerns raised by Chesterfield in 1737 were repeated frequently throughout the period. His claims that dramatic censorship was nothing less than an attack on fundamental liberties, that the play examiner would receive unprecedented powers and that the stage would be singled out for extraordinary repression were repeated by playwrights and managers as diverse as Shee, Shaw and even Charles Kemble, who later took up the role of examiner himself.[25] Even calls for the abolition of dramatic censorship were heard throughout the period, although those who made these arguments were compared to the anarchically republican French. The association of the abolition of censorship with a Jacobinical attack on the crown, a connection forged in France during the Revolution,[26] was often enough to silence critics of play licensing.[27] So effective was this association of the protection of censorship with the protection of the crown that it is still evident in Pigott's memorandum:

> In no country and in no age except during revolutionary crises, when despotic anarchy has usurped the seat of law, have theatrical entertainments been exempt from the supervision and control of the authorities responsible for public peace. Absolute free trade in theatres and theatrical representations may be left to the advocacy of disciples of Jack Cade whose political economy is a sort of Benthamism burlesqued. These purveyors of theatrical scandals are equally in favour of absolute free trade in disorderly houses and houses of ill fame.[28]

Pigott's provocative association of free trade in theatre with legalized prostitution may raise eyebrows, but such strategies were often effective in distracting opponents from principles and focusing their attacks on personalities. Those critical of censorship certainly responded in kind to Pigott's insults. They argued that the examiners themselves, with their absurdities and interferences, were their best weapon in the fight for the abolition of censorship.[29]

As an example of the official attitude towards censorship, Pigott's 1883 memorandum is illuminating. It asserts the examiner's indulgence, liberality and complacency and denies the existence of discontent, but its tone is defensive. It thus provides a paradigm for understanding the strategies used to soothe the criticisms the Lord Chamberlain's office feigned not to notice. The memorandum is also significant for the blithe confidence with which it expects its startling version of nineteenth-century censorship history to go undisputed. Pigott's own desire to emphasize an historical precedent for an overwhelmingly moralistic censorship surgically removes the eighteenth-century government's concern about political references in the theatre and puts in its place an anxiety about moral continence. The memorandum therefore appears to be predicated on the knowledge that few, including the Lord Chamberlain's Office itself, really understood the roots of theatrical censorship. Based on that supposition, Pigott appears to have felt free to rewrite its history, safe in the knowledge that no one would notice the shift in principles upon which nineteenth-century theatre censorship now operated.

Censorship: 1737–1901

Pigott's assumption of general ignorance about the history of theatre censorship appears to have been well founded. Attempts made by play examiners, comptrollers of the Lord Chamberlain's Office, and members of the theatrical profession to produce a useful narrative of censorship reveal widespread confusion about how the Lord Chamberlain came to have such power over the theatre. In 1832 the stage manager James Winston admitted, 'I cannot ascertain what his powers are' when asked about the role of the Lord Chamberlain 'with respect to licensing'.[30] Ponsonby was repeatedly forced to give the vague answer 'I have heard so' when questioned in 1866 about specific aspects of the statutes enshrining the Lord Chamberlain's control over play licensing. In 1892 Pigott himself showed a superb misunderstanding of pre-1737 censorship when he asserted that: 'Shakespeare himself was a member I believe, at some time, of the Lord Chamberlain's company and that did not prevent his plays being written.'[31] It is clear that many of those who administered or experienced dramatic censorship failed to understand the reasons for its introduction, the principles by which it was governed, or the extent of the Lord Chamberlain's powers. Perhaps given the confusion of kings and prime ministers on the same point, this is understandable.

Prior to the 1660 Restoration of Charles I, when the king issued patents to two courtiers that trampled over the traditional mechanics of dramatic censorship, the licensing of plays was administered by a host of officials. At different times, civil and ecclesiastical authorities, mayors, justices of the peace, the Lord Chamberlain, the Bishop of London,[32] the Privy Council and the monarch involved themselves in censorship, and continued to do so even after 1581 when the Master of Revels emerged as the functionary in charge of play licensing.[33] In addition to planning and supervising court masques, overseeing the safekeeping of costumes and inspecting rehearsals, the Master of Revels would, for a steadily increasing fee, read, sign and return plays to companies. This aggrandizement of power of the Master of Revels' part was not duplicated by the nineteenth-century censors. When, in 1859, Queen Victoria decided that it would be appropriate to cast the play examiner as a modern Master of Revels and asked Donne to oversee the production of plays at her theatre, Donne was horrified. 'I am in for a load of most unlooked for responsibility and care,' he grumbled to Fanny Kemble.[34]

Although Donne lamented the elision of his role with that of the Master of Revels, other points of contact between these officials existed. Most notable is the way in which Masters such as Henry Herbert recorded their work. Herbert, who acted as Master of Revels between 1623 and 1673, faithfully kept an office book of his dealings with theatre companies,[35] and requested that copies of plays should be lodged with him so that he might 'show what he had allowed or disallowed'.[36] His records and play collection are the forefathers of the daybooks and licensed play collection amassed by the nineteenth-century examiners.

Herbert's enjoyment of his post later caused him to protest loudly when Charles I gave the new patent holders, Davenant and Killigrew, the right to censor the plays performed by their companies. The patents were, Herbert complained, 'an unjust surprise and destructive to the powers of the Master of Revels'.[37] Although a court case and an agreement with Killigrew in 1662 protected the Master of Revels' power to an extent, the office was described as 'enervated' by confusion over who had control over censorship.[38] It was against this backdrop that the Lord Chamberlain, as head of the royal household and thus the Revels Office, began to take a more central role in mediating between the Master, the patent holders and their successors in the late seventeenth and early eighteenth century.[39]

In 1737 the Lord Chamberlain's role in the theatre was formalized when Prime Minister Robert Walpole rushed through Parliament a bill that placed the responsibility for licensing plays in the Lord Chamberlain's hands. The Licensing Act required playwrights and managers to submit plays to his office fourteen days before a first performance, and promised financial penalties if unlicensed plays were acted.[40] The Act also reserved spoken drama for the patent theatres and placed strict limits on the licensing of other places of entertainment within twenty miles of the City of Westminster. It distinguished, in other words, between patent and non-patent theatres, and created a culture of theatrical illegitimacy that, as the following section on nineteenth-century censorship makes clear, produced numerous opportunities for managers, actors and playwrights to flout the Lord Chamberlain's censorial authority.[41]

Critics have argued over the exact spur to Walpole's busy activity in May and June of 1737. Some suggest that Fielding's plays *Pasquin* and *Historical Register* (both 1736) laid the groundwork for Walpole's haste, and that an anonymously written and politically outrageous script entitled *The Golden Rump* tipped the balance. Certainly Hansard's record of Parliament's discussion suggests that the bill was proposed after a concerned manager brought a copy of the non-extant *Golden Rump* to the government's attention.[42] Others contend though that blaming or crediting individual plays or playwrights with the formalization of a dramatic censorship that lasted for a further 230 years oversimplifies a more diffuse series of concerns about the theatre.[43] Unfortunately for Pigott, few dispute the association of the Licensing Act with the suppression the theatre's political caricatures and satires.

Concerns raised by Lord Chesterfield shortly before the Licensing Act was passed ranged from fears that it was simply a precedent for reintroducing censorship of books and the press which had been abolished in 1695, to a polite boggling that anyone imagined that the stage could overturn the government.[44] Yet although Chesterfield's complaints were focused on issues of liberty, politics and government, those charged with the operation of censorship in both the nineteenth and twentieth centuries chose to interpret the Licensing Act as being founded upon the protection of public morality. Both Pigott and, later, John Johnston, whose book on censorship was written after his retirement from the role of comptroller of the Lord Chamberlain's Office, take this stance. Johnston even suggests that 'By the early 1800s in fact, public opinion had become so keen on moral propriety in plays that the Lord Chamberlain had little censoring to do.'[45]

It is certainly the case that by the early nineteenth century the work of play examiners had become associated with the policing of public morality, but it is equally clear that censors still scrutinized scripts for awkward political references. During the nineteenth century a series of parliamentary investigations into aspects of censorship and isolated contests between playwrights and examiners enable a closer scrutiny of the development of play licensing. In 1832, for example, at a time when several MPs thought that the House of Commons could spend its time more profitably on the reforms already in hand,[46] a Select Committee was convened to examine the state of dramatic literature. As is the case in subsequent Select Committees, its investigations included interviews with the examiner, comptroller, playwrights, actors and managers. The section of the report concerned with censorship produced several conclusions for the committee. It reassured them that audiences had developed methods to make it unpleasant and unprofitable for managers to introduce immorality on the stage; it gave them the opportunity to ridicule the incumbent examiner, Colman, for his scrupulous excision of words such as 'Heaven' and 'angels'; but it also caused them alarm about the extent to which political references were still introduced in the theatre.[47] Despite Pigott's and Johnston's claims to the contrary, the 1832 Select Committee questioned its interviewees most closely on issues of political rather than moral censorship.

Faced with general dismay at the state of British drama, the 1832 Select Committee made Colman the scapegoat for censorship's failures and absurdities. It criticized him for his prurience, his choice of expressions and his vigorous pursuit of fees. Nevertheless, in 1843 radical changes to theatrical law actually extended the Lord Chamberlain's and thus the examiner's control over play licensing.[48] This Act abolished the distinction between patent and non-patent theatres, enabled all licensed theatres to play spoken drama[49] and required every play performed to be submitted to the examiner for licensing. Although the Act created new distinctions between theatres and music halls that led to the revival of arguments about legitimacy and illegitimacy throughout the rest of the century,[50] it greatly increased the examiner's role.

In spite of sharp criticisms of certain decisions and further calls for the abolition of censorship, the efficacy of the newly extended censorship was commended by the

1866 Select Committee report into theatrical licences and regulations.[51] Criticisms of examiners, however, began to be made more publicly thereafter. In 1872 Donne was attacked in a number of daily newspapers when details of his zealous practice of deleting topical references from pantomimes was exposed. Finding himself ridiculed in the daily press, Donne noted, 'Little did I think to live to be one of the most celebrated and unpopular men of the day.'[52]

Twenty years later however, at the time of the 1892 Report on theatres and places of entertainment, Pigott still claimed that discontent with censorship was felt only by the few. He argued that William Archer, who had delivered a strong attack on censorship, was alone in believing that censorship had a malign effect on the development of drama.[53] Although characterized as a unique voice of complaint, Archer's reasons for launching his attack in 1892 were characteristic of *fin de siècle* critics and writers. He argued that the time to release the theatre from the Lord Chamberlain's shackles had arrived because there was finally the prospect that serious new drama was being written.[54] Based on the familiar contention that the majority of nineteenth-century drama was degraded but that a 'new dawn' approached in the 1880s and 1890s, Archer's attacks on censorship prefigured the later strategies of Shaw and Harley Granville Barker during the 1909 Select Committee on stage censorship.

This history of censorship looks very different from that offered by Pigott in his 1883 memorandum. What unites them, however, is the preoccupation of parliamentary committees, theatre statutes and censorship's critics with the figure of the examiner. Examiners such as Colman and Redford were scapegoated by the Lord Chamberlain to defend the broader work of censorship. Others such as Donne were praised, their assiduity in their reading serving as an advertisement for censorship's successes. However quickly such views of examiners shifted during the period, it is clear that they represented the human face of the censorial institution. Tracing attitudes towards them therefore provides an insight into the changing fortunes of censorship during the nineteenth century.

The characteristics of play examiners

Although Shaw once observed that he would struggle to find someone to criticize the play examiner,[55] the most positive descriptions emanated from the Lord Chamberlain's Office itself. In 1866 Ponsonby argued that examiners were never severe in making their decisions and by 1892 Pigott claimed that the only mistakes ever made by the Office were errors of extreme indulgence.[56] Yet W. S. Gilbert in particular tested the censor's habit of indulgence in *The Realm of Joy* (1873) and *Utopia Limited* (1893). In both plays, Gilbert dared the examiner to intervene by putting the Lord Chamberlain onstage. Although the Lord Chamberlain's primary crime in his role in *Utopia Limited* was to pass only plays that were three hundred years old and in blank verse, in *The Realm of Joy* his characterization as the Lord High Disinfectant was more difficult to overlook.

Written shortly after the post-performance banning of Gilbert's *The Happy Land* (1873), *The Realm of Joy* seems to serve as an attempt to sting the examiner into abandoning his much-vaunted indulgence. The play, which deals with the audience's activities during an unseen onstage performance of *The Happy Land*, makes repeated reference to the Lord Chamberlain. As the boxkeeper explains to a party of eager theatregoers:

> The authority of the most generally esteemed and unmistakably indispensable of all our court functionaries – I allude to the Lord High Disinfectant – is publicly set at naught and his office is declared night after night to be nothing better than an unnecessary mockery – Society is furious . . . It regards [the Lord High Disinfectant] as a discreet and loving father who shall decide what it is fit for them to hear.[57]

In this play, the description of the Lord Chamberlain as a father doubles as an insult. The only other father in *The Realm of Joy* is a marvel of moral contradiction. Although he brings his two daughters to the play for fear of leaving them unchaperoned in their hotel, Jellybag forgets to send them out of the box when the most disgraceful parts of the play begin. When he remembers his attempt to protect their innocence, he sends them out into the theatre's corridor where they are subjected to the lascivious attention of two young men. By providing his audience with a reprehensible example of patriarchal protection, Gilbert suggests by analogy the Lord Chamberlain's failings in his role as theatre's 'discreet and loving father'.

Letters exchanged between the harassed examiner and the Lord Chamberlain reveal their confusion about how they should react to Gilbert's attack. The Lord Chamberlain decided to continue with his stance of lofty indulgence but left Donne, his examiner, to deal with the playwright. Having received a request to make 'the usual corrections' to Gilbert's play, Donne expostulated, 'What "the usual corrections" can be in a piece so utterly incorrigible . . . passes my understanding.'[58]

Gilbert's baiting of the Lord Chamberlain's office also gives an insight into the examiners' boasts about their work ethic. Although this is mocked by Gilbert in *Rosencrantz and Guildenstern* (1891), evidence elsewhere indicates that after the increase in the number of scripts to be licensed in 1843, and the requirement that the safety of theatres should be checked from 1857 onwards, examiners were extremely hard pressed. Donne's private correspondence provides a woeful account of 'no small amount of correspondence and book keeping', laments for cancelled holidays and prognostications that he will soon be 'dead and buried' from his exertions.[59]

Not all were impressed by descriptions of such assiduity. Shee, writing in response to Colman's treatment of *Alasco*, described the examiner as 'the judicious Dogberry of the Dramatic Police', intent on 'active molestation'.[60] Yet despite the examiners' hard work they were often criticized for radical inconsistencies in their practice. Donne's scrupulous attention to detail, which manifested itself in his desire to see a description even of mute performance, looks very different from George Redford's more casual approach. When asked if he read the stage directions written into the scripts sent to him, Redford, examiner between 1895 and 1912, replied 'Oh dear no'.[61]

As Boucicault told the Select Committee in 1866, it was primarily the discrepancies of practice and attitude that caused the theatre profession most confusion:

> We have been greatly disturbed in consequence of the Lord Chamberlain having different opinions on the same subject, both with regard to plays and to theatres. Some plays have been licensed and have been withdrawn after eight or ten years; others have been refused and then licensed after ten or thirteen years; we do not know when a piece will be refused or on what grounds it will be refused.[62]

Critics of censorship turned evidence of such inconsistent practice to their own advantage however. Findlater expressed relief at the fact, arguing that if Edmund Tilney worked according to subsequent licensing principles, Elizabethan drama would be in shreds. Shaw, in contrast, denied any inconsistency at all, arguing that the examiner was fixed on one principle: that drama should never present new ideas.[63]

The procession of nineteen Lords Chamberlain and six examiners between 1824 and 1901 also prompted interest in the qualifications of those newly appointed. This was particularly the case with examiners who had experience in the theatre. Like Ben Jonson, who applied for the post of Master of Revels after a career of conflict with the office, these 'poachers turned gamekeepers' discovered that they were made to suffer for their previous careers.[64] In 1832 Colman was confronted with extracts of his own scurrilous plays by members of the Select Committee and was forced to admit that: 'I was in a different position at that time, I was a careless immoral author, I am now the examiner of plays.'[65] Charles Kemble, examiner between 1836 and 1840, was criticized for returning for a twelve-day run on the stage while still examiner and his son John Mitchell Kemble, putatively examiner between 1840 and 1857, was accused of being prejudiced in favour of plays to be performed at his father's theatre.[66] Those without links to the theatre were equally maligned. Shaw argued in his 'eulogy' to Pigott that the late examiner's only qualifications for his post were hysteria and intellectual confusion, and doubted that Redford's experience as a bank clerk suited him for his new role.[67]

Whatever their qualifications, examiners were almost universally criticized for their incompetence and ineffectuality. After a series of complaints against Colman for being too rigorous in his cutting, the examiner was rebuked for failing to notice a potentially embarrassing caricature of the French ambassador in a play by Alfred Bunn. The Lord Chamberlain was so incensed that he privately offered Colman's job to Theodore Hook, who had himself engaged in a highly publicized fracas with an earlier examiner.[68] Pigott made equally humiliating blunders at the latter end of the nineteenth century. In 1894 he circulated a memorandum to managers of music halls asking to see copies of unlicensed plays, but, after being reminded by the Home Office that the Lord Chamberlain had no jurisdiction over the halls, Pigott was forced to recall his circular and apologize for his mistake.[69]

Claims that examiners were incompetent, unfit for their post and ineffectual were less insulting than other criticisms, however. Shee, for example, pointed out that Colman's propensity to see any depiction of corrupt politics as an attack on the government was nothing less than unpatriotic.[70] Others, examiners included, wondered whether being filthy minded might not be a prerequisite of their job. Donne gloomily described himself as 'the devil's archdeacon', wallowing daily in a pool of degradation: 'I descend into the bowels of the earth: . . . I inhale evil smells; . . . and all for £500 a year, besides injuring my mind by reading nonsense and imperilling my soul by reading wickedness.'[71]

Such was the examiners' association with dirty mindedness that in the 1889 play *Lady Godiva* performed at George Sanger's theatre, William Muskerry cast him as Peeping Tom, spying on Godiva's nakedness in order to condemn her for immodesty. After catching the Peeping Tom staring at her with his opera glasses, the outraged lady informs him that censorship should be left in the hands of the 'true' audience:

> Our judges are the true patrons of drama
> Not modern maw-worms who with lengthy faces
> Would like to regulate our skirts and laces.[72]

Accused of a lack of patriotism and an excess of prurience, censors also had to face repeated questions about their greediness. Although complaints about the censors' pursuit of fees and status are traditional, with Buc, Herbert and Larpent emerging as particular culprits in the history of censorship,[73] Colman faced particularly close questioning about his financial dealings. The 1832 Select Committee heard that Colman had sought to extend his right to fees by announcing that lectures, oratorios and even Charles Mathews' famous unscripted 'monopolylogue' required a licence.[74] Yet perhaps more damaging was the revelation that Larpent and Colman had stored copies of licensed scripts and viewed them as their own property. In 1832 J. P. Collier informed the Select Committee that he had bought 'all the plays that ever came into the licenser's hands' from Larpent's widow.[75] The Lord Chamberlain did not share the sanguine response of the Select Committee to this news. When in 1836 Colman's impoverished widow requested permission to sell her husband's fourteen-year run of scripts, he pointed out that they were not hers to sell. She was so dismayed by this revelation that the Lord Chamberlain eventually gave her £100 to recompense her for the shock.[76]

However financially grasping the censors and their wives were, the most risible insult levelled against examiners was that they were lunatics. Findlater gleefully noted that Buc was relieved of his post after he went mad, leaving it up to the reader to imagine how many years had gone by before anybody had noticed his condition. He also asserted that a similar malaise afflicted both Larpent and Colman, arguing that 'their reigns in the censor's throne are speckled with a lunacy which helps account in part for the puerility of the English drama in the period'.[77] In 1892, however, the examiners' sympathizers argued that the experience of reading the material sent to be licensed was enough to 'drive any man into a lunatic asylum'.[78]

It emerges from this account of attitudes towards play examiners that Pigott's 1883 claim that there was 'no murmur of opposition' to censorship was far from the case. Although the criticisms levelled at examiners were often ludicrous, it is clear that references to the censors' indulgence, liberality and protection of the dramatic heritage were greeted with derision. It is also worth noting that it was the examiner rather than the Lord Chamberlain who tended to serve as the focus of such criticisms. The reasons for this become clear when the relationship between Lord Chamberlain, examiner, comptroller, playwrights, managers and audience members is examined more closely.

The mechanics of censorship

Although Shaw described the Lord Chamberlain as the 'Malvolio of St James' Palace',[79] there is little doubt that he exercised real power over the theatre. Whether out of diplomacy or for self-preservation, beleaguered examiners plaintively reminded anyone who would listen that it was the Lord Chamberlain rather than themselves who was in charge of censorship. When Colman suffered some sharp questioning on his methods and decisions in 1832, he was careful to insist, 'I have not the power to license or prohibit anything', emphasizing instead his status as a 'deputy' and 'subordinate'.[80] Despite these modest claims, Colman went on to argue that the Lord Chamberlain had no power to remove him from his post, an observation that led the committee to recommend that: 'it should be clearly understood that the office of the censor is held at the discretion of the Lord Chamberlain'.[81] A later Lord Chamberlain showed that this advice had been heeded, for he issued a memorandum in 1895 to George Redford that pointedly reminded him of his subordinacy.[82]

Occupying the space between the examiner and the Lord Chamberlain was the comptroller who, in any Select Committee investigation, invariably criticized the former and protected the latter if it seemed that censorship was under attack. When Colman was questioned about the records of his fees in 1832 for example, he confidently asserted that his facts would be corroborated by the comptroller, Thomas Baucott Mash. 'Mr Mash stated he knew nothing of your fees or of the power under which you exacted them,' Colman was informed.[83] When the relationship was easy, however, the comptroller would act as a conduit between the examiner and Lord Chamberlain. Ponsonby described this ideal process in 1866:

> Before a play is performed it is sent to . . . the Examiner of Plays; he looks through that play and if he sees nothing objectionable in it he sends, for the Lord Chamberlain's signature, a form of license for that play; if he sees anything which to his mind is objectionable he sends it to me and it is then brought to the notice of the Lord Chamberlain who gives his directions on it.[84]

In practice it appears that it was the comptroller and examiner who investigated objections and came to decisions about a play. Presumably the examiner found it necessary to convince the comptroller of the significance of his concerns before the comptroller would pass a play to the Lord Chamberlain. Indeed, as the Lord Chamberlain's correspondence indicates, it was frequently Ponsonby rather than either the Lord Chamberlain or the examiner who responded to complaints about plays or sought clarification from managers about objections. Through such communications, the comptroller was able to wield more power than his position as buttress between Lord Chamberlain and examiner might suggest.

Even within the confines of the Lord Chamberlain's office, however, those charged with the responsibility of play licensing often requested advice from outside authorities. Conolly enjoys the fact that the Earl of Hertford, Lord Chamberlain between 1766 and 1783, frequently consulted his cousin, Walpole's son, about whether certain plays were objectionable. Other critics note with a mixture of amusement and dismay the input of Larpent's theatre-loving wife, and that of Donne's children in making decisions about what to censor.[85]

Whatever the relationship between the Lord Chamberlain's office and its circle of advisers, playwrights believed that the examiners' decisions were final. Several, unaware of the role of comptroller and other advisers, bewailed the fact that the examiner seemed to be the only official able to determine the fate of particular plays. James Kenney, whose *Masaniello* (1829) caused political consternation when it was interpreted as a caution to George IV to take better care of his subjects, argued that the job of reading plays should be undertaken by committee.[86] He objected to a situation that enabled an examiner to license or reject plays according to his personal prejudices. By the end of the nineteenth century, Kenney's concerns about the power of examiners had grown into a more general fear that they could launch attacks on any play without explanation and without offering any opportunity for the playwright to appeal.[87]

The examiners' right to prohibit plays without explaining their reasons to their authors constituted one of the key objections to the censors' seemingly insuperable authority. Playwrights protested that they were obliged to guess why their work had fallen into official disfavour when their plays were censored. Shaw for instance, who presumably cannot have been surprised when Redford refused to license his play about a prostitute, *Mrs Warren's Profession*, objected loudly to the fact that the examiner was not required to account for his decision.[88] Such reticence was traditional, however. Both the Lord Chamberlain and examiner had similarly refused to explain to Brooke, the author of the first post-1737 prohibited play, why *Gustavus Vasa* was unacceptable, a fact which led Samuel Johnson to remind his readership that official silence was one of the more enjoyable prerogatives of public office: 'Unhappy would it be for Men in Power were they always obliged to publish motives of their conduct', Johnson explained. 'What is power but the liberty of acting without being accountable?'[89]

Some examiners did explain their difficulties with scripts. Shirley Brooks informed the 1866 Select Committee that he received an invitation from the examiner to discuss his proposed adaptation of Disraeli's *Coningsby* (1845):

> . . . we agreed to go through the piece, act by act, if not scene by scene, and the singular objections that were taken by the examiner to points in that piece which appeared

perfectly harmless astounded me. After a tenth or twelfth effort to get over some of the small points which he raised I very nearly gave it up as a hopeless business.[90]

Such behind-the-scenes discussions with playwrights were underpinned by the examiners' reliance on the cooperation of the theatre managers with whom they communicated more regularly. Donne notes with pleasure testimonials and gifts of wine from grateful managers, and commended managers who checked plays before sending them for licensing.[91] This relationship led playwrights to view with extreme scepticism the level of support they would receive from managers should their plays fall foul of the examiner.

After a play was licensed, however, nineteenth-century Lords Chamberlain and examiners seem genuinely unsure of their role in post-production censorship. Newspaper reviews and letters sent to the Lord Chamberlain from outraged members of public alerted examiners to problems, but few were sure of the extent to which they should routinely check productions. When Colman was asked if he troubled about 'what passes in the theatre' after a licensing script left his hands, he replied, 'Not in the least'. To do otherwise would make a spy out of the examiner, he suggested.[92] The correspondence of later examiners indicates that Colman's lassitude could not always be emulated. Donne admitted that he was sometimes required to attend potentially mischievous productions but said in 1866, 'it is not three times in the year that there is any occasion for it'.[93]

It was this routine failure to translate pre-production examination into post-production censorship that became one of the main stumbling blocks for the examiner in the early twentieth century. The 1909 Select Committee was treated to the familiar argument that it was impossible to imagine in performance the effect of a written text, and such was the force of this argument that the Lord Chamberlain's office was made to acknowledge that limiting censorship to the act of reading was problematic. Yet this reading process, whether transcribed into reports or confided to friends in letters, reveals official interpretations of nineteenth-century plays. Examining these texts certainly lends credence to the playwrights' contention that reading the script alone placed censorship in a precarious position, but they do more than this. These texts make possible fresh insights into the effect of the censor on the development of British drama. They enable a consideration of the pressures that could be brought to bear on examiners required to read plays for a career, and they reinforce the fact that for the government at least nineteenth-century theatre could still be threatening.

NOTES

1 [Samuel Johnson], *A compleat vindication of the Licensers of the stage from the malicious and scandalous aspersions of Mr Brooke, author of Gustavus Vasa, with a proposal for making the office of the Licensers more extensive and effectual* (London: C. Corbett, 1739), p. 25.

2 The Select Committee examination of censorship in 1909, discussed by Steve Nicholson in Part 2, prompted the publication of several splenetic works. See George Bernard Shaw, 'Preface', in *The*

Shewing up of Blanco Posnet (1909), *The Works of Bernard Shaw*, vol. 12 (London: Constable, 1930), pp. 361–433, and Henry Arthur Jones, *The Censorship Muddle and the Way Out of It* (London: Samuel French, 1909). Richard Findlater's similarly wrathful *Banned! A Review of Theatrical Censorship* (London: MacGibbon & Kee, 1967), was published during the year in which theatre censorship was abolished.

3 John Russell Stephens, *The Censorship of English Drama 1824–1901* (Cambridge: Cambridge University Press, 1980), p. 1. A similarly measured critique of censorship is provided in Steve Nicholson's *The Censorship of British Drama 1900–1968*, vol. 1 (Exeter: Exeter University Press, 2003).

4 See Archer's evidence to the 1892 Select Committee and Shaw's well-known 'eulogy' for Edward F. Smyth Pigott: *Report from the Select Committee on Theatres and Places of Entertainment, together with the proceedings of the Committee, minutes of evidence, appendix and index. Reports from Committees* (London: HMSO), vol. 18. 19 February–28 June 1892, pp. 257–8 q. 3951; Shaw, 'The Late Censor', 2 March 1895, in *Our Theatres in the Nineties*, *The Works of Bernard Shaw*, vol. 23 (London: Constable & Co. Ltd., 1931), pp. 50–57.

5 Findlater, *Banned!*, p. 51. Those who disagree with Findlater's latter claim include Robert D. Hume: *Henry Fielding and the London Theatre 1728–1737* (Oxford: Clarendon Press, 1985), p. 260 and the MP Mr Hume, Parliamentary debate, Hansard's Parliamentary Debates, vol. 16, 1 March–1 April 1833 (London: Baldwin & Craddock, 1833), p. 565.

6 Shaw, 'Review of *The Leader of Men*', 16 February 1895, in *Our Theatres in the Nineties*, pp. 38–43.

7 Spencer Ponsonby-Fane, *Report* 1892, p. 14, q. 390. For an example of managerial pre-censorship, see the references to Ellis's practice in John Russell Stephens, 'William Bodham Donne: some aspects of his later career as examiner of plays', *Theatre Notebook* 25.1 (Autumn 1970), p. 27.

8 For official resistance to communication with playwrights, see the Lord Chamberlain's upbraiding of Martin Shee for seeking an explanation of the fate of his play, discussed below, pp. 30–1.

9 William Bodham Donne in *Report from the Select Committee on Theatrical Licenses and Regulations together with the proceedings of the Committee, minutes of evidence and an appendix, Reports from Committees* (London: HMSO), vol. 11, 1 February–10 August 1866, p. 88 q. 2413. See also George Colman in *Report from the Select Committee on Dramatic Literature with minutes of evidence. Ordered by the House of Commons to be printed 2 August 1832, Reports from Committees* (London: HMSO), vol. 7, session 6, December 1831–16 August 1832, p. 66 q. 970; and Pigott in *Report* 1892, p. 330 q. 5184. As will be noted from the title of the 1866 *Report* and in various extracts throughout this book, the distinction between 'licence' (noun) and 'license' (verb) was often overlooked.

10 Martin Archer Shee, 'Preface', in *Alasco. A Tragedy in Five Acts. Excluded from the Stage by the Authority of the Lord Chamberlain* (London: Sherwood, Jones & Co., 1824), p. 26.

11 Mary Russell Mitford, Letter to Rev. William Harness, 9 October 1825 in Rev. A. G. L'Estrange, *Life of Mary Russell Mitford in Three Volumes*, vol. 2 (London: Richard Bentley, 1870), p. 214.

12 Mitford, Letter to George Colman, 16 December 1825, ms 42873, f. 413.

13 Hume, Parliamentary debate 1833, p. 565.

14 George Colman, quoted in Richard Brinsley Peake, *Memoirs of the Colman Family*, vol. 2 (London: Richard Bentley, 1841), p. 438.

15 Pigott, Memorandum, 15 March 1883, General Letters (Theatres) for 1890, LC 1: 546, f. 31, p. 2.

16 Ibid., p. 4, 3.

17 Ibid., pp. 6–7. Pigott put this more bluntly when he pointed out that audiences who rushed 'all over town for some doggrel [sic] buffoonery or some wild dance or song', should not be trusted to exercise judicious censorship. Pigott in *Report* 1892, p. 333 q. 5205. Pigott was not the only examiner to doubt the abilities of the audience. See Donne, 'Letter to Fanny Kemble', 8 July 1858, in Catharine Johnson (ed.), *William Bodham Donne and his Friends* (London: Methuen, 1905), pp. 224–5.

18 Edward Bulwer Lytton, 'Dramatic performances', *The Times*, 13 March 1833, p. 4.

19 Shaw, 'The censorship of the stage in England', *North American Review*, 169 (August 1899), reproduced in *Shaw on Theatre*, ed. E. J. West (London: MacGibbon & Kee, 1958), p. 73.

20 Pigott, Memorandum 1883, p. 7.

21 Ibid., p. 3. Pigott also objected when the examiner's reliance on information from the public was described as 'surveillance'. See Pigott in *Report* 1892, p. 333 q. 5212.

22 Ponsonby in *Report* 1892, p. 313 qq. 4903–4; Pigott, ibid., p. 328 q. 5178.

23 Coxe, author of Walpole's memoirs, later argued that the repetition of Chesterfield's arguments gave the impression of 'a violent opposition to the measure' where none existed. See the footnote to Lord Chesterfield's 'Speech to the House of Lords,' 20 May 1737, *The Parliamentary History of England from the Earliest Period to the Year 1803*, vol. 10, 1737–1739 (London: T. C. Hansard, 1812).

24 Shaw, 'The author's apology', in *Mrs Warren's Profession, The Work of Bernard Shaw*, vol. 7. (London: Constable, 1930), p. 151.

25 Chesterfield in Hansard 1737, pp. 330–1. See above for details of Shee's and Shaw's protests. Kemble's complaints can be found below, p. 36.

26 F. W. J. Hemmings, *Theatre and State in France 1760–1905* (Cambridge: Cambridge University Press, 1994), pp. 49, 53; Nicholas Harrison, 'Colluding with the censor: theatre censorship in France after the Revolution', *Romance Studies* 25 (Spring 1995), pp. 10–11, 13–14. Calls for abolition continued to prompt analogies with France, *Report* 1866, p. 14 q 391.

27 *The Times*, 29 September 1832; p. 2 Sir Charles Wetherell, Parliamentary debate, 31 May 1832, Hansard, vol. 13, p. 249.

28 Pigott, Memorandum 1883, p. 5.

29 See *New Monthly Magazine* 2 (1824), pp. 554–9, which argued that Colman's appointment would lead to the abolition of censorship, and Edward Fitzgerald's 8 September 1874 letter to Donne on his retirement in which he predicts that the office will not last long in Pigott's hands, Johnson, *Donne*, p. 299.

30 James Winston in *Report* 1832, p. 18 q. 190. John Payne Collier, who took over as examiner from Colman while he was on holiday, in fact proved to be the best informed about the history of censorship. Collier, ibid., pp. 21–36 qq. 245–443, and especially p. 41 q. 549.

31 Ponsonby in *Report* 1866, p. 1; Pigott in *Report* 1892, p. 329 q. 5183.

32 The Bishop of London continued to involve himself during the nineteenth century. See his intervention on the issue of *The Israelites in Egypt, The Times*, 19 February 1834, p. 5.

33 Evelyn May Albright, *Dramatic publication in England 1580–1640: a Study of Conditions Affecting Content and Form of Drama* (New York/London: D. C. Heath & Co./Oxford University Press, 1927), p. 19.

34 Donne, Letter to Fanny Kemble, 20 November 1859, Johnson, *Donne*, p. 233. See also 20 January 1860, ibid., p. 237.

35 Herbert's notes have been edited by Joseph Quincy Adams, *The Dramatic Records of Sir Henry Herbert, Master of the Revels 1623–1673* (New Haven: Yale University Press, 1917). Herbert also quotes from the non-extant office books of his predecessors Edmund Tilney and George Buc, see ibid., p. 9.

36 Herbert, quoted by Albright, *Dramatic Publication*, p. 58.

37 Herbert, quoted by Adams, *Dramatic Records*, p. 86.

38 Edward Heywood, quoted by Adams, *Dramatic Records*, p. 132. Killigrew later took over the role of Master of Revels on Herbert's death, thus eliding and further complicating the relationship between Master and patent holder. See Matthew J Kinservik, 'Theatrical regulation during the Restoration period', in Susan J. Owen (ed.), *A Companion to Restoration Drama* (Oxford: Blackwell, 2001), pp. 36–52.

39 The presence of licensed theatres after 1695 confused the issue further.

40 According to Findlater, the subsequent appointment of play examiners to read these scripts was made because the incumbent Lord Chamberlain was virtually illiterate. Findlater, *Banned!*, p. 42. The text of the Licensing Act can be found at 10 Geo II.c.28 (London: His Majesty's Stationery Office, 1737).

41 See below pp. 47–50. Further guides to the significance of these changes to theatre licensing are offered by Watson Nicholson, *The Struggle for a Free Stage in London* (London: Archibald Constable & Co., 1906); Jane Moody, *Illegitimate Theatre in London, 1770–1840* (Cambridge: Cambridge University Press, 2000).

42 Critics who credit or blame Fielding with the Licensing Act can be found in the notes to the Hansard record of the Act, Hansard 1737, pp. 322–4; 'Origin of Dramatic Censorship', *The Times*, 7 September 1825, p. 3; Findlater, *Banned!*, p. 35.

43 Those who argue that there were other issues at stake include Hume, *Fielding*, p. 249; Vincent J. Liesenfeld, *The Stage and the Licensing Act 1729–1739* (New York: Garland, 1981). pp. ix–x; P. J. Crean, 'The stage licensing act of 1737,' *Modern Philology* 35 (1937–8), pp. 247–8.

44 Chesterfield in Hansard 1737, p. 331, 340.

45 Pigott, Memorandum 1883, p. 3. John Johnston, *The Lord Chamberlain's Blue Pencil* (London: Hodder & Stoughton, 1990), p. 29. For an excellent examination of eighteenth-century censorship see L. W. Conolly, *The Censorship of English Drama 1737–1824* (San Marino, CA: The Huntington Library, 1976).

46 Even Bulwer Lytton, who proposed the investigation, said he did so with 'diffidence' seeing as 'the public mind was so much occupied with the most important affairs'. *The Times*, 1 June 1832, p. 1.

47 *Report 1832*, p. 51 q. 708, pp. 59–60 qq. 852–7, p. 66 qq. 967–968.

48 An Act for Regulating Theatres, 6 & 7 Vic.c.68, *The Statutes Revised 1836–1844*, vol. 4, 3rd edn (London: Her Majesty's Stationery Office, 1844).

49 This rule had been flouted for more than fifty years. See Dewey Ganzel, 'Patent wrongs and patent theatre: drama and the law in the early nineteenth century', *PMLA* 76.4 (1961), pp. 384–96.

50 See in particular *Report 1892*, pp. 215–217 qq. 3244–300.

51 *Report 1866*, p. iv.

52 Donne, Letter to J. W. Blakenley, 18 January 1782, p. 278. See also *The Era*, 14 January 1872, p. 12.

53 Pigott in *Report 1892*, p. 332 q. 5204.

54 Archer ibid., pp. 257–8 q. 3951.

55 Shaw, 'Preface,' *Plays Unpleasant*, in *The Works of Bernard Shaw*, vol. 7 (London: Constable, 1930), p. xvi.

56 Ponsonby in *Report 1866*, p. 2 q. 40; Pigott in *Report 1892*, p. 330 q. 5184.

57 W. S. Gilbert, *The Realm of Joy, being a free and easy version of Le Roi Candaule*, LCP 53128E, lic. 1873, pp. 3–4.

58 Donne, quoted in Jane W. Stedman, *W. S. Gilbert: a Classic Victorian and his Theatre* (Oxford: Oxford University Press, 1996), pp. 109–10. For the correspondence see Donne's letter to Everett, 10 October 1873, Donne to Lord Sydney, 13 October 1873; Donne to Ponsonby, 15 October 1873; General Letters (Theatres), LC 1: 276.

59 Donne, Letter to R. C. Trench, 16 December 1853; Letters to Fanny Kemble, 9 September 1858 and 31 July 1858, Johnson, *Donne*, pp. 193, 226, 225.

60 Shee, 'Preface,' pp. 3, 12.

61 Donne in *Report 1866*, p. 78 q. 2124; Redford, *Report from the Joint Select Committee of the House of Lords and the House of Commons on the Stage Play (Censorship), British Sessional Papers* 8 (1909), p. 509.

62 Boucicault in *Report 1866*, p. 142 qq. 4041–2. Archer subsequently denied 'the possibility of a fixed authority with no fads', *Report 1892*, p. 263 q. 4011.

63 Findlater, *Banned!*, p. 71; Shaw, 'Censorship', p. 76.

64 Richard Burt, *Licensed by Authority: Ben Jonson and the Discourses of Censorship* (Ithaca: Cornell University Press, 1993), p. 12.

65 Colman in *Report 1832*, p. 60 q. 860.

66 *Report 1866*, p. 81 q. 2225; Mary Vernon, '*Mary Stuart*, Queen Victoria and the censor', *Nineteenth-Century Theatre Research* 6.1 (1978), pp. 35–40.

67 Shaw, 'Late censor', p. 52; 'Censorship,' p. 67.

68 J. F. Bagster-Collins, *George Colman the Younger 1762–1836* (New York: King's Crown Press, 1976), pp. 300, 319, 321.

69 Johnston, *Lord Chamberlain's Blue Pencil*, p. 50.

70 Shee, 'Preface,' p. 18, 20. See also below, pp. 22–3.

71 Donne, Letter to Fanny Kemble, 9 September 1858, Johnson, *Donne*, p. 227.

72 William Muskerry, *Lady Godiva; or George and the Dragon and the seven champions of Christendom*, LCP 53443L, lic. 26 December 1889, p. 21. The examiners' preoccupation with the length of skirts is discussed below, p. 46. See also figure 3 on p. 40.

73 Findlater, *Banned!*, pp. 27, 29, 54; Kinservik, 'Theatrical regulation', p. 38.

74 Colman in *Report* 1832, p. 63 qq. 898, 900, 903.

75 Collier ibid., p. 29 q. 343.

76 John Russell Stephens, 'The Lord Chamberlain's Plays: rescuing the George Colman archive', *Notes and Queries* 34 232.1 (March 1987), pp. 30–32.

77 Findlater, *Banned!*, pp. 28, 53.

78 Fardell in *Report* 1892, p. 5 q. 53.

79 Shaw, 'Censorship,' p. 66.

80 Colman in *Report* 1832, p. 59 qq. 848–50.

81 *Report* 1832, p. 4. Two years later the Lord Chamberlain attempted this removal by asking Hook to replace Colman as examiner, see above p. 13.

82 Memorandum 13 March 1895, quoted in Johnston, *Lord Chamberlain's Blue Pencil*, p. 266.

83 *Report* 1832, p. 63 q. 914.

84 Ponsonby in *Report* 1866, p. 7 q. 186.

85 L. W. Conolly, 'Horace Walpole, unofficial play censor', *English Language Notes* 9.1 (September 1971), pp. 42–5, and 'The censor's wife at the theatre: the diary of Anna Margaretta Larpent, 1790–1800', *Huntington Library Quarterly* 35.1 (November 1971), pp. 19–28; Johnson, *Donne*, p. 298.

86 Kenney in *Report* 1832, p. 230 q. 4114.

87 Archer in *Report* 1892, p. 256 q. 3936.

88 Shaw, 'Censorship', p. 70.

89 [Johnson], *Vindication*, p. 16.

90 Brooks in *Report* 1866, p. 158 q. 4480. For the political significance of *Coningsby* see Robert O'Kell, 'Disraeli's *Coningsby*: political manifesto or psychological romance?' *Victorian Studies* 23.1 (Autumn 1979), pp. 57–9.

91 Donne, Letter to Fanny Kemble, 28 May 1856, 31 July 1858, Johnson, *Donne*, pp. 197, 225; Stephens, 'William Bodham Donne', p. 27.

92 Peake, *Memoirs*, vol. 2, p. 436.

93 Donne in *Report* 1866, p. 79 q. 2138.

CHAPTER 2

Before Readers' Reports

WITHIN a month of being appointed the Lord Chamberlain's play examiner in January 1824, George Colman made his presence felt by demanding radical changes in *Alasco*, a tragedy written by first-time playwright Martin Shee.[1] His action quickly disabused the theatrical profession of any hope that Colman's earlier career as a scurrilous playwright and an artful manager would lead him to be a lenient examiner.[2] Many, hearing of the 'rage of red ink' on Shee's script, began to suspect that Colman had embarked instead on a new profession of 'petty tyranny'.[3] At the other end of the century, however, W. S. Gilbert proved himself singularly more adept than Shee at negotiating the censorship process.[4] He saw his burlesque *Rosencrantz and Guildenstern* licensed despite the fact that he had given the censor a walk-on part.[5] The two cases demonstrate central truths about nineteenth-century theatre censorship. Firstly, that, far from being rooted on fixed principles, censorship adapted according to the whims of each examiner. Secondly, that in some cases this changefulness could be predicated on the fame, or in Gilbert's case the pugnacity, of the playwright. And finally, perhaps most importantly, that no one could predict the censor's reaction to a play.

The responses elicited by the very different provocations of Shee's and Gilbert's plays may seem to emphasize nothing more than the capriciousness of censorship, but in fact both plays are united by an idiosyncratically nineteenth-century use of Shakespeare's *Hamlet* to reflect on the process of play licensing. Shee's lengthy preface to the published version of *Alasco* turns wrathfully to Shakespeare in order to characterize the examiner as an anxious Hamlet. Whether consciously or unconsciously, Shee's approach harks back to Lord Chesterfield, who in 1737 accused the government of paranoia for seeing plays as mousetraps for catching its guilty conscience.[6] For Shee, Colman personified this guilty paranoia. He nervously scrutinized every political nuance, fearful that the theatre was on the verge of exposing institutionalized corruption. Shee writes:

> He [Colman] pays the government under which he lives and by which he has been so judiciously selected for the post he enjoys, the happy compliment to suppose that, if tyranny be but mentioned, oppression alluded to, or usurpation exposed, it is a 'palpable hit' at our constituted authorities . . . he proceeds to prove, that he considers our public functionaries as so many political culprits writhing under the consciousness of crime.[7]

Shakespeare's Hamlet may set out to trap Claudius with the representation of Gonzago's murder, but Shee's systematically mutilates scripts with the opposite intention. He seeks to ensure that he will never be accused of failing to protect guilty kings and government ministers from feeling the pressure of their consciences when they visit the theatre.

Gilbert's use of *Hamlet* is less obviously accusatory than Shee's, perhaps because it focuses on the censorship of indecency rather than on the suppression of political commentary. Gilbert's play revolves around Rosencrantz's attempt to trick Hamlet into staging a deeply unsuccessful drama written and subsequently embargoed by the touchy Claudius. Having searched in vain for an extant copy of Claudius's play, Rosencrantz sends Ophelia into 'her father's den', knowing that Polonius, the Lord Chamberlain, would have the licensing copy of the piece. Ophelia returns from her expedition, '*white with terror, holding a heavy MS*', and describes the nightmarish underworld she has visited:

> The clock struck twelve, and then – oh horrible! –,
> From chest and cabinet there issued forth
> The mouldy spectres of five thousand plays,
> All dead and gone – and many of them damned!
> I shook with horror! They encompassed me,
> Chattering forth the scenes and parts of scenes
> Which my poor father wisely had cut out.
> Oh horrible – oh! 'twas most horrible! (*Covering her face*)
> ROSENCRANTZ: What was't they uttered?
> OPHELIA (*severely*): I decline to say.
> The more I heard the more convinced was I
> My father had acted *most judiciously*;[8]

Ophelia's account of her father's work sounds surprisingly sympathetic. Admittedly the censor's daughter uncovers a mausoleum of five thousand plays secreted away from the public, but she leaves her father's office convinced that he has acted sensibly in protecting the state from the indecencies offered by these 'damned' plays. Whether Gilbert intended it or not, the speech realizes onstage an illustration of the earlier examiner, William Bodham Donne, tormented in his sleep by the characters he has censored.[9]

These depictions of the censor's lot reflect the contemporary perception of the examiner's work as a nightmarish experience. Gilbert's play goes on to examine the censor's role in a more sustained way, using the burlesque of *Hamlet* to flesh out its critique. The very fact that Polonius plays the part of the censor in *Rosencrantz and Guildenstern*, for instance, undermines the approving tone with which Ophelia describes his work. Gilbert tactfully stops short of staging the brutal slaughter of Polonius by Hamlet but he subjects the play's censor to a fate that is almost worse. Such is this Lord Chamberlain's insignificance that his name is omitted from the play's dramatis personae.

1. 'The Censor's Dream'; unsigned illustration of the nightly haunting of William Bodham Donne's dreams by the characters of the plays he has censored.

Although Gilbert condemns Polonius to obscurity, his play, unlike Shee's preface, accuses the examiner of nothing more malevolent than incompetence and irrelevance. Polonius appears onstage in time to witness the performance of Claudius's play in the third tableau, but once there he is singularly ineffective either in realizing that the play being performed has been banned, or in stopping its representation. In addition to being burdensome, this censor's work is ineffectual.

Yet perhaps what is most important for this chapter about *Rosencrantz and Guildenstern*'s representation of censorship is the fact that the play casually elides the distinctions that existed between the nineteenth-century Lord Chamberlain and his play examiner. Unlike Gilbert's Polonius, who is referred to as a Lord Chamberlain but does the work of a play examiner, the real Lords Chamberlain had very little to do with the actual reading of plays. Their signatures appeared on licences and their names were invoked when letters were sent to inform managers that plays had been prohibited or needed amendment, but in the nineteenth century it was the play examiners who recorded what the Lord Chamberlain regretted.

Readers' reports?

While Parts II and III of this book reproduce and critique the reports written by a committee of readers about particular plays, this chapter looks significantly different. As Part II explains, the practice of writing readers' reports on plays was not required of examiners until 1911, and even then the incumbent play examiner, George Redford, protested that: 'It would be physically impossible for any man to make a précis of every stage play submitted for licence.'[10] Redford's dismay at the addition of this new task should not be taken to mean that no earlier examiner had written a critique of a play he was asked to license. As the 1909 Select Committee inquiry demonstrated, Redford managed to ignore and 'forget' many of the job specifications that had been written into his memorandum of appointment.[11] Nevertheless it is clear that before 1911, there was no consistent requirement for examiners to provide the Lord Chamberlain or his comptroller with a report on the plays he read.[12]

George Colman, it seems, was the only nineteenth-century examiner to count the writing of reports as part of his official duties. In his evidence to the 1832 Select Committee on Dramatic Literature, Colman described his responsibilities as including the composition of reports.

> The Lord Chamberlain is the licenser, to whom the Examiner forwards an outline and sends his opinion, of the entertainments which he has officially perused, and then the Lord Chamberlain signs, or does not sign the form of licence as he may think proper. I may observe here, that as to sending an outline, that is a voluntary act, because my predecessor never sent any outline; but I thought it might be more satisfactory, and I have gratuitously sent it, that the Lord Chamberlain might see what the subject of the play was.[13]

Although Colman makes tantalizing references to the fact that he is enclosing 'short remarks' or 'outlines' of *Alasco* and Mary Russell Mitford's *Charles the First* in his private correspondence, neither these nor any other reports are to be found.[14]

John Payne Collier, who stood in as examiner while Colman went on holiday, reiterated the fact that Colman was unusual in producing reports on the plays he licensed. Collier, who is best known now for buying the plays licensed by Larpent from his widow despite the fact that they were not hers to sell,[15] revealed in his evidence to the 1832 Select Committee that he had a different understanding of the examiner's duties. He said, 'I believe the examiner always sends in writing a statement of the parts of the play to which he objects. I don't think he gives his reasons, but he distinctly states what he objects to.'[16]

The discrepancy of practice between Colman and his contemporary is only heightened when one looks at censors working later in the nineteenth century. Donne's and Pigott's descriptions of their duties to the 1866 and 1892 Select Committees respectively, make no reference to compiling anything resembling a reader's report.[17] As we have seen, George Redford clearly viewed this as no part of his working practice either.[18]

The absence of nineteenth-century readers' reports does not mean that any attempt to gauge an 'official' insight into particular plays is futile. In fact, nineteenth-century examiners left a wide range of texts that record their reading of plays. By using these it is possible to construct a narrative of censorial interpretation and response that links the practice of nineteenth-century examiners to that of their twentieth-century counterparts.

Recording the examiners' response

One of the best sources for discovering a nineteenth-century examiner's interpretation of plays is the collection of daybooks now held at the British Library.[19] These daybooks were compiled in an effort to record the examiners' response to all plays submitted for licensing during the nineteenth century. Despite this aim, it takes only a cursory glance to realize that in the later volumes in particular certain plays are omitted. While early volumes make a note of all plays submitted whether licensed or not, the later volumes obliterate prohibited plays from official memory by refusing to record their arrival at St James's Palace or the response that greeted them. At the back of the second volume, for example, is a list of nine plays that were refused a licence even though these plays are not referred to in the main body of the daybook. In a censorial version of *damnatio memoriae*, plays prohibited later in the century fail to achieve an entry at all.[20]

Those plays included in the daybooks are ordered alphabetically, with more or less information entered under the headings of title, genre, the theatre at which the play was to be performed, date of licensing, date of entry, and, most importantly for this chapter, the words and passages to be omitted in representation. The first daybook, 1824–1852, is much more lightly marked than the later volumes. Although as in several others someone, probably Donne, has pasted into the back of the volume copies of letters in which problem plays are discussed, it is notable that in later volumes the final column is more richly annotated with letters, rebukes and even press announcements of the play's first night. This column, which purports to be reserved for prohibited words, comes to function as an archive of correspondence and pre-production interpretation collated by the examiner.

The reference to correspondence in the daybooks is significant. Figure 2 (p. 27) taken from the first daybook, reproduces George Colman's entry for Mary Russell Mitford's banned *Charles the First*. The final column tantalizingly refers the reader to the relevant letters exchanged during the discussion of the play's fate.[21] Such letters, many of which are to be found amongst the Lord Chamberlain's papers in the Public Record Office, represent the closest thing there is to a nineteenth-century reader's report. One of the best-known examples of this correspondence appears in the 1892 volume of General Letters, and records the correspondence and scandalized delight of Pigott, who wrote to inform Ponsonby of his objections to Wilde's *Salome*. The letter, which has been reproduced elsewhere,[22] includes, alongside a brief précis of the play, the famous description of it as 'a miracle of impudence . . . half-biblical, half- pornographic'.[23]

2. Examiner George Colman's daybook entry for Mary Russell Mitford's *Charles the First*.

The letters exchanged between the examiner and the comptroller or Lord Chamberlain form the core of this chapter. This official correspondence is glossed by additional letters circulated between the examiner and a range of recipients: theatre managers, playwrights and outraged members of the public. These texts offer invaluable insights into particular responses to plays and the examiner's reasons for requesting alterations. For instance, a letter from Ponsonby provides unique evidence to prove that there were political reasons to prohibit *War*, which was planned for performance at the Surrey Theatre in August 1870. Another letter, in which a theatre manager vehemently denied the performance of the can-can, exposes the examiner's attempts at censoring dance. Yet another records an impassioned appeal from a member of the Fulham Branch of the National Vigilance Association that the Lord Chamberlain should investigate a theatre manager for breaching rules of decency and nudity.[24]

The examiners' mode of reading can also be deduced by looking at the British Library's collection of plays for the period. Notes on the title pages and in the margins, and even the increasingly wrathful range of squiggles and exclamation marks made in pencil or in red ink according to the examiner's fancy, flesh out the process of censorship. Further insights into the examiners' reading styles can be gleaned from contemporary parliamentary reports on the theatre. During these investigations successive examiners were questioned about their decisions on individual plays: in 1832, for example, we find a record of Colman's explanation of his treatment of *Charles the First*; in 1866 Donne describes the principles governing his treatment of pantomime, and in 1892 Pigott superbly delivers himself of his interpretations of Ibsen.

The final source for investigation of examiners' reading processes can be found in the prefaces of plays, particularly those that fell foul of the censor. Shee's preface to *Alasco* and Shaw's 1902 'Author's apology' for *Mrs Warren's Profession* (1894) lie at opposite ends of the period covered in this chapter but each couple highly coloured representations of the examiner's reading with references to otherwise unrecorded exchanges between author, manager and censor. If, as in the case of *Mrs Warren's Profession*'s first outing to St James's Palace, we rely solely on the examiner's note that the play was read, we lose the preface's reference to Redford's generous offer to attempt to forget the experience of that first reading if Shaw chose to submit a revised version later.[25]

Taken together, daybook entries, correspondence, marginalia, parliamentary reports and prefaces enable an attempt at creating a form of readers' report for certain nineteenth-century plays. The material may not be so neatly presented as twentieth-century reports, but cumulatively it offers an insight into the examiner's reading process. This insight benefits from the fact that it derives from multiple accounts of the examiner's response to particular plays. What the examiner emphasized when explaining a decision to the Lord Chamberlain can often differ dramatically from the reasons he gave when explaining himself to the theatre manager, playwright or to more or less hostile members of a parliamentary Select Committee. The reports that can be constructed from these sources record the examiners' attempts at diplomacy, rebuke and vindication. Unlike the later readers' reports, they also shed light on the strategies used by examiners to retreat from or consolidate the validity of their first interpretations of the plays they encountered. The next section of this chapter sets about constructing readers' reports from the array of material available. It cites two instances when George Colman, the examiner most noted for report-writing, articulated his interpretation of plays for a range of audiences.

The plays chosen for closer scrutiny, Shee's *Alasco* and Mitford's *Charles the First*, are well-known staging posts in nineteenth-century theatre history. Colman suggested such vigorous changes to the former that Shee withdrew his play from the licensing process in a rage. The Lord Chamberlain prohibited the latter. The texts that describe Colman's reading of these plays, and the response these texts elicited, are collated from a number of sources, but they bring us as close as it is possible to get to a nineteenth-century reader's report.

Reconstructing readers' reports: *Alasco* and *Charles the First*

In the absence of Colman's précis of *Alasco*, the fullest account of the examiner's reading of the play appears in his letter to Sir William Knighton.[26] The very fact that Knighton had requested an explanation of Colman's decision about a play by an unknown playwright is significant given that he was the king's private secretary. As there is no evidence that Knighton wrote a similar letter to the Lord Chamberlain, his request for an explanation firmly characterizes the examiner as solely responsible for the furore, a charge that Colman vehemently sought to deny later in his career.[27]

Colman's response to Knighton's request for information reads:

> Mr Colman presents his compliments to Sir William Knighton, and is much gratified by Sir William having expressed a wish to see his short remarks on *Alasco*, a copy of which he has the pleasure to enclose. [Remarks missing] Although the ferment of the times has greatly subsided, still plays which are built upon conspiracies and attempts to revolutionize a state stand upon ticklish ground and the proposed performance of such plays is to be contemplated with more jealousy when they pourtray [sic] the disaffected as gallant heroes and hapless lovers. Thus drawn *ad captandum vulgus*, their showy qualities and tender distresses of the heart throw a dazzle and an interest round their sedition, while they preach up the doctrine that government is tyranny and that revolt is virtue and that rebels are the righteous.
>
> Alasco, in the tragedy of the same name, is a character of the above description and Walsingham is set up against him as a contrast whenever these two meet. There is an effusion of claptrap sentiments between them, in the alternate expression of loyalty and radicalism; and they prove in a pro and con dialogue, vying with each other speech for speech by turns like a couple of contending swains in an eclogue. In respect to their good and evil influence over an audience they are the bane and antidote of the tragedy; and from a tragedy that needs so much counter-poison, for the chance only of neutralizing its arsenic, the deducement to be made as to its dangerous tendency is very obvious.
>
> It is my opinion that the objections against acting this play may be removed by the erasures which I have made; in which, should the managers think proper to acquiesce, I will (at their altering the manuscript and again placing it in my hands) submit the play to the Lord Chamberlain for his licence.[28]

Colman's letter to Knighton confirms that he recognized in Shee's play a parallel with the contemporary political situation, even if he seems to suggest that the point of reference may no longer be as obvious as it once might have been. He may have simply objected to Shee's characterization of Prussia, Britain's ally during the Napoleonic war, as the tyrannical oppressor of Alasco's Poland, but, as the reviewer for *Blackwood's Magazine* suggested, it is more likely that Colman thought the play's themes referred too pointedly to the current state of Anglo-Irish relations.[29] Certainly Covent Garden's stage manager George Bartley was not surprised at the examiner's lengthy list of omissions in *Alasco* as: 'there were some strong political allusions contained in it, and there were some political events then pending which that play bore upon, and when I read it, the impression upon my mind was that I did not wonder the licence had been refused'.[30]

Colman's letter goes beyond the simple identification of historical context. He is explicit about why he finds these allusions subversive. For Knighton's benefit he specifies the dangers attached to Shee's effort to court sympathy for Alasco's political agenda. He points to the particular 'dazzle' of the character, the adeptness of his speech in comparison with the more dour Walsingham and the 'effusion' of Alasco's 'claptrap sentiments'. In effect, Colman not only parades before Knighton what he sees as his sophisticated and necessary art of paranoid play reading, he also leaves the king's secretary in no doubt that Shee intends the most 'ticklish' of these readings.

Colman's representation of Shee as subversive, a reading which the author vehemently denies in his lugubrious protestations of patriotism, honour and Britishness in the footnotes of his published play,[31] serves another purpose. It directs the responsibility for *Alasco*'s fate elsewhere. By reminding Knighton that he has simply suggested cuts rather than banning the play outright, Colman draws attention to Shee's response, which was to refuse this customary 'socialization' of his text and to withdraw his play from Covent Garden's rehearsals. Colman thus neutralizes Shee's careful representation of himself as a victim and emphasizes his own flexibility and generosity in offering to see a revised version of the play. He also astutely reminds Knighton that it is the Lord Chamberlain rather than himself who ultimately decides the fate of individual plays: 'I will (at their altering the manuscript and again placing it in my hands) submit the play to the Lord Chamberlain for his licence.'

Colman's representation of the roles played by himself, Shee and the Lord Chamberlain in determining *Alasco*'s fate is further illuminated by the Lord Chamberlain's own correspondence with the dissatisfied playwright. This letter appears in Shee's preface to *Alasco*, thereby adding to the impression that the entire published edition was designed not only as a monument to the author's outraged dignity, but also as an archive of Shee's dispute with censorship. Despite the Lord Chamberlain's apparent unwillingness to intercede on Colman's behalf during Knighton's enquiry into the play's treatment, he responded to Shee's request for further explanation. Unlike Colman, who examined the specific dangers of Shee's play, the Lord Chamberlain contents himself with a more general expression of *Alasco*'s subversiveness:

Thinking Mr Colman a very sufficient judge of his duty, and as I agree in his conclusion (from the account he has given me of the tragedy called *Alasco*) I do conclude that at this time, without considerable omissions, the tragedy should not be acted; and whilst I am persuaded that your intentions are upright, I conceive that it is precisely for this reason (though it may not strike Authors) that it has been the wisdom of the legislature to have an Examiner appointed and power given to the Chamberlain of the Household to judge whether certain plays should be acted at all, or not acted at particular times.

I do not mean to enter into an argument with you Sir, on the subject; but think that your letter, conceived in polite terms to me, calls upon me to return an answer, shewing that your tragedy has been well considered.[32]

Disconcertingly, the Lord Chamberlain's letter reads like a straight-faced version of lofty officialdom satirized by Samuel Johnson in his *Compleat vindication of the Licensers of the stage*: 'Is it for a Poet to demand a Licenser's reason for his proceedings? Is he not rather to acquiesce in the Decision of Authority, and conclude that there are Reasons which he cannot Comprehend?'[33] In accordance with such principles, Montrose informed Shee that he had breached the etiquette of play licensing by writing a play such as *Alasco* and by questioning the examiner's decision. He assured Shee that the problems unravelled by the censors are too profound for a playwright to understand on a case-by-case basis, and that censorship is instituted to protect the body politic from the infections that even unwitting or 'upright' playwrights might introduce. Montrose reminded Shee that it was unusual for any author to involve him or herself in a play's censorship, and pointed out more particularly that Shee transgressed his status as playwright by appealing, however politely, to the Lord Chamberlain.[34]

When read alongside the observations made by Shee, a reviewer and Covent Garden's stage manager, Colman's and the Lord Chamberlain's letters construct an account of the play's censorship that approximates a British Library file on a twentieth-century play. What this material fails to record, however, is the fact that the extensive analysis of *Alasco*'s appropriateness for performance did not prevent it from being staged in London. The gap in the Lord Chamberlain's jurisdiction over non-patent theatres, that is, all those other than Drury Lane, Covent Garden and the Haymarket, meant that Shee was able to see his play staged at one of the so-called 'illegitimate' playhouses. *Alasco* was performed at the Surrey Theatre in April 1824, a fact that irked Covent Garden's stage manager almost a decade later:

You have never been able to get over the strong instance of *Alasco*? – Yes, that renders it a hard case on the patent theatres, that while they conform to what they understand to be the laws of the country, and while they pay every attention to the dictation of the higher powers, a minor theatre will start up like the Coburg theatre and get a licence; and yet that theatre, on a play being published, can take that play and act it, in defiance of the patent theatres, the Lord Chamberlain and his licenser.[35]

The only other example of texts that can, when collated, parallel the insights produced by twentieth-century readers' reports, relates to Mitford's historical tragedy *Charles the First*. Unlike *Alasco*, this play was prohibited outright by the Lord

Chamberlain,[36] although it too was subsequently staged without his permission at one of the illegitimate theatres.[37] In this case the primary record of the examiner's reading of the play comes in Colman's letter to Montrose, in which he asks for the Lord Chamberlain's advice on whether the play should be licensed.

My Lord,

As a point of duty, I forward the enclosed form of license; but it will surprise me if your Grace should think proper to sign it. It refers to a Play the very title of which – *Charles the First* (of England) – brings instantly to mind the violent commotions and catastrophes of that unhappy monarch's reign, and, in following closely the historical facts previous to his death, the dramatis personae (as far as Cromwell and his adherents are concerned) exhibit the fanatical manners and utter all the puritanical cant [common] in their times. – Consequently, the Piece abounds (blasphemously I think) with scriptural allusions and quotations and the name of the Almighty is introduced and invoked over and over again by the hypocrites and regicides.

If it be in keeping thus to delineate the morals and religion of the Cromwell party, the political part of this dialogue is, by the same rule, dramatical; more insulting to Charles in particular, and to the Monarchy in general.

I submit an outline of the play giving its prospective conduct, Act by Act. [Outline missing]

I think this can be but an impartial opinion upon the nature of this Drama. At all events, I certainly cannot assure to the Lord Chamberlain that 'it does not contain anything immoral or otherwise improper for the stage'.[38]

This letter suggests that Colman was primarily concerned with the play's 'immorality'; its frequent allusions to God and to the scriptures. As is well known, these faults alone could be enough to alienate many a nineteenth-century examiner. However, Colman's other letters and his later response to the 1832 Select Committee place his anxieties elsewhere, for although Mitford's play stops short of representing the actual act of execution onstage, it comes dangerously close to it. Act V scene ii is set in '*The banqueting house at Whitehall, glass folding doors opening to the Scaffold which is covered with black. The block, axe &c, visible*'. After the king is led away his queen rushes onstage and treats her audience to her tortured vision of what is taking place offstage: 'They murder him; the axe falls on his neck; / The blood comes plashing; —'.[39] At the time, Colman merely warned the theatre manager seeking the play's licence that it had been sent to the Lord Chamberlain to consider 'the propriety of licensing the representation of a Drama so peculiar in title and incidents.'[40] Subsequently he observed that *Charles the First* 'amounted to everything but cutting off the King's head onstage'.[41]

However much Colman may have elided the fact in his various letters about *Charles the First*, it is clear that his primary concern was not that the play was blasphemous, but that it dramatized regicide at a time when many were deeply disenchanted with George IV. This certainly seemed to have been John Payne Collier's reading of the motive for banning the play: 'The reason why the license was refused for *Charles the First* I suppose (not knowing anything decisively of the fact) was, because there was something in the state of the times, a disposition to think lightly of the authority of Kings, or some public feeling of that kind, which rendered it then objectionable.'[42]

Colman's initial letter to Montrose appears to have been written with the aim of providing the Lord Chamberlain with a different reason for prohibiting the play. By citing its blasphemies, Colman perhaps sought to avoid referring openly to its allusions to criticisms of the king. Montrose appears to have had little time for such tact: '[I] cannot think that it is fit for representation on the stage; more I think it not necessary to say.'[43] Taking his cue from Montrose, Colman's subsequent letter to the theatre manager adopted a similar tone of irritation: 'I have less regret in communicating this intelligence [the play's prohibition] as I think you might have anticipated it; and when there could have been little hope of permission there can be little disappointment in a refusal.'[44]

Although Mitford's private correspondence reveals that she was aware that she was embarking on a perilous project in producing a play about Charles I,[45] she sought further illumination about the examiner's decision once the prohibition was announced. Unlike Shee, Mitford was alert to the importance of etiquette, so she persuaded a friend to elicit further information from Colman on her behalf. She reproduced Colman's response in her own correspondence with Revd William Harness:

> I followed your advice and requested Mr Rowland Stephenson to ask Mr Colman if *Charles* could not be altered so as to be made licensable, and today's post brought me a packet from Mrs Stephenson enclosing the following from Mr Colman to her brother in law …

> My dear Sir,

> … My official opinion of her tragedy is certainly unfavourable to the author's interests. I was however so far from wishing it to prejudice the Lord Chamberlain that the play was submitted to his perusal at my suggestion. He therefore formed his own judgement upon it and decidedly refused to license its performance.

> As to alterations – the fact is that the subject of this play and the incidents it embraces are fatal in themselves – they are an inherent and incurable disease – the morbid matter lies in the very bones and marrow of the historical facts and defies eradication. Indeed it would be a kind of practical bull to permit a detailed representation of Charles's unhappy story on the public stage when his martyrdom is still observed in such solemn silence that the London theatres are actually closed and all dramatic exhibition whatever suspended on its anniversary.

> I give Miss Mitford full credit for the harmlessness of her intentions but mischief may be unconsciously done, as a house may be set on fire by a little innocent in the nursery …

At the close of this transcribed letter, Mitford observed, 'Now, is this not a precious *morceau*?'[46]

Colman's explanation of his motive for banning *Charles the First* is significant for its abandonment of any pretence that the fate of the play could be laid at the door of its blasphemy or 'immorality'. However much Colman may have pointed out the contradiction of a theatre staging Charles I's death on one night and closing in honour of his memory the next, it was the fact that the play dealt with the history of this murdered king that disbarred it from performance. His letter to Mitford's friend reveals that Colman was astonished that any playwright should dramatize Charles I's execution. In fact, such was the audacity of Mitford's play that it encouraged Colman to embark on what appears to have been a rare course of research to check whether hers was the first attempt to dramatize the regicide. On the back of a page of the licensing script, Colman cites the *Biographica Dramatica*'s reference to an earlier version, noting: 'It is to be remembered that the above play was acted before the Lord Chamberlain's control over drama was established by the Act of George II.'[47] Had Colman researched further he would have realized that this earlier version was one of the two scurrilous plays whose production Lord Chesterfield lamented in his speech against the proposed Licensing Bill in 1737. Like Mitford's, this version caused considerable offence by drawing parallels between Charles and the reigning monarch, George II.

> There have but very lately been two plays acted which one would have thought should have given the greatest offence . . . In [*King Charles the First, a tragedy*], a most tragical story was brought upon the stage, a catastrophe too recent, too melancholy, and of too solemn a nature to be heard of anywhere but from the pulpit. How these pieces came to pass unpunished I do not know; if I am rightly informed, it was not for want of law, but for want of prosecution, without which no law can be made effectual. But if there was any neglect in this case, I am convinced it was not with a design to prepare the minds of the people, and make them think a new law necessary.[48]

Had Colman been aware that there was an historical precedent for finding theatrical representations of regicide unsavoury, he might have been less cautious in stating his reasons for refusing to license the play.

Like the material that glosses Colman's interpretation of *Alasco*, the letters that passed between the examiner, Lord Chamberlain, theatre manager and playwright on the subject of *Charles the First* can be read as a proxy reader's report of the play. The remainder of this chapter, however, deals with more piecemeal responses. Accordingly the close reading of individual plays must be exchanged for a broader view of the examiners' interpretations of nineteenth-century drama. This work does not parallel the detailed responses given to twentieth-century theatre by its official readers, but in sifting through the material that critiques the plays, it provides an insight into the characteristics of the examiners' responses to nineteenth-century theatre.

Much existing scholarship on nineteenth-century censorship has concentrated either on the examination of well-known or notorious plays performed professionally in the capital, such as *Jack Sheppard*, *Oliver Twist* and plays by Ibsen,

Wilde and Shaw,[49] or on the practice of particular censors, with William Bodham Donne emerging as a particularly rewarding source of study.[50] This chapter is intended as a complement to this scholarship. It concentrates instead on the censorship of less familiar works produced around the country during the tenure of all six examiners working in the 1824–1901 period. It also shifts attention away from plays that were prohibited or aggressively censored, looking instead at the piecemeal 'eternal interference' of examiners. It thus focuses on the different examiners and their methods of reshaping plays according to their own idea of what was appropriate for the nineteenth-century stage.[51]

With six volumes of daybooks, marginalia, correspondence and parliamentary evidence to scour, the job of surveying examiners' responses to nineteenth-century plays would be difficult without the formulation of a framework for analysis. The study that follows is predicated on the material that each examiner found to be objectionable. Some examiners were anxious about suppressing allusions to current events, and others sought to prevent satire on well-known institutions. Some worried about protecting actors and audiences from dangerous stage effects and others paid little attention to the plays in performance. All were concerned to varying degrees with political allusions, references to real people and crimes, blasphemies, indecencies and lewdness. By collating the censorship of this material it becomes possible to make sense of how different examiners read the plays they censored.

What follows, then, is structured according to a typology of examiners' responses. Like all surveys based on typologies, the examination produced contains flaws. Some reports record acts of censorship that fall outside the parameters of the research. For instance, plays could be censored simply because it was decided that the Lord Chamberlain's Office should make a stand against bad playwriting. As Ponsonby observed to Donne after reading *The Wrath's Whirlwind* (1853): 'a license should be refused in the case of *The Wrath's Whirlwind* as it is highly desirable to elevate the tone of the drama and it is specially necessary in the case of the saloons to prevent as much as possible the representation of any pieces which have a tendency to lower the morals and excite the passions of the classes who frequent these places of resort'.[52] Such comments, which fall outside the normal rules governing examiners' decisions, expose the latitude with which censors could approach their work. They also indicate why the theatrical community found it so difficult to anticipate the fate of the plays they submitted to the Lord Chamberlain's Office. The other main difficulty with organising the examiners' responses according to this typology emerges when plays fall into more than one category. The examiner's stern prohibition of allusions to Queen Victoria's thighs in *Girolfe Girolfa* (1874), for example, could appear comfortably either amongst the 'reference to real people' plays, or in the 'indecent dramas' collection.[53]

Nevertheless, reading the daybooks, correspondence and other resources with this typology in mind helps to clarify the shape of examiners' responses to nineteenth-century plays. What follows is intended as an examination of the censor's process of play reading that takes account of changing perceptions of what was and was not appropriate for performance at different points in the nineteenth century. Yet, as becomes clear, the nineteenth-century theatre's ability to circumvent and even ignore the examiners' carefully penned objections to certain plays must also be considered. Thus the final part of this chapter acknowledges the alternative history of nineteenth-century censorship. It will look not just at the predilection of pre-1843 illegitimate theatres and post-1843 music halls for staging unlicensed pieces, but also at the other modes of suppression instituted by both government and theatre managers to contain subversive activity.

Examiners' responses

Standing upon ticklish ground: political allusions

The appropriateness and frequency of political allusions in nineteenth-century plays was much disputed during the period. Speaking as the theatre manager involved in attempts to stage *Alasco* and *Charles the First*, the future examiner Charles Kemble glumly observed that censors seemed to be primarily concerned with seeking out political nuance.[54] In 1883, however, Kemble's assumption was contradicted when Pigott actively played down the association between censorship and the suppression of political commentary. In a memorandum written to brief anyone likely to face questions about the principles or practice of censorship, Pigott produced a skewed version of its history by describing the political plays of the early eighteenth century as being merely the 'somewhat trivial incident' which led to the Licensing Act;[55] he claimed instead that from the outset the censor's real role was to preserve the dignity and morality of the stage.[56]

The nineteenth century also saw corresponding shifts in the examiner's interpretation of what constituted unacceptable political references. Where Colman in 1832 defined as such 'anything that may be so allusive to the times as to be applied to the existing moment and which is likely to be inflammatory', sixty years later Pigott had trained his eye to notice only those that were 'disloyal'.[57] Furthermore, it appears that examiners working in this period sought to suggest either that such allusions were on the wane or that censors were more indulgent towards them. Donne remarked that at the outset of his association with the Lord Chamberlain's Office he cut political allusions 'frequently', but by 1866 there had been 'not many lately' to catch his eye. By 1892, Pigott coolly suggested that the need to censor political commentary even in pantomimes was now 'a thing of the past'.[58]

Whatever the shifts of policy underway in St James's Palace, other commentators raised doubts about whether examiners were able to suppress political allusions even if they wanted to. In 1832 Thomas Morton appropriated the French audience's technique of locating 'applications'[59] for the British when he asserted that no censor could be expected to predict the audience's process of interpreting a play topically:

> I think it is worthwhile to remark, I am sure every playgoer would agree with me, that there is a tendency in the audience to force passages never meant by the author into

political meanings . . . There are two recent instances to show the danger of a theatre being a place for political discussion. The first I will mention is the visit His Majesty paid to the theatre soon after his accession to the throne, and when the Revolution of Paris broke out. Immediately it was known His Majesty commanded *Masaniello*, handbills were printed about the town to induce the public to assemble in the theatre, not to partake with His Majesty in the social enjoyment of the drama, but to teach him, through the story of Masaniello, the danger to his throne if he disobeyed the wish of his people, and the King was advised to change the play in consequence of that.[60]

The examination of Colman's daybook and the licensing copy of *Masaniello* certainly indicates that he did not anticipate this response to the play. The lack of any notes in the daybook entry suggests that he licensed the play without qualms, and although there are numerous pencil and ink squiggles on the licensing script, these appear to be notes marking up the play for production at Drury Lane rather than records of Colman's censorship.[61]

As the century progressed, the account of political cuts in the daybooks begins to look very different from the considered critiques of subversiveness written by Colman about *Alasco* and *Charles the First*. Concerns about 'applications' and parallels are rarely articulated in the daybooks. Instead 'political' cuts revolve around explicit references to particular situations. Donne, for instance, notes that the lines 'Talking of Parks my night there has been a tried one / But I have found my way there, that was a Hyde one' should be omitted from the performance of *Harlequin Cock Robin and the Children at the Wood* (1866), clearly believing that the playwright intended a reference to the recent Hyde Park riots. Although there is a corresponding mark for a cut in the licensing script, there is no evidence that Donne addressed himself further to the interpretation of the play's topicality.[62] He is similarly brief in refusing to allow the New Adelphi Theatre in Liverpool to perform *The Last Slave*, but it is not until he added a note to the entry in 1867 that the reasons for his concern are made clear: 'A license can now be granted in consequence of a change in American affairs.'[63] Perhaps the most ironic of the political cuts recorded in the daybooks can be found in Donne's entry for a one-act burlesque, *William Tell*, performed at the Strand theatre in 1857. Noting that the play's 'political allusions are inadmissible and quite out of place on the stage', Donne recorded his excision of the hero's promise that he will:

> follow the Debates – watch every Bill
> They smuggle through our Liberties to kill;
> Scan o'er the estimates with careful Eye,
> And when the Imbeciles who make our Laws
> For Insurrection give us valid cause
> This Life preserve to some trusty friend
> By parcels company prepaid we'll send.[64]

Unsurprisingly Donne offers no acknowledgement of the comedy inherent in his decision to cut William's determination to safeguard his 'liberties'.

These meagre references to topical allusions do not indicate the full range of the examiners' work in rendering plays appropriate for the nineteenth-century stage. The 1872 furore over political references in pantomime alone, discussed in Chapter 1 above, suggests that Donne at least was more zealous than the daybooks imply. In fact, what is most surprising about the evidence of the daybooks is the extent to which plays that we view as highly politicized passed through the examiners' hands without eliciting more commentary or censorship. One explanation for this is provided by Colman in 1832. Citing his advice to a theatre manager that he should cut the word 'reform' in a play if he wished to avoid 'a hubbub', Colman revealed an unexpectedly superficial search for the 'inflammatory'. By confining himself to cautioning against certain vocabulary, Colman displays a startling failure to acknowledge that a play featuring the word 'reform' might register political nuance on a deeper level.[65]

The historicist bent of much that has been written about nineteenth-century theatre has uncovered numerous instances of overt and covert political commentary both in melodramas and in other kinds of play,[66] but the evidence of the daybooks suggests that in some cases the examiners' first realization of this may have come from reading reviews of plays in performance, or from receiving letters from concerned members of the public.[67] Such a conclusion may seem to say more about the material written into the daybooks than the examiners' reading processes, but these texts nevertheless show the censors' tendency to record only their response to specific and explicit political allusions. This tendency is nowhere more apparent than in plays that introduce references to, and even personifications of, a 'living person' on stage.

Plays referring to 'living persons'

Given the notoriety of the highly satirical dramatic portraits of Walpole and the monarchy shortly before the passing of the Licensing Act, it is not surprising to see the pressure placed on examiners to check plays for personal allusions. In 1737, however, Lord Chesterfield argued that the dramatization of living persons on stage represented one of his main concerns about the proposed Licensing Act. He warned in his speech to the House of Lords that:

> the person against whom the application is made will think himself injured and will, at least privately, resent it: at present this resentment can be directed only against the author; but when an author's play appears with my Lord Chamberlain's passport, every such resentment will be turned from the author and pointed directly against the Lord Chamberlain!

Chesterfield may have been unsuccessful in convincing Parliament to reject the Licensing Bill on these grounds, but his concerns appear to have communicated themselves to subsequent Lords Chamberlain. Their anxiety is best demonstrated in the care taken to cut references to the royal family. A sample of the deletion of royal allusions recorded in one daybook alone, ms. 53703, indicate the censor's removal of simple references, *The Betting Boys from the Counting House to the Hulks* (p. 19), *The Charade* (p. 45); inappropriate comic business, as in *Jack and Jill* when Harlequin conjures a fully grown uniformed Prince of Wales from inside a large nut (p. 247); and even the overblown expressions of patriotism in *The Horse Will Be Sold to Pay the Expenses* (p. 289). Indeed, the policing of references to any real person became so embedded in the process of nineteenth-century censorship that general cautions were written into the annual licences issued to theatre managers: 'No offensive person or representation of living persons, nor anything calculated to produce riot or a breach of the peace.'[68] Despite this, numerous plays that made explicit references to living people still reached the censor, and examiners routinely recorded their excision of references in weary tones: 'To represent a member of the British embassy at St Petersburg as a secret leader of the Nihilist conspiracy is obviously a scandalous inconvenience not excusable on the grounds of its absurdity';[69] 'The name Lord Hatherby, this being the title of the Lord Chancellor of England, must be exchanged for some other; especially as the Lord Hatherby in this drama is a card sharper';[70] 'All mention of and all representation of Miss Nightingale and her companions must be omitted . . . Miss Nightingale is wholly out of place and improper in pantomime business'.[71]

The most notorious example of the clash between censors and the theatre over references to living persons comes not from the daybooks but from newspaper reports that recorded the examiner's failure to anticipate the introduction of caricatures of leading politicians on the stage. Gilbert's *The Happy Land* (1873), which featured three actors made up to resemble Gladstone, Ayrton and Lowe, produced an example of post-performance censorship. The play exposed not just Donne's naive reading of the play but also the manager's failure to submit a true written copy of the planned production.[72] The incident was so embarrassing to the censor that in a contemporary illustration of Donne at work, the appearance of a poster for *The Happy Land* was enough to suggest the irony of the central sign, 'Ye Great Censor' (see Figure 3 (p. 40)).[73]

In addition to day-to-day allusions to well-known figures, both daybooks and correspondence suggest that examiners were galvanized to closer scrutiny by newspaper reporting of *cause célèbre* cases. In July 1871, for example, Donne wrote a letter to the Lord Chamberlain alluding to what appears to be one of a tranche of plays dealing with Roger Tichborne. Having travelled from Australia to England to argue that he had not been drowned at sea, the so-called 'Tichborne Claimant' launched a court bid to restore himself to his position as the rightful owner of an extensive property, much to the dismay of the unconvinced majority of his family. On reading a farce called *Disguises*, Donne wrote to Viscount Sydney:

> . . . I entertain a great objection to a considerable portion of its contents. In the cadre of some older farce is inserted a kind of parody of the Tichborne case.
>
>   A court of justice with accompaniments – Judge, Jury, barrister etc. is put on the stage – and that has been done before on many occasions – but the drift of the piece

3. 'The Censor at Work'; illustration of William Bodham Donne surrounded by the memorabilia of censored plays.

is to represent the late forensic duel between the Solicitor General and the claimants under a broadly comic light . . .

There is nothing in *Disguises* immoral in the ordinary sense of the word. But in my opinion amusement should not be extracted from an undecided case – a very momentous one to the parties concerned in the final verdict – and moreover I doubt whether too close a parody of the forms of court is altogether wholesome for audiences.[74]

When collated with entries for other Tichborne related plays, Donne's response to *Disguises* reveals that there was something about this play that he found particularly reprehensible. His concerns are not evident elsewhere. The manager of the Grecian theatre was informed that *Sick or Good out of Evil* (1871) would be licensed as long as it heeded Donne's warning: 'It will be advisable wherever the name "Australia" occurs to substitute for it some other word, Indiana or Illinois for example', and a year later the Pavilion's manager was informed that his play would be passed if he replaced all allusions to Tichborne with the phrase 'the Claimant'.[75] The licensing copy of *Harlequin Hop o' My Thumb* (1872) confirms that once again the examiner was concentrating only on the more obvious allusions to the case. He missed other numerous references to it in the play, including the allusion to Hop's 'form so monstrous', which referred to the radical difference in size between the slight Tichborne youth and the enormously fat Claimant. Donne also left untouched the play's references to the fact that Hop came from the East End, as did Arthur Orton, the person many suspected the Claimant to be; and he also overlooked the scene in which Hop's mother fails to recognize him, a dramatic moment which alluded to the courtroom's astonishment on being told that Tichborne's late mother had accepted the Claimant as her son.[76]

It seems that *Disguises* stood out from these plays not simply because it was performed at a critical moment in the Tichborne trial, but because it brought the trial onstage.[77] In common with other nineteenth-century examiners, Donne's anxiety about the theatre's ability to sway public opinion clearly increased when there was a possibility that the processes of law might be affected.

Plays to do with crime

> The prison inspectors alluded to the existence of the number of minor theatres in Liverpool . . . They found that several youthful criminals ascribed to these low theatrical representations their first initiation into crime. M.S. aged 18 states, 'I have been eight times in prison and twice discharged. I cannot tell how many times I have been at the Sanspareil, I have been there so often. I have seen *Jack Sheppard* performed, and am sure, if anything, it encouraged me to greater crimes. I thought that part the best where he robbed his master and mistress.'[78]

The much-discussed concern that theatres had become schoolrooms for criminals may have peaked during the mid nineteenth century,[79] but examiners continued to be careful when they encountered references to crimes and court cases. The daybook entries for *Achora Maetree* (1867) and *Hearts* (1883) indicate that examiners were concerned about references to courtroom business, particularly when it referred to announcements of the death penalty. 'Omit stage business of Judge putting on black cap and the words of the sentence "and may the Lord have mercy on your soul", Pigott requested in 1883.[80] The examiners offered no explanation for such cuts, but further research into some of their decisions reveals that there were times when it simply became inappropriate to acknowledge the undeniable theatricality of courtroom business, or to hold up its workings to wider public scrutiny. This is best illustrated by *Eliza Fenning, or the Victim of Circumstance* (1855), the play that recounted the true story of the execution of Eliza, a maid accused of poisoning her employers. Given the public doubt over the safety of Eliza's conviction and the appropriation of her case by those championing the abolition of capital punishment, it is hardly surprising that the examiner noted that 'there must be no representation of an execution on the stage' in the daybook entry for this play.[81]

Although references to execution, court cases and pickpocketing were routinely deleted, licences for plays dealing with murders were refused outright. In response to a request for advice about three murder plays submitted in 1844, the Lord Chamberlain expostulated: 'I confess I am astonished at the *audacity* of the managers . . . in soliciting a License for *Such Pieces*. Pray have the goodness to take the necessary steps to prevent the performance of the same.'[82] Later in the century the Lord Chamberlain Viscount Sydney gave a more detailed explanation of the official reasons for censoring murder plays. Thirty years after the illegitimate plays based on the notorious Weare murder of 1823 nearly caused a miscarriage of justice, the Lord Chamberlain found himself confronted with another play from the same stable, *The Gypsy of Edgware* (1862). In response to a letter from Donne requesting advice, Sydney wrote:

All such representations of recent murder on the stage appear to me to be very undesirable. It only gives the Public a morbid feeling and encourages mischievous ideas in their minds. The manager I think should be warned not to submit this style of play especially as in this case there is scarcely any disguise of the Thurtell and Weare murder.[83]

Although the Lords Chamberlain expressed serious concerns about the dangers of staging or reviving crimes and their punishment in the theatre, their anxiety about the 'morbid feelings' and 'mischievous ideas' of the public was piqued when they encountered the dangers inherent in other kinds of plays.

Home truths and dangerous effects

The extension of the examiners' duties to include safety checks on theatres licensed in the capital in 1857 seems to have alerted censors to the potential for danger lurking in numerous nineteenth-century plays. Pigott's nervous note, 'It is to be distinctly understood that there is to be no vitriol throwing', is one of several cautions issued by nineteenth-century examiners against dangerous onstage effects.[84] In 1866 Spencer Ponsonby told a shocked Select Committee that since a man had been killed by a lion during a performance at Astley's Theatre, the Lord Chamberlain had decided to withhold licences for any further exhibitions of 'wild animals' on the stage. Despite the end of this lively tradition of nineteenth-century performance and the Committee's plaintive question, 'Wild beasts are not allowed now?',[85] playwrights and managers continued to introduce effects likely to cause injuries and incite 'mischievous ideas' in the audience.

In 1877 Pigott expressed understandable concern about a shooting stunt in *Bob Bretton; the Dead Shot of the Bush*:

BOB: Hang up that piece of wood (*he points to prepared wood on ground*) over there. (*She does so. He loads*) Now take the sword and I will endeavour to split the bullet against the edge – Hold it horizontally across the wood – the edge towards me – Now if I divide the bullet there will be two holes in the wood. Steady . . . (*fires and two holes seen in the wood*).

Plainly unconvinced by the licensing copy's explanatory note that 'The wood is prepared for hanging – two holes are bored through with two pieces of wire', Pigott requested that the entire stunt should be omitted in representation.[86]

Fears about the physical safety of performers and audiences extended to a more politicized anxiety about the theatre's ability to damage the reputation of key social institutions. Some of the lengthiest entries in the daybooks are devoted to plays that purport to expose wrongdoing in a particular profession, or that simply lambast certain institutions. In the late 1860s, for example, Donne not only rebuked the manager of the Marylebone Theatre for submitting a play that was highly critical of the guardians of workhouses, *The Casual Ward of Workhouse Life* (1866),[87] he also complained when the manager of the Royal Alfred requested a licence for its scurrilous attack on policemen, *Gulliver's Travels, or Harlequin Lilliput* (1869). Although Donne admitted in the latter case that some of the observations made about the dishonesty of policemen merely reflected contemporary concerns about the force, he refused to accept that such criticisms were appropriate for a Christmas pantomime. Having read Mrs Gulliver's lament that a simple stroll along a street would most likely end with her being arrested for a spurious crime and forced to listen to policemen 'commit honest-faced perjury' during her trial, Donne wrote to the manager: 'There may have been recently some cases of gross misconduct in policemen; but to stigmatise an entire body of public servants with habitual perjury passes the bounds of even pantomime satire, and is very unjust to the force generally.'[88]

Donne's admission that policemen in the 1860s provoked unforgivable satire is paralleled in 1884 by Pigott's acknowledgement that the 'eccentricity' of the Salvation Army could prompt inappropriate amusement. Thirty years before Shaw's *Major Barbara* (1905), the examiner leapt to the defence of the Salvation Army in his daybook entry for *Baffled* (1884):

> Omit in representation all allusions to the Salvation Army. It is not permissible to insult and vilify a considerable number of people who are perfectly well meaning and worthy of respect, however eccentric in some of their manifestations, by identifying them with a felon and a heartless hypocrite as in this piece. Nor is it desirable in the interests of the stage that the religious feelings of any portion of the public should be offended. Although the Blue Ribbon Army may be considered hostile to the trade of a publican, it is not desirable that a licensed theatre should be used as a platform for advocating intoxication and sneering at temperance. This pandering to vicious tastes and habits is a degradation of the stage.[89]

Pigott's commentary on the insult offered to the Salvation Army by the theatre comes close to being a report not only on *Baffled* but also on his sense of what was appropriate on the stage. To an extent, Donne's and Pigott's observations on the 'home truth' plays simply represent an extension of their responses to other aspects of the censors' work. Their notes to managers connect the attacks on professions, institutions and even 'philanthropists' to their work in seeking out allusions to living persons, but their critiques register one significant difference: rather than simply identifying the allusions, the examiners sought to contextualize the insult of the theatre's attack. Where Donne's remarks on *Gulliver's Travels* focused on a social wrong, Pigott's daybook criticism approaches *Baffled* on moral grounds.

Plays blasphemous, lewd and indecent

This chapter's earlier discussion of 'ticklish' political plays introduced the debate about whether censorship was formalized to combat politics or licentiousness. By 1883 there appears to have been no doubt in Pigott's mind that censorship, historically, was instituted to safeguard the morals of a vulnerable public from the scurrilous stage.[90] It would be a mistake to conclude that this emphasis on the protection of moral scruples was a late-nineteenth-century development, however. Each examiner may have had idiosyncratic responses to the need to protect audiences from the potential depravity of the theatre, but all paid attention to the blasphemous, lewd or indecent.

The daybooks' record of cuts of 'hell', 'damme', references to God and other kinds of swearing upholds criticisms of the examiners' practice of cutting plays and inserting safer alternatives. Indeed, in 1866 one member of the Select Committee, Mr Locke, proposed to Ponsonby that the censor's job had devolved to the point where he simply had 'the objectionable parts struck out and something more stupid put in'. 'That is a matter of opinion,' replied Ponsonby.[91] It is certain, though, that there were inconsistencies of practice in dealing with blasphemy. When examiners insisted that playwrights should replace 'God' with 'Heaven' it seemed strange that they later argued that: 'A scenic representation of heaven and the heavenly host would be calculated to shock the sensibilities of English audiences'.[92] Detractors keen to demonstrate the absurdity of censorship further seized on the 1832 Select Committee's ill-concealed mockery of Colman for finding 'angel' unacceptable, and the examiners' insistence that there was blasphemy even in phrases such as 'lamb to the slaughter' and 'judgement day'.[93] Only one examiner, Donne, seemed to appreciate that his practice as censor made him a hypocrite. In a letter to Fanny Kemble during the early 1870s when Donne was being attacked for being too scrupulous, he gloomily confided, 'Yesterday only eighteen letters! I began to swear terribly at the fifteenth and yet (hypocritically) I cut "d—ns" out of the plays!'[94]

The examiners' very different attitudes to censoring blasphemy may have been communicated only to parliamentary committees or to personal friends, but they were united in condemning the use of religious icons or Bible stories onstage. Yet the cluster of plays censored for using crucifixes, altars or religious statues as stage props suggests at once censorial implacability and odd reasoning. Donne's insistence on the omission of any such attempts at scene-setting throughout his career became more flexible in 1870 when he suggested an idiosyncratic distinction between the unacceptable 'ivory crucifix' that 'gives offence to many spectators' and the 'plain cross' which did not.[95] Pigott was much sterner. He notes in his entry for *Bella* (1879), 'Omit statue of the Virgin and stage direction (*lays pistol on pedestal, lights a cigarette and leans lazily against Helen*). There is no humour in blasphemy and it is not permissible to insult the Religious feelings of any portion of a mixed audience.'[96]

Taking care of the religious feelings of the audience was sometimes achieved only through compromise. In response to a plea from Donne in 1858 that a play based on the story of Judith and Holofernes might be licensed, Ponsonby wrote:

> The Lord Chamberlain . . . has come to the conclusion that he cannot grant the licence in question without rendering it almost impossible for him or any future Lord Chamberlain to refuse a licence to any play founded on any historical incident to be found in the Bible. It is true that in this case the story is taken from the Apocrypha and not actually from the Bible itself but his Lordship is of the opinion that in the minds of many the story is so closely . . . associated with the actual Bible that its representation on the stage would not fail to give offence while the enemies to the Stage would take advantage of the circumstance to say that profanity was now added to the immorality of the theatre.
>
> It is true again as you say that in foreign countries the plots for the stage are as frequently taken from the Bible as from other sources but the Lord Chamberlain cannot admit that that argument would avail in this country . . . He agrees with you however as to allowing as much liberty as possible to dramatic authors in the choice of their subjects and would regret much to deprive the Public of the opportunity of seeing Madame Ristori in a favourite play of which the plot is in no other way objectionable. He would therefore make no objection to the representation of Judith under some other name, the names of the Dramatis Personae also of course change . . . and His Lordship conceives that a story might without difficulty in History be found the main facts of which would tally with those of the story in question. He would not of course wish this to be publicly announced, but he desires me to request you to convey unofficially to the author of Judith . . . that while he must decline to licence a play founded on a Biblical story of Judith and Holofernes, he would not be unwilling to take into consideration a play the plot of which might closely resemble this story.[97]

This letter from Ponsonby is a revelation about the covert negotiations of censors. It demonstrates that on certain occasions, examiners wanted to bend the rules to license plays they thought valuable. In this case, as in the earlier case of *Myrrha* (1856) which John Mitchell Kemble had championed vehemently, the examiner's primary motive for wishing the play to be licensed appears to be his enthusiastic desire to see Ristori playing as many of her famous roles as possible in London.[98] With this in mind, Donne sketched out a series of defences for a positive decision from the Lord Chamberlain. He indulges in hair splitting in his argument that the story comes from the Apocrypha rather than the Bible; he calls upon the Lord Chamberlain's respect for dramatic writing in a plea for the artistic freedom of authors and actresses; and he characterizes the British as overly pious by pointing out that British censorship was out of step with European practice. Ponsonby's reply in contrast indicates what drove the Lord Chamberlain: a fear that his flexibility on one play might make a rod for the backs of his heirs, and concern that any sign of flexibility might give 'enemies of the stage' a better standpoint for criticizing his decisions.

The compromise offered in Ponsonby's letter is also instructive. That Ponsonby should advise a private conversation with the playwright and a hasty scouring of history to find an alternative 'story' indicates both official flexibility on the matter of blasphemy on the stage and its collusion in shaping plays so that they might appear appropriate for performance. What is similarly illuminating is Donne's private letter to Fanny Kemble in which he writes: 'to please the thick-skulled superstitious British public, I have been obliged to find [Ristori] a new name for the tragedy, and new titles for the characters . . . When shall we be wiser people?'[99]

Donne appears to have needed no such private outlet for his frustration with the censorship of lewdness. He was equally implacable on major and minor examples, although perhaps his decisions were variably effectual. He deletes the allusions to finger squeezing in *Bibb and Tucker Comedy* (1873), for example, but marks for omission only the actual struggle of an onstage attempted rape in *Mathilde and the Mulatto* (1861).[100] In his preoccupation with moments of physical contact, Donne leaves untouched the sound of Mathilde being locked in a room, the rapist's revelation that he has drugged her tea, 'before ten minutes you will be entirely at my mercy!', and the note observing that Mathilde *'grows languid'*.[101] The difference between what Donne found acceptable in *Mathilde* and in *Bibb and Tucker Comedy* therefore indicates that he saw lewdness only in inappropriate onstage touching; he saw nothing lewd in making entertainment out of the threat of sexual violence.

Policing indecency onstage was equally fraught with difficulty, not least because examiners disagreed over the stance they should take towards public morality. While Pigott believed this to lie at the heart of his duties, Redford earned himself a public remonstrance for claiming in 1900 that 'I am not in any sense a censor of morals.'[102] Most examiners shared concern over the indecency of costume, as the anxious measuring of the muse's skirt in Figure 3 above (p. 40) indicates. They deleted references to nightgowns and bedtime scenes, to unacceptably short ballet dresses, and to cross-dressing: 'the disguise is not necessary'.[103] Particular problems emerged when theatre managers attempted to put Lady Godiva on the stage. The fact that a stage illustration for the Astley's 1872 production of *Lady Godiva* appeared as the frontispiece of a periodical associated with pornography indicates the difficulties faced by examiners.[104] In 1890 the Lord Chamberlain was greeted with a letter from the National Vigilance Association complaining about Godiva's nudity at Sanger's Theatre.[105] Pigott had already cut portions of the play; his pencil marks can be seen in the margins of scene three 'TABLEAU. What the moon saw through the parted curtains of my Lady's chamber'. However, his failure to cut the later scene in which Godiva peeps round the edges of her curtains before making a naked dash for her horse provoked a hostile response.[106]

The greatest difficulties in checking plays for indecency occurred once London discovered its taste for the can-can.[107] In 1870 the *Observer* announced that 'British morality . . . has drawn the line at the cancan and we confess it was certainly high time that the line should be drawn somewhere'.[108] Yet examiners seeking to purge the theatre of the dance were forced to confine their pre-production activities to cutting explicit references to it.[109] Authors and managers capitalized on examiners' ignorance about dance to the point where, in 1871, the manager Charles Morton convinced the Lord Chamberlain that his informer was wrong in saying that his dancers were performing the cancan:

> The dance appears to have been described to your Lordship as the cancan but this is not the case – it is merely a dance introduced into Offenbach's opera bouffe *Genevieve* and is simply an exhibition of ballet dancing.[110]

The censors' difficulty in recognizing or preventing the performance of the cancan was also exploited at the music halls that lay beyond the Lord Chamberlain's control. In 1870 Frederick Strange, who had repeatedly been disciplined for breaking the terms of his licence by producing plays at his music hall, introduced a can-can into 'the innocuous divertissement' *Les Nations* at the Alhambra.[111] Alerted by the alarmist language of a review of the production in *The Day's Doings* of 22 October 1870, a police constable protested to the magistrates who had convened to sign the Alhambra's annual licence for music and dancing, and observed that:

> The dance on the whole is indecent, especially on the part of one . . . who raised her foot higher than her head several times towards the public and which was much applauded.[112]

The magistrates refused to pass the licence and Strange's dancers and theatre staff were put out of work.[113]

Owners of music halls exploited the censors' difficulty in proscribing the performance of the cancan. Yet as Strange's experience shows, mechanisms were in place to check the lawlessness of those places of entertainment operating on the edges of the Lord Chamberlain's jurisdiction. This conclusion reveals the existence of an alternative history of nineteenth-century theatre censorship. The previous pages have suggested the range of readings offered by examiners when confronted with the political, indecent, blasphemous and insulting onstage, but the authority of each of these commentaries is undermined by the fact that nineteenth-century theatre offered opportunities for interested parties to ignore the censors altogether. The ingenuity with which the play examiners attempted to circumvent such opportunities offers perhaps the most forceful evidence of their insistence upon their rights as censors.

An alternative historiography of nineteenth-century censorship

Confusion about how and even whether the 'illegitimate' theatres and music halls of the nineteenth century were censored was common not only amongst examiners and the Lords Chamberlain, but amongst the theatrical profession as a whole. Whether the censors understood it or not, it was possible for illegitimate theatres of

4. 'Reading the Magistrates' Decision'; newspaper illustration of Frederick Strange's soon to be unemployed company, reading the news that magistrates have refused to renew the Alhambra's music hall licence; reproduced in Ivor Guest, *Ballet in Leicester Square: the Alhambra and the Empire 1860–1915* (London, 1992) from *The Day's Doings* of 11 November 1870

all descriptions to risk staging unlicensed plays or performing unexpurgated versions of censored pieces. Before 1843 the censors' authority extended only over the patent theatres and over those scripts submitted by illegitimates who coveted the sense of security gained from having licences for their plays. After 1843, when the Lord Chamberlain's control was broadened, only music halls and entertainment venues offering music and dancing remained able to take advantage of this position. Throughout the century, therefore, there existed opportunities for playwrights and actors to stage unaltered plays that the examiner had amended or prohibited, or those which had not been officially licensed at all.

Although many of those subject to the Lord Chamberlain's jurisdiction complained bitterly about the lawlessness of illegitimate theatres and music halls, it is a mistake to think that there was no alternative mode of censorship in place. In 1823 for example, when plays based on the Weare murder were staged without the Lord Chamberlain's licence at the Surrey and the Coburg, mechanisms were in place to darken the theatres. The manager of the Surrey Theatre was visited shortly before the play's first performance by a local magistrate who expressed concern after receiving a playbill for the production; two days later, lawyers for the accused murderer entered a criminal information (a complaint) against the theatre, and shortly afterwards the theatre was forbidden to perform the play. Finally, in October

1824, when the Surrey was required to appear before magistrates to request the renewal of its annual licence, its manager was forced to promise never to stage a play of a similar ilk again unless he wished to have future licence applications rejected.[114]

At the other end of the century, the manager of the Liverpool Adelphi discovered that even distance from London did not protect him from prosecution when he staged a provocative, unlicensed play. The Lord Chamberlain's correspondence for 1892 records its receipt of newspaper notices of a play based on the serial murderer Frederick Deeming.[115] On noticing the reviews of *Deeming; or Doomed at Last*, Ponsonby instructed a lawyer to issue a summons against the Liverpool Adelphi's lessee and ordered the magistrates to revoke the theatre's licence. As both the correspondence and *The Era* report, the subsequent suit against the theatre manager was prosecuted with such speed that within twenty-one days he had been stripped of his licence, ordered to return the profits of the performances and required to pay a fine. In fact, the magistrates reinstated the Liverpool Adelphi's licence two weeks later, but the manager's punishment, even though it was short lived, showed that the examiner kept a careful post-production eye on what was performed in the provinces, and that there were systems in place for the swift punishment of unlicensed performances.[116] Given enough provocation, it was entirely possible for plays to be censored even when they were performed beyond the Lord Chamberlain's jurisdiction or outside London.

Although Pigott in particular was uncomfortable with the idea that the Lord Chamberlain operated a system of espionage to ensure that the rules of censorship were not breached,[117] he acknowledged that the work of the examiner went far beyond play reading. The requirement that the censor should scan newspapers and correspondence for signs of inappropriate performances in venues beyond the Lord Chamberlain's control placed a heavy burden on the examiner. However, as Penelope Summerfield has argued in her excellent account of the evolution of London music hall, the censor was increasingly able to rely on others to lighten the load for them.[118] By retaining the power to instruct magistrates, and later the London County Council, to revoke the licences of music halls when they disobeyed the established rules of censorship, play examiners were able to manipulate proprietors by threatening their profits. Thus we find the proprietors first pleading with the Lord Chamberlain to take over the job of censoring music hall, and subsequently issuing guidelines to performers that duplicated almost exactly the principles upon which examiners censored plays:

> No offensive allusions to be made to any Member of the Royal Family; Members of Parliament, German Princes, police authorities, or any member thereof, the London County Council or any member of that body; no allusion whatever to religion, or any religious sect; no allusion to the administration of the law of the country.

Summerfield is disappointed by the 'culture of consolation' that encouraged music hall proprietors to play the part of examiners. Nevertheless this proxy censorship shows that examiners, when faced with no other means of containing the subversive potential of the music hall, would apply pressure to its proprietors. It becomes clear that the Lord Chamberlain's examiners made use of whatever tool lay at hand to implement the laws governing play censorship. They also left behind meticulous records of the strategies used for controlling the theatre, whether undertaken by proxy or in person. It is rare that these records come in the form of readers' reports on individual plays, but daybook entries, marginal marks, a prolific correspondence and, at times, a refusal to acknowledge the existence of an objectionable play, accumulate to document the censors' determination to perform their role.

NOTES

1 Martin Archer Shee, *Alasco. A Tragedy in Five Acts. Excluded from the Stage by the Authority of the Lord Chamberlain* (London: Sherwood, Jones & Co., 1824).

2 For these signs of optimism, see *Morning Post*, 14 February 1824; concern that this optimism was unfounded can be seen six days later: *Morning Post*, 20 February 1824. Colman was the first of six examiners working between 1824 and 1901: George Colman (January 1824–October 1836); Charles Kemble (October 1836–February 1840); John Mitchell Kemble (February 1840–March 1857); William Bodham Donne (March 1857–August 1874); Edward F. Smyth Pigott (August 1874–February 1895); George Redford (March 1895–January 1912). It should be noted that J. M. Kemble fulfilled much of his father's duties and Donne performed most of J. M. Kemble's from 1849 onwards.

3 Shee, *Alasco*, p. 63. Richard Brinsley Peake, *Memoirs of the Colman Family*, vol. 2 (London: Richard Bentley, 1841), p. 429.

4 One extreme example of Gilbert's 'negotiation' was his claim that he ignored the censor's alterations of his plays altogether. See *The Era*, 14 January 1872, p. 12.

5 Examiner E. F. Smyth Pigott's decision to license *Rosencrantz and Guildenstern* represents a considerable shift in policy since 1873 when William Bodham Donne cut the line 'I wonder the Lord Chamberlain permits it' in a one-act farce. See his entry for *Seeing Toole*, Daybook, Register of Lord Chamberlain's Plays, vol. 4, 1873–1876, ms. 53705 (London: British Library), p. 102.

6 Lord Chesterfield, 'Speech to the House of Lords,' 20 May 1737, *The Parliamentary History of England from the earliest period to the year 1803, 1737–1739*, vol. 10 (London: T. C. Hansard, 1812), p. 333.

7 Shee, Preface to *Alasco*, pp. xx–xxi.

8 W. S. Gilbert, *Rosencrantz and Guildenstern, Original Plays by W. S. Gilbert*, vol. 3 (London: Chatto & Windus, 1903), p. 83.

9 Donne continued the nightmare theme by describing his working life as a descent into an underworld. See his letter to Fanny Kemble, 9 September 1858 in Johnson, *Donne*, p. 227.

10 George Redford, Letter to Frederick Stanley Osgood, November 1911, LCO *Theatre Files*, not catalogued; original Lord Chamberlain's Office reference 344/11, London: British Library.

11 See the contradictions between Redford's description of his post, and that offered by the Lord Chamberlain's comptroller. *Report from the Joint Select Committee of the House of Lords and the House of Commons on the Stage Plays (Censorship) together with the proceedings of the Committee, minutes and appendices* (London: HMSO, 1909), pp. 11–21; 41–50. Steve Nicholson provides a compelling reading of the Lord Chamberlain's use of Redford as a fall guy in *The Censorship of British Drama 1900–1968*, vol. 1 (Exeter: Exeter University Press, 2003), pp. 64–7. For an excerpt from Redford's memorandum of appointment, see John Johnston, *The Lord Chamberlain's Blue Pencil* (London: Hodder & Stoughton, 1990), pp. 266–7.

12 Nicholson's statement that earlier readers would 'write a report recommending (or otherwise) the script for licence, and noting any cuts and changes' perhaps overstates the detail provided in

correspondence and daybooks by examiners in the nineteenth century. Nicholson, *Censorship of British Drama*, vol. 1, p. 4.

13 George Colman, *Report from the Select Committee on Dramatic Literature with minutes of evidence. Ordered by the House of Commons to be printed 2 August 1832. Reports from Committees*, vol. 7, session 6 December 1831–16 August 1832, p. 59, q. 850.

14 George Colman, Letter to William Knighton [private secretary to the King], 29 February 1824, in Peake, *Memoirs*, vol. 2, p. 400; Letter to the Lord Chamberlain, the Duke of Montrose, 29 September 1825, ms. 42873, vol. 2, f. 408, London: British Library. For more on Colman's response to these plays, see below pp. 29–34.

15 Collier's revelation that he owned this material drew no comment from the Select Committee. See *Report 1832*, p. 29 q. 343. The ambiguous ownership of licensed plays has been more fully discussed above, p. 24.

16 Collier in *Report 1832*, p. 33 q. 400.

17 See William Bodham Donne's evidence and that of the Lord Chamberlain's comptroller, Spencer Cecil Brabazon Ponsonby in *Report from the Select Committee on Theatrical Licenses and Regulations together with the proceedings of the Committee, minutes of evidence and an appendix, Reports from Committees*, vol. 11, 1 February–10 August 1866, p. 82 q. 2250; p. 7 q. 186, and the evidence of the examiner, Pigott, *Report from the Select Committee on Theatres and Places of Entertainment, together with the proceedings of the Committee, minutes of evidence, appendix and index, Reports from Committees*, vol. 18, 19 February–28 June 1892, p. 329 q. 5183.

18 There is no evidence that either Charles or John Mitchell Kemble produced such reports during their time as play examiners.

19 Daybooks, Register of Lord Chamberlain's Plays, vols. 1–6, 1824–1897, mss. 53703–53707 (London: British Library). James Stottlar's superb article, 'A Victorian stage censor: the theory and practice of William Bodham Donne', *Victorian Studies* 13.3 (1970), pp. 253–82, makes excellent use of this resource, as does John Russell Stephens's, *The Censorship of English Drama 1824–1901* (Cambridge: Cambridge University Press, 1980).

20 There is no reference to Wilde's *Salome* in the relevant daybook for example.

21 This correspondence is discussed below pp. 31–4.

22 See for example Stephens, *Censorship of English Drama*, p. 112.

23 E. F. Smyth Pigott, Letter to Spencer Ponsonby, 27 June 1892, LC 1: 582, f. 79.

24 Spencer Ponsonby, Letter to Mr Farrier, 11 January 1871, LC 1: 248, f. 6; Charles Morton, Letter to Viscount Sydney, 19 December 1871, LC 1: 247, f. 282; Mr Norris of the Fulham Branch of the National Vigilance Association, Letter to the Lord Chamberlain, 31 January 1890, LC 1: 546, f. 10; George Sanger, Letter to the Lord Chamberlain, 15 February 1890, LC 1: 546, f. 15.

25 G. B. Shaw, 'The author's apology,' *Mrs Warren's Profession*, in *The Works of Bernard Shaw*, vol. 7 (London: Constable, 1930), pp. 156–7.

26 Colman footnoted his letter: 'The foregoing summary remarks were written by me, as Examiner of Plays; and I communicated them to Mr Charles Kemble, manager of Covent Garden Theatre, when the tragedy of *Alasco* was under my official consideration.' Peake, *Memoirs*, vol. 2, p. 401.

27 Colman doggedly insisted that it was the Lord Chamberlain rather than himself who was responsible for the decision to license or prohibit plays. Colman in *Report 1832*, p. 39 q. 848.

28 Colman, Letter to Sir William Knighton, 29 February 1824, reproduced in Peake, *Memoirs*, vol. 2, pp. 400–401.

29 T. Tickler, 'Pike, prose and poetry', *Blackwood's Magazine* 15 (1824), p. 595; Stephens gives further details of the contemporary nuances of *Alasco* in *Censorship of English Drama*, pp. 39–41.

30 George Bartley in *Report 1832*, p. 181 q. 3249.

31 See Shee's footnotes to *Alasco*, pp. 27, 40.

32 Montrose (Lord Chamberlain), Letter to Mr Martin Archer Shee. 19 February 1824, reproduced in Shee, Preface to *Alasco*, p. liv.

33 [Samuel Johnson], *A compleat vindication of the licensers of the stage . . .* (London: C. Corbett, 1739), p. 16.

34 This problem emerged more than once during the nineteenth century. When Alfred Bunn objected to Charles Kemble's appointment as play examiner in October 1836, he sent his next play directly to the Lord Chamberlain for licensing. Kemble was subsequently instructed to remind Bunn of the appropriate protocol. Jane Williamson, *Charles Kemble, Man of the Theatre* (Lincoln: University of Nebraska Press, 1964), p. 219.

35 Bartley in *Report 1832*, p. 181 q. 3244. Bartley has mistaken the Coburg Theatre for the Surrey in this statement, an error which he later corrects. This exploitation of the loophole in censorship laws will be explored more fully later.

36 Entry for *Charles the First*, ms. 53702, p. 26.

37 In her later preface to the play Mitford displays considerable anxiety that this illegitimate production offended the censor: 'I beg most earnestly and sincerely to disavow having been influenced [to stage the play at the Victoria Theatre] by anything like a spirit of defiance towards the licenser or his office.' Mitford, 'The original preface to *Charles the First*', in *Dramatic Works of Mary Russell Mitford*, vol. 1 (London: Hurst & Blackett, 1854), p. 244.

38 Colman, Letter to the Lord Chamberlain, 29 September 1825 [marked 'copy'], ms. 42873, vol. 2, f. 408. I would like to acknowledge the help of the entire staff of the British Library's manuscripts reading room in deciphering Colman's letter.

39 Mary Russell Mitford, *Charles the First, An Historical Tragedy in Five Acts* (London: John Duncombe, 1834), pp. 68, 79.

40 Colman, Letter to Charles Kemble, 10 October 1825, ms. 42873, f. 407.

41 Colman in *Report 1832*, p. 66 q. 972.

42 Collier ibid., p. 30 q.362.

43 Montrose, Letter to George Colman, 13 October 1825, ms. 42873, f. 410.

44 Colman, Letter to Charles Kemble, 15 October 1825, ms. 42873, f. 411.

45 On announcing her intentions to William Elford, she asked: 'Should you ever have suspected your poor little friend of so adventurous a spirit? . . . Do you think I shall succeed? . . . I fear, I greatly fear.' Mitford, Letter to William Elford, 21 August 1823, Revd A. G. L'Estrange (ed.), *Life of Mary Russell Mitford*, vol. 2 (London: Richard Bentley, 1870), pp. 106, 107.

46 Mitford, Letter to Revd William Harness, 1 December 1825, ibid., pp. 215–16.

47 Colman's annotation, *Charles the First*, ms. 42873, f. 480.

48 Lord Chesterfield, Speech to the House of Lords, 20 May 1737, *Parliamentary History*, vol. 10, p. 330. This earlier version of *King Charles the First* is discussed by Vincent J. Liesenfeld in his Introduction, to *The Stage and the Licensing Act 1729–1739* (New York and London: Garland, 1981), pp. xx–xxii.

49 John Russell Stephens's book and articles on censorship have been invaluable not only in tracing the censors' response to such plays, but also in making evident the range of resources available for such research. See both his *Censorship of English Drama* and his article, '*Jack Sheppard* and the licensers: the case against Newgate plays', *Nineteenth-century Theatre Research* 1.1 (1973), pp. 1–13.

50 See Stephens, 'William Bodham Donne: some aspects of his later career as examiner of plays', *Theatre Notebook* 25.1 (Autumn 1970), pp. 25–32 and Stottlar, 'A Victorian stage censor,' pp. 253–82.

51 Nicholson, *Censorship of British Drama*, p. 10. As I also pointed out in Chapter 1, the 'eternal interference' of censorship also affected plays before they were even submitted to the examiner, but it would be impossible to include such works in this chapter.

52 Ponsonby, Letter to William Bodham Donne, 13 October 1853, transcribed in the daybook, ms. 53703, p. 314. See also the script, *The Wrath's Whirlwind or the Neglected Child, the Vicious Youth and the Degraded Man*, LCP 52942U, lic. refused 13 October 1853. *Tita of Tibet* was banned for the same reason, ms. 53706, p. 300.

53 Entry for *Girolfe Girolfa*, ms. 53705, p. 44.

54 Charles Kemble in *Report 1832*, p. 51 q. 708.

55 Although many would agree that the significance of Fielding's plays in particular has been overstated in accounts of Walpole's dash to pass the Licensing Act, few would suggest that they were of trivial importance. See Robert D. Hume, *Henry Fielding and the London Theatre 1728–1737* (Oxford: Clarendon Press, 1985), p. 249; Liesenfeld, *The Stage and the Licensing Act*, pp. ix–x; P. J. Crean, 'The stage licensing act of 1737', *Modern Philology* 35 (1937–8), pp. 247–8.

56 Pigott, Memorandum, 15 March 1883, LC 1: 546, p. 31. Pigott reproduced much of this memorandum almost verbatim during his later evidence to the 1892 Select Committee. See my later discussion of blasphemous, lewd and indecent plays for a closer consideration of Pigott's argument, pp. 44–7.

57 Pigott, *Report* 1892, p. 333 q. 5211. Both examiners resisted attempts to associate their 'loyalty' with contemporary party politics.

58 Donne in *Report* 1866, p. 88 q. 2408; Pigott in *Report* 1892, p. 333 q. 5211.

59 For a discussion of the French audience's 'applications', see Nicholas Harrison, 'Colluding with the censor: theatre censorship in France after the Revolution', *Romance Studies* 25 (Spring 1995), p. 16.

60 Thomas Morton in *Report* 1832, p, 219, qq. 3945–6.

61 Entry for *Masaniello*, ms. 53702, p. 128; [James Kenney] *Masaniello*, lic. 25 April 1829, ms. 42895, ff. 100–159.

62 Entry for *Harlequin Cock Robin and the Children of the Wood*, ms. 53704, p. 55; LCP 53064, lic. 24 December 1866.

63 Entry for *The Last Slave*, ms. 53703, p. 175. Apparently the state of American affairs required no such care to be taken over the licensing of a play called *Ku Klux Klan; or the Secret Death Union of South America*, ms. 53704, p. 69.

64 Entry for *William Tell*, ms. 53703, p. 317.

65 Colman in *Report* 1832, p. 66 q. 968.

66 See my interpretation of *Caste*'s engagement with the Second Reform Act in Miriam Handley, 'Performing dramatic marks: stage directions and the revival of *Caste*', in Joe Bray, Miriam Handley and Anne C. Henry (eds), *Ma(r)king the Text: The Presentation of Meaning on the Literary Page* (Aldershot: Ashgate, 2000), pp. 253–70, or the chapter 'Murder, madness and reform,' in Handley, *Directions in Nineteenth-Century British Theatre* (Oxford: Oxford University Press, forthcoming). Of the numerous works which critique the political significance of melodrama see Simon Shepherd, 'Melodrama as avant-garde: enacting a new subjectivity', *Textual Practice* 10.3 (1996), pp. 507–22; Elaine Hadley, *Melodramatic Tactics: Theatricalized Dissent in the English Marketplace, 1800–1885* (Stanford: Stanford University Press, 1995); Julia Swindells, *Glorious Causes: the Grand Theatre of Political Change, 1789–1833* (Oxford: Oxford University Press, 2001).

67 See the response when Charles Kemble failed to notice the significance of Bulwer Lytton's *The Duchesse de la Vallière*. Richard Foulkes, 'Censure and censorship', in his *Church and Stage in Victorian England* (Cambridge: Cambridge University Press, 1997), p. 30.

68 One example of the general warnings can be found in Samuel Tolhurst's licence to run the Novelty theatre, LC 1: 564, f. 58.

69 Entry for *Doomed*, ms. 53707, p. 55. For Pigott's censorship of the script, see *Doomed*, LCP 53446J, lic. 17 July 1890. The greatest concentration of crossings out, underlinings and excision marks appear on Claud's speech: 'I often think ~~you must regret having married a fellow like me~~ with no visible means of subsistence as they say of vagabonds', p. 3. Presumably this was an inappropriate statement for a British Ambassador to make.

70 Entry for *Lily Dale*, ms. 53704, p. 78. Other plays brought the chancellor of the exchequer and the lord mayor of London onstage. See entries for *Little Bo Peep*, ms. 53705, p. 72, and *Harlequin and Tom Thumb*, ms. 53703, p. 122.

71 Entry for *Robin Hood, Little John and Friar Tuck; or the Goblin of Menderstone Moore, with the Castle of one hundred gates*, ms. 53703, p. 244. A further cluster of Florence Nightingale allusions occur in plays submitted during her time in the Crimea: entries for *Harlequin Fury Candle and the Emperor Flashlight; or the Fairy Queen of the Regions of Light*, ms. 53703, p. 125; and *Jack and Jill; or Harlequin and King Mustard and Four and Twenty Blackbirds baked in a pie*, ms. 53703, p. 141.

72 Elwood P. Lawrence, ' "The Happy Land": W. S. Gilbert as political satirist', *Victorian Studies* 15.2 (1971–2), pp. 161–83; Edward Righton, 'A suppressed burlesque: "The Happy Land" ', *Theatre* 28 (August 1896), pp. 63–6.

73 The can-canning dancer and the measuring of the muse's skirt are discussed below, pp. 46–7.

74 Donne, Letter to Viscount Sydney, 26 July 1871, LC 1: 247, p. 152.

75 Entries for *Sick or Good out of Evil*, ms. 53704, p. 66; and *Harlequin Hop o' My Thumb*, ms, 53704, p. 60.

76 *Harlequin Hop o' My Thumb* 53115P, lic. 19 December 1872, pp. 3, 4, 5, 12.

77 The Tichborne Claimant's civil case began in May 1871. By June–July, when *Sick or Good out of Evil* and *Disguises* were submitted to Donne, the Claimant had already given extremely contradictory testimony in the trial, although it took until December 1871 for the jury to conclude that he was not Tichborne. By the time *Harlequin Hop o' My Thumb* was performed, the Claimant had been found guilty of perjury and was awaiting trial in the criminal courts. For more on the Tichborne trial see Michael Gilbert, *The Claimant* (London: Constable, 1957), and Douglas Woodruff, *The Tichborne Claimant: a Victorian Mystery* (London: Hollis & Carter, 1957).

78 Debate on the drama, 1842. Hansard's Parliamentary Debates, vol. 64, 17 June–11 July 1842 (London: Baldwin & Cradock, 1842), p. 793.

79 See Stephens, '*Jack Sheppard* and the licensers', pp. 1–13. In 1854 Donne argued that 'The theatre indeed, at the present moment, is in more danger from the social and sentimental corruptions of the French stage than from exhibitions of open ruffianism or the coarser species of vice and crime.' *Essays on the Drama and on Popular Amusements* (London: Tinsley Brothers, 1863), pp. 130–31.

80 Entries for *Achora Maetree*, ms. 53704, p. 2, and *Hearts*, ms. 53706, p. 89.

81 Entry for *Eliza Fenning; or the Victim of Circumstance*, ms. 53703, p. 78. The omitted business is described in scene vii of the licensing copy, LCP 52956E, lic. September 1853. Fenning's fate was still being discussed years later: *The Times*, 21 July 1857, p. 9. Stottlar mistakenly gives this play as *Elijah Jenning*, which indicates the difficulty of reading some of the handwriting in the daybooks, Stottlar, 'A Victorian stage censor', p. 274.

82 Delaware, Letter to J. M. Kemble, 23 August 1844, ms. 53702, p. 226. The plays banned were *The Murder House; or the Cheats of Chick Lane*, *The Thieves' House; or the Murder Cellar of Fleet Dirch* and *George Barrington; or the life of a pickpocket*.

83 Viscount Sydney, 'Letter to William Bodham Donne,' 20 August 1862, General Letters (Theatres) LC 1: 112, f. 38. The licensing script for this play is not extant. A discussion of the legal problems posed by the performance of the illegitimate Weare plays can be found in Handley, *Directions in Nineteenth-Century British Theatre*.

84 Entry for *The Turtle Doves*, ms. 53706, p. 202; LCP 53241J, lic. 15 November 1880.

85 Question posed to Ponsonby, *Report 1866*, p. 13 qq. 350–51. Handley, *Directions in Nineteenth-Century British Theatre*, looks in greater detail at lions on the nineteenth-century stage.

86 [George Warriner], *Bob Bretton; the Dead Shot of the Bush*, LCP 53189D, lic. 11 July 1877, p. 25; entry in daybook, ms. 53706, p. 12.

87 Stephens notes that Donne also visited the Marylebone Theatre to assure himself that the offensive lines had been cut in performance. Stephens, 'William Bodham Donne', p. 26.

88 Entry for *Gulliver's Travels*, ms. 53704, p. 51. For the offensive speech, see the licensing script LCP 53081R, pp. 22, 23. Donne appears not to have cared that the veracity of Mrs Gulliver's statement might have been undermined by the fact that she gets into an unprovoked fight almost as soon as her speech is over. For a similar example, see Pigott's daybook entry on the insult offered to the British army in *Called to the Front*, ms. 53706, p. 59.

89 Entry for *Baffled*, ms. 53706, p. 21.

90 Pigott, Memorandum 1883, p. 31.

91 *Report 1866*, p. 14 q. 392.

92 Entry for *Mephistofele*, ms. 53706, p. 127.

93 Colman's evidence in *Report* 1832, pp. 59–60 qq. 852–7; see also entries for *What's Your Game*, ms. 53703, p. 318, and [Title not recorded], ms. 53703, p. 319.

94 Donne, Letter to Fanny Kemble, 21 May 1874, Johnson, *Donne and his Friends*, p. 295. Earlier censors such as Colman failed to see the problem. Peake, *Memoirs*, vol. 2, p. 430. Colman's friend, Theodore Hook, refuted this attack, 'Recollections of the late George Colman', *Bentley's Miscellany* 1 (1837), p. 11.

95 Entry for *Twixt Axe and Crown*, ms. 53704, p. 128.

96 Entry for *Bella*, ms. 53706, p. 16.

97 Ponsonby, Letter to Donne, 2 June 1858, LC 1: 51, f. 344.

98 John Mitchell Kemble's plea about the French-language play *Myrrha* was prompted by his wish to see 'one of Alfieri's finest tragedies and one of Mme. Ristori's finest pieces of acting'. He was unsuccessful in his bid to persuade the Lord Chamberlain to overlook the play's thematic treatment of incest, however. Entry for *Myrrha*, ms. 53703, p. 184. No such special pleading was offered by subsequent examiners for plays that featured incest. See Donne's entry for *The Waiter at the Eagle* (1863), ms. 53703, p. 321.

99 Donne, Letter to Fanny Kemble, 8 July 1858, Johnson, *Donne and his Friends*, pp. 224–5.

100 Entries for *Bibb and Tucker Comedy*, ms. 53705, p. 6, and *Mathilde and the Mulatto*, ms. 53703, p. 190

101 *Mathilde and the Mulatto*, LCP 53005U, lic. 10 August 1861, pp. 23–5. Donne's pencil marks can be seen only on a small portion of p. 24.

102 Redford, quoted in Samuel Smith, *Plays and their Supervision* (London: Chas. J. Thynne, 1900), p. 18.

103 Entries for *Harlequin and the World of Flowers*, ms. 53703, p. 121; *The Album of Beauty*, ms. 53706, p. 4; *Lantern Light*, ms. 53704, p. 84. Tracy Davis argues for the association of cross-dressing and pornography in 'The actress in Victorian pornography', *Theatre Journal* 41.3 (October 1989), p. 298, but she is referring to women dressing as men. By 1892 Pigott was claiming that he felt himself to be ill-equipped to censor any issues of costume, *Report* 1892, p. 334 q. 5223.

104 Davis refers to the frontispiece of *The Day's Doings*, 10 February 1872, 'Actress in Victorian pornography', p. 304.

105 Mr Norris of the Fulham Branch of the National Vigilance Association, Letter to the Lord Chamberlain, 31 January 1890, General Letters (Theatres), LC 1: 546, f. 10.

106 *Lady Godiva*, LCP. 53443L, lic. 26 December 1889, pp. 2, 16. Sanger not only protested about the cost of Godiva's 'nude' outfit, he also suggested that the author of the complaint might be 'a person who was discharged for being in a helpless state of drunkenness'. Sanger, Letter to the Lord Chamberlain, 3 February 1890, LC 1: 546, f. 15. The censor's difficulties were heightened by the popularity of tableaux vivants of 'nude statues' in the 1890s. See *The Times*, 3 February 1897.

107 See Donne on the difficulties of understanding references to dance in the licensing scripts, *Report* 1866, pp. 78–9 q. 2131.

108 *Observer*, 16 October 1870, p. 5.

109 See entries for *Ixion Rewheel'd*, ms. 53703, p. 57 and LCP 53143N, lic. 20 November 1874, pp. 9, 65; *Sleeping Beauty*, ms. 53705, p. 106 and LCP 53143O, lic. 18 December 1874, p. 48.

110 Charles Morton, Letter to the Lord Chamberlain, 19 December 1871, LC 1: 247, f. 282.

111 Emily Soldene, 'How the Alhambra was shut', *The Sketch* 9 (30 January 1895), p. 53.

112 *The Times*, 14 October 1870, p. 12.

113 Ivor Guest, *Ballet in Leicester Square: the Alhambra and the Empire, 1860–1915* (London: Dance Books, 1992), pp. 21, 24. Strange was subsequently granted a theatre licence from the Lord Chamberlain.

114 *Morning Chronicle*, 18 November 1823, p. 3; *Observer*, 23 November 1823, p. 1; *The Times*, 21 October 1824, p. 3. See Handley, 'Murder, madness and reform', for a full account of the illegitimate Weare plays.

115 *The Era*, 11 June 1892, p. 10.

116 See the correspondence between Ponsonby and the appointed solicitor, LC 1: 582, especially f. 66. Developments in the case were reported in *The Era*, 25 June 1892, p. 6; 2 July 1892, p. 9; 16 July 1892, p. 7.

117 Pigott in *Report* 1892, p. 333 q. 5212.

118 Penelope Summerfield, 'The Effingham Arms and the Empire: deliberate selection in the evolution of music hall in London', in Eileen Yeo and Stephen Yeo (eds), *Popular Culture and Class Conflict 1590–1914. Explorations in the History of Labour and Leisure* (Sussex: Harvester Press, 1981), pp. 224–37.

PART II

Getting Away With It:
Strategies and Practice, 1902–1944

This luckless department . . .

IN May 1938 the Lord Chamberlain received an angry protest from the United Commercial Travellers' Association concerning the punchline in a comic sketch involving a dairymaid: 'her mother calls from the house and asks, has she milked the cow. She replies: – No, but that she is talking to a Commercial Traveller. Whereupon the mother calls to her "Come into the house at once and bring the cow with you".' The complaint was made by the Executive Council of the Association on behalf of its members:

> I would like to make it perfectly clear that there is no objection to humorous satire at the expense of Commercial Travellers. What we do object to is the obscenity of the whole thing, and the association of the name of a Commercial Traveller with practices that can be characterised by no other name than immoral.

The assistant comptroller in the Lord Chamberlain's Office, Brigadier Sir Norman Gwatkin, sought to reassure them that 'it was not the intention of the author that the "joke" at the end of this scene should indicate "pervertion", [sic] but merely that the cow could not be left unattended'; nevertheless he accepted that the way in which the gag was played did indeed encourage 'a rather more doubtful construction', and he instructed the manager to remove any suggestion that the cow was 'in danger of an immoral assault'. The mother's line was duly amended to 'Come inside at once and put the cow in the barn', and the Executive Council thanked the Lord Chamberlain for his action.[1]

At almost the same time, Gwatkin was also engaged in discussion with the Foreign Office about an anti-Nazi play called *Lorelei*, a 'ponderous and treacly drama' which had been submitted by Cedric Hardwicke for production in the West End; the official Reader's Report had expressed concern about the 'many references to German persecution and cruelty', and on 5 May Gwatkin sent the script to the FO for general advice:

> I can foresee that we shall receive an increasing number of plays bearing on Germany and the Nazi regime so it would be a help to us if you could give – not so much a ruling, but some hints as to subjects and situations which it will be well to avoid.
>
> We do not want to be too rigid as the conditions vary from time to time.
>
> It is 'la verité qui blesse' in most cases of this sort, but the playwrights have to be treated fairly gently and given consideration, otherwise this luckless department will merit the abuse which is heaped upon it, and which I really believe is not fully deserved at the moment.

The FO responded with a specific recommendation:

We have, of course, had to consider this point on several occasions in the past, often as the result of a protest from the German embassy. We have always taken the line with the embassy that it is impossible in this country to censor plays dealing with Nazi ideology in general, merely on the ground of their underlying theme and general tendency. On the other hand it is clearly important that we should do what we can to give Herr Hitler, as the head of the German state, the protection which is afforded to heads of states by international practice. The Germans are very touchy about criticism of Herr Hitler and they have often pointed out that in Germany the greatest care has always been taken to prevent the appearance of any objectionable references to the British Royal Family. We should therefore welcome it if, in dealing with plays about Germany you were able to remove all references to Herr Hitler and passages which might be considered derogatory to his dignity as Head of the German state.

Gwatkin informed them that it was standard practice to 'remove anything unpleasant about Heads of any States', though he added: 'I fear that some times they are inclined to be guyed on the Music Halls over which we have no control'. Meanwhile, he spoke to Hardwicke's business partner:

<u>Lorelei</u>

Mr Leslie Banks came to see me about this play today, as he is in some sort of partnership with Sir Cedric Hardwicke, who owns the play.

Mr Banks asked me straight out if the feeling in this Office was that England would be better served by not putting on such plays during this time of international stress, and I had to tell him that I doubted if they do much good, even if they do not do much harm.

Mr Banks then said, that, as the father of children, he did not consider it advisable to put on the stage, or to make money out of anything that might possibly prejudice the future lives of people in this country, and he is putting this point before his Management.

I pointed out to him that such high-mindedness was rare and said that if he did not put on this play, some one else would probably do so.

On the question of Ruritanianizing the play, as he pointed out, even if the places and names were altered it would still be possible to recognize what country was meant, but I said that if it was Ruritanianized, we could at least answer the German Government in these terms, and it would be evident that we had done our best to take the label away from them.

Gwatkin

21st July 1938

The application was not pursued, and the script remained unlicensed and presumably unperformed.[2]

Taken together, these not untypical examples offer several insights into the practice of theatre censorship. First, there is the contrast between the triviality and the magnitude of issues with which the institution was typically dealing; then there is the remarkable degree of significance attributed to theatre, not just by the censors themselves but by others. They also demonstrate that although power and authority were ostensibly located in the Lord Chamberlain, he was subjected to considerable external pressures; indeed, in the second instance the Foreign Office – itself casting at least an eye over its shoulder at the German embassy and government – is all but invited to dictate policy. Finally, it is important to note that although in neither case was a licence officially refused, in each case the script (or the element complained of) was not performed. The Lord Chamberlain almost never withdrew a licence once it had been issued – to do so would have been to concede that he had been wrong and to court controversy and ridicule – but few managers wanted to risk getting on his wrong side. There is more than one way to skin a cat.

I have charted elsewhere some of the primary routes through the history of theatre censorship between 1900 and 1945, focusing on significant policies, strategies and the intricacies of daily practice in relation to recurring themes and issues.[3] By contrast, the main aim here is to allow the reader direct and extensive contact with specific documents in relation to the censorship of a selection of texts – though it is necessary to touch on some of the contexts through reference to other correspondence, plays and events. We should remember, too, that what is presented here is no more than the tip of an iceberg; for every playscript cited and document reproduced, there are many others which vied for inclusion. Moreover, the process of selection itself reflects an imperfect attempt to combine a number of criteria; it seems appropriate to traverse the period and to include a range of subject areas and different 'types' of script – pantomime and revue sketches, 'commercial' as well as 'highbrow' plays, for example. Moreover, without wishing to impute value judgements and suggest that the 'best' and most important plays are necessarily those which have survived, I have also focused on a number of texts which retain theatrical importance for us today. And inevitably, one looks also to examples where the rulings and the debates allow us to glimpse a new perspective not just on theatre censorship, but also on the history of British theatre in the first half of the twentieth century.

Hunting the censor: the 1909 enquiry

In 1909, the government of Herbert Asquith established a Joint Select Committee Of Enquiry to investigate the history and current practice of theatre censorship, and to make recommendations as to its future. It was set up very largely as the result of pressure brought about by a vigorous campaign for the abolition of censorship, and during twelve sittings between 29 July and 24 September, the Committee – the composition of which incorporated conflicting views on the subject – interviewed playwrights, managers, critics and members of the Lord Chamberlain's staff before producing a report and a series of proposals.[4] With few exceptions, playwrights spoke against the system and managers in favour of it. As George Redford, the

Lord Chamberlain's Reader of Plays, confidently claimed in a letter of June 1909, the latter

> have a very shrewd idea of the proscribed limits, and are only too glad to avail themselves of an independent and recognised authority as a buffer between themselves, and the advanced school of irreconcilable Dramatists who would, if unrestrained, drive out of the theatre a very large proportion of their paying public.

Redford had little respect for playwrights or for those who challenged the censorship:

> There is seldom any difficulty with the Managers. The opposition to all, and any authority, is confined to an insignificant clique of Dramatic Authors who prefer to advertise themselves, rather than yield to any kind of restraint. Each member of the little band has now been given an opportunity of airing his supposed grievance.[5]

When the Committee published its report in November, by far the most potentially important recommendation was that obtaining a licence for public performance should become optional; managers who wanted its security (and most felt they benefited from the shelter it afforded them against possible complaint or prosecution) would still have been able to submit their scripts to the Lord Chamberlain for royal approval. But those willing to take the risk of proceeding without the written protection of the king's representative would have been free to do so. Had this proposal been enacted, the story of theatre censorship – and British theatre in the twentieth century – might have been vastly different. But the Lord Chamberlain's Office was horrified by the implications, as an internal memorandum demonstrates:

> The recommendations of this Committee, if carried into effect, will completely destroy the position of the Censor and turn it into ridicule. No one need submit a play for license [sic] unless he chooses.
>
> The Lord Chamberlain thus remains the Censor in theory but not in practice. The playwright can ignore his authority whenever he chooses, and yet, in the eyes of the Public the Lord Chamberlain is still the person responsible . . .
>
> The theatrical Manager also is in an impossible position, for he becomes his own Censor.
>
> The troubles and pitfalls created in the future for the Censor, were these proposals to become law, are so evident that no one with due regard to the dignity of a high public office could accept them . . . It is in fact proposed to retain for him the difficult and delicate duties appertaining to the Censor, and to multiply a thousandfold those difficulties, while depriving him of all power to enforce his authority. He is in future to be the target, the buffer for abuse, without the power to remedy abuses of which he himself is cognisant.[6]

The Office was adamant there must be 'no drastic change' to existing practice, and it secured the support of the king by pointing out that since the Lord Chamberlain was the head of the royal household, to tamper with the system in this way would be to sacrifice a part of the royal prerogative. With the Home Office and the Director of Public Prosecutions also opposing such reform, there was no chance that legislation would be introduced or properly debated in Parliament.

Given that none of its proposals became law, it would be easy to assume that the enquiry had little impact. But in fact the Committee's attempt to enshrine the grounds on which the Lord Chamberlain might legitimately reject a script established a list of conditions which became widely imbued with the status and authority of an unwritten law. The terms of definition envisaged were wide, and never became officially binding, but they created reference points which were hard to deny:

It should be his duty to license any play submitted to him unless he considers that it may reasonably be held –

(a) To be indecent;
(b) To contain offensive personalities;
(c) To represent on the stage in an invidious manner a living person, or any person recently dead;
(d) To do violence to the sentiment of religious reverence;
(e) To be calculated to conduce to crime or vice;
(f) To be calculated to impair friendly relations with any foreign Power; or
(g) To be calculated to cause a breach of the peace.[7]

Furthermore, some of the questions raised during the enquiry, and especially some of the inadequate answers given by Redford to those questions, had exposed the incompetence, the arbitrariness and the indefensible bias which were rife in the system. If the censorship had not subsequently contrived to reinvent (or re-present) itself by tightening its procedures, ridding itself of the discredited Redford and establishing an Advisory Board to offer supposedly expert opinions to the Lord Chamberlain, the system might even have passed away.

In as much as the censorship did manage to convince people that it had reformed itself, the credit was due less to the incumbent Lord Chamberlain, Viscount Althorp (1905–12), than to Sir Douglas Dawson, who had become comptroller in charge of his Office in 1907. Dawson was largely responsible for introducing procedural changes and alterations in both policy and personnel, though in many ways these constituted little more than a smokescreen designed to shield the lack of real concessions. Redford – deliberately hung out to dry by the comptroller and left to take as much of the blame as possible – had been exposed by the enquiry as vague, incompetent, inconsistent, arrogant, ignorant of the law, at odds with his employers and ready to act with an authority not bestowed on him. In answer to the Committee's first question about licensing plays he had told them that it was 'impossible to say on what principles I proceed' and that 'there are no principles that can be defined'. His evidence went downhill from there onwards.[8] Dawson and the Lord Chamberlain privately found fault with Redford during and after the enquiry – it was not difficult to do – and the comptroller effectively instituted a campaign to drive him from office.

One innovation which resulted from the enquiry (Dawson slightly spuriously claimed it had been scheduled to occur in any case) was the inauguration of an Advisory Board whose members would consider controversial decisions. However, while several witnesses – and some of the Committee – believed the Board should be independently appointed and enjoy an authority which matched or exceeded that of the Lord Chamberlain, the terms on which Dawson contrived to introduce it allowed the Lord Chamberlain to choose and appoint its members, and left it entirely up to his discretion when and in what circumstances he should seek its advice, and whether he should take any notice of such advice. What the comptroller had in mind was not so much a sharing of power as a fig leaf, and for the most part that is what he got.

Dawson's instinct was in fact to centralize control at St James's Palace. He suggested to Althorp that the existing practice whereby scripts were submitted by theatre managers direct to the reader was 'subversive of the Lord Chamberlain's authority', and had resulted in 'the majority of the Public being under the impression that Mr Redford is the Censor of Plays'.[9] Meanwhile, Dawson plotted to get rid of Redford by bringing in additional readers under the guise of helping him to deal with his workload, while dividing the reader's original salary accordingly. In October 1911 he informed Redford:

> It has been decided therefore to create a syndicate to carry out the duties of Reader of Plays, and the Lord Chamberlain has under consideration the appointment of two other gentlemen who will collaborate with you in these duties.
>
> This will naturally effect the emoluments which you have hitherto received from your office.[10]

Dawson must have known that this would be financially crippling and unacceptable to Redford.

A couple of weeks later he wrote to Lord Stamfordham, the king's private secretary, explaining his plan:

> I spoke to H.M. about it, and mentioned the possible introduction of two gentlemen to assist Mr Redford.
>
> The Lord Chamberlain is advised by the Home Office to begin, at any rate, with only one besides Mr Redford. Mr Brookfield is so essentially the man required that the Lord Chamberlain ventures to put his name forward . . . It will be a great advantage to have the office of Reader here under the Lord Chamberlain . . . The rooms in St James's Palace recently occupied by Lord Esher shall be constituted the office of the Reader of Plays.[11]

In November Redford was instructed that as part of the new conditions of service, readers must in future produce a summary of every stage play submitted; in future, he was also to be bound to seek the advice of the department before corresponding with managers or authors. After such a double whammy Redford knew his days were numbered, and he overlapped only briefly with Brookfield before resigning and taking on a new role as the first president of the Board of Film Censors. But rather than signalling any kind of concession to the anti-censorship brigade, Brookfield's appointment was like a red rag to them. Indeed, Brookfield was a declared enemy of Ibsen and 'intellectual' drama, and himself the author of a farce in which he mocked Granville Barker and *Waste* by referring to an author called Bleater and his play *Sewage*.[12] No wonder Barker declared:

> in view of Mr Brookfield's recently published opinions on the Modern Drama this action of the Lord Chamberlain's is but further proof, if further proof were needed, that he is hopelessly out of touch with the theatre over which he exercises despotic control and that the continuance of his legalised tyranny is inimical to the Drama's welfare and its good name.[13]

In February 1912 Brookfield was joined by Ernest Bendall, a former theatre critic who enjoyed the support of many managers. Dawson described him as 'an ideal man for the post', since he was 'a favourite with all connected with [the] theatrical profession', excepting only 'the extremists with whom no appointment would be popular'.[14] However, Brookfield's reign was short-lived; he died in 1913 and was rather surprisingly replaced by George Street, an enthusiastic supporter of Ibsen and Wilde, and a man of rather more progressive theatrical tastes. Perhaps this appointment was due in part to the influence of Lord Sandhurst, who had replaced Althorp in 1912.

The campaign to abolish censorship had not been silenced by the 1909 enquiry or its aftermath. In November 1911 a question was asked in Parliament about the government's intention to legislate; Dawson, clearly on the defensive, warned the Home Office privately:

> You know there is more in this than meets the eye. It is in fact part of an organised plan, by a very small but noisy section of the community to hunt the censor and bring about his abolition. My belief is that the abolition of the censor would mean ruin for all connected with the drama, the authors included, for the only alternative is action by the police, <u>after the harm has been done</u>, and where international questions are at issue this would involve great risk.[15]

He also wrote to the MP Sir Edward Carson, himself a member of the Lord Chamberlain's Advisory Board:

> It appears possible that (though I can hardly believe it) Mr. R. Harcourt may be able to get up a debate tomorrow ABOUT Mr Brookfield's appointment as 'Joint Examiner of Plays' . . .
>
> There are four or five authors whose plays have been rejected in the last ten years, and four or five MPs who are I hear disappointed authors. These eight or ten people are on the warpath to abolish the censor. They are very violent, noisy, and have prolific pens, and the ear of the Press . . . The General Public who are all for the retention of the censor are misled by their statements, which are usually mis-statements of fact.[16]

On 30 November an MP did indeed ask, in relation to the Lord Chamberlain,

> whether means exist within his power of checking the alleged tendency to the encouragement of plays of a low intellectual and moral character at the expense of drama opening up new vistas of thought in social, political, and ethical matters.[17]

This was the old complaint.

The good, the bad and the unhealthy: Shaw, Barker and Brieux

Waste

It had long been one of the main grievances of the so-called 'advanced school' of playwrights and managers that the censorship was more lenient towards the light and frivolous than towards the thoughtful and intelligent. You could (to some degree) *joke* about sexual relationships and construct farces (such as Brookfield's) on a structure of immorality, but to explore such subjects in a serious context was impossible. In their view, the practical effect of the censorship was to ensure that the British theatre remained primarily a grubby and exploitative commercial enterprise rather than aspiring to the level of an artform. Granville Barker told the 1909 enquiry that censorship had 'retarded the advancement and especially the development of English drama', because the expression of 'any original or unusual point of view' was almost certain to be banned: 'I regard the extreme narrowness of the English drama as being distinctly influenced and brought about by the operation of the Censorship'.[18]

Similar claims were repeatedly advanced by the authors who gave evidence, including some who declared that they eschewed the dramatic genre precisely because of the unique restrictions beneath which it laboured. The refusal to license Barker's *Waste* in 1907 had been the starting point for a renewed campaign, in which seventy-one British playwrights appealed directly to the prime minister for a change in the law. Moreover, that play's rejection, and the energy Barker subsequently devoted to the campaign against censorship, were crucial factors in the collapse of his co-management of the Court Theatre, where his aim had been nothing less than to offer a model for a future National Theatre.

At the centre of *Waste* is a married woman who becomes pregnant after a brief affair with a Tory politician, and then dies while having an abortion; the politician commits suicide when the prime minister excludes him from his cabinet for fear of adverse publicity. The surviving evidence suggests that it was primarily the subject of abortion – and particularly the suggestion that a qualified doctor would be prepared to conduct an illegal operation – which upset the censorship; indeed, Barker had apparently been invited by Redford to 'moderate and modify the extremely outspoken references to sexual relations', and to remove 'all reference to a criminal operation'.[19] He had declined to do so, and *Waste* was deemed unacceptable for the public stage. When the play was resubmitted in 1911, Dawson, commented:

I have no hesitation in saying that, however cleverly written the play is, I consider the procuring of abortion, by cabinet ministers or anyone else, to be a subject which is, to say the least, unnecessary and undesirable to produce on the public stage, even in these days.[20]

With one exception, the Advisory Board supported this view, and it was a further nine years before even Dawson capitulated by reluctantly conceding that the original version should finally be licensed:

If we must have this subject introduced on the stage it certainly could not be less offensively treated. On the whole I feel that our moral senses must by now have become so blunted, and acclimatised to plots dealing with venereal disease, brothel keeping, etc that the Censor may survive the issue of a licence even to 'Waste'.[21]

Mrs Warren's Profession

One play which suffered an even longer wait was *Mrs Warren's Profession*, Shaw's attack on capitalism which showed prostitution as an industry rooted in economic factors rather than in sin, and some of its most successful entrepreneurs enjoying positions well up the social scale. First submitted in 1898, a licence for public performance was eventually granted over a quarter of a century (and five Lords Chamberlain) later, and Shaw lived in a permanent state of philosophical and ideological conflict with the Lord Chamberlain's Office. He was also more adept than most at needling the censors, usually preferring mockery to overt confrontation, and pretending to be amused rather than angered by their actions; but this does not always mask his frustration at the extent to which his work was muted. It is true that – as even the Lord Chamberlain's Office admitted – the ban did not entirely prevent Shaw's voice from being heard, for the text was published and received several nominally 'private' productions in theatre clubs. Arguably, then, the retention of the ban was more symbolic than practical, but the more Shaw's play became a focal point in the campaign against censorship the harder it became for the Lord Chamberlain to back down.

In October 1916 the management of Plymouth Repertory Theatre – with the playwright's encouragement – resubmitted his script to the 'more enlightened censorship' now in control. They also submitted a fee for re-reading it:

The theme of the play, admittedly an uncommon one on the stage, is treated seriously by the author; it is essentially a play for women, to whom it conveys a great moral lesson, and as now, with the bulk of our manhood on war service, the theatre is largely patronised by women, this seems to me an appropriate time to ask for further consideration of a play that is sincere in purpose and moral in tendency.[22]

But Street could see no likelihood of the ban being overturned:

I do not think this play should have a licence for general performance. My opinion is based not on the dialogue or incidents – given the theme – but simply on the theme itself, which is the question of the advantages and disadvantages of prostitution as a profession for women, as compared with other professions, and which involves the presentment of a brothel-keeper as the chief character. Such a discussion and such a character are not fitted for casual audiences of various ages . . . no doubt the theme is important and can be rightly discussed in the press. But the theatre is not the place, except before an audience well knowing what it is to expect and of a special kind, as is the Stage Society.

Bendall agreed: 'The more cleverly Mrs Warren defends prostitution the more objectionable does it seem to me that she should be allowed to do so on the public stage.' Since the play was not to be reconsidered, the fee for reading it was duly returned. This allowed Shaw to revel in a mocking and lightly veiled attack on the Lord Chamberlain, which he sent on 8 October:

Dear Lord Sandhurst,

A point has just arisen with reference to a play of mine, as to which I have to take a mean advantage of our personal acquaintance because, being merely an author, I have no <u>locus standi</u> in your office, and I do not care to leave the matter to a manager. The point is quite a technical one; and as its settlement in the sense I think the right one will not help me personally in the least, and will bring additional reading fees to your office, you will perhaps forgive me for raising it in a way which will protect me from the mere official rebuff that I do not exist for the purposes of your department.

The facts are these. About twenty years ago I wrote a play with certain public objects that were then considered quite outside the scope of the theatre. I wanted to show what was the real character of what is now called the White Slave Traffic, and how it was boldly defended morally by the people who profited by it. Also how its real root was in the refusal to secure higher wages for virtue than for vice. Incidentally also to shew the objection to what was called politely (by 'advanced' people) Group Marriage: namely, that when the children of such marriages grew up and fell in love with one another they were confronted with the impossibility of determining the questions of consanguinity raised by the marriage law.

All this happened long before your time, you will not mind my saying that the play simply horrified the Reader of that day, just as he would have been horrified by the White Slave agitation, the Minimum Wage Board legislation, and the treatises of Westermarck and Havelock Ellis. He refused to license it, with very serious consequences to me, which I need not trouble you with. The play has now been worn out on the American and Continental stages, and is, besides, so old fashioned by this time, that at one of the so-called private performances which took place in London a few years ago, Mr Granville Barker and I could do nothing but laugh at its technique. I now take no personal interest in it, though the lesson it conveys is, I am sorry to say, as much needed as ever.

Now for my technical point. The other day a Plymouth manager, wishing to add the play to the Repertory of his theatre, which aims at doing work of a special class, sent in the play for licence, with the usual fee. The official reply was that you regret that you cannot see your way to altering your decision not to license *Mrs Warren's Profession* for public performance on the stage, and that the Office therefore returns the script <u>and the reading fee</u>. That underlined (by me) passage is the crux of the case. The statement that you do not see a way to alter a decision that you never made is only a form: Heaven forbid I should hold you responsible for the things that were done by your predecessors in those dark days! But the return of the fee, which brought the whole transaction to my knowledge because I promised to reimburse the management when I knew what it intended to do, implies a refusal to re-read the play.

I contend that your Reader should have read the play again; pocketed my two guineas; and, if he felt still in the eighteen-nineties about it, reported against licensing it exactly as if it were a new play. I quite recognise that the return of the fee was an act of consideration, outside the official routine, for which the manager should have felt obliged, as no doubt he did. And I appreciate it myself. But you will see the position it creates. If the Reader reads the play again he has no right to return the fee: the auditor, if you have an auditor, ought to surcharge him. If he refuses to read the play, he is putting your Office in the position of governing the stage by the Dead Hand, and giving me an excuse for agitating for a Statute of Mortmain against you. I need not elaborate the argument . . .

By the way, I of course do not contend that it would be reasonable to send the play in every month – though for the life of me I do not see why the Reader should object at two guineas a time – but a reasonable interval has passed in this instance since the last attempt, which, if I recollect aright, was made some years ago by Miss Gertrude Kingston. Probably some other enthusiast will return to the charge later on, and will consult me on the subject. I always say 'You can try if you like'; but I have not said that the play will not be read again. Only the other day a play of mine was reconsidered and licensed after seven years of suppression. Why is Mrs Warren beyond consideration? Please do not misunderstand me: I am not pleading for a licence for Mrs Warren: it would rather embarrass me nowadays, except in its old capacity as a stick to beat your department with. What I do want to know is whether there is any provision in the office rules for reconsidering a decision which was arrived at in view of the state of public opinion on matters subject to change . . . anything like a rule of Once stopped always stopped would be outrageous . . . I still regard it as nothing short of a crime that suitable legislation on the White Slave Traffic was burked, and a miserable Act for the flogging of souteneurs and the protection of Mrs Warren substituted because I was not allowed to educate public opinion as to the real nature of that traffic. Some day you will have a Reader of Plays with some knowledge of the subject and some conscience as to the guilt of the nation in the business. We shall both be dead by that time probably . . .

I am not keeping a copy of this letter . . .

Forgive the inordinate length of this letter. Our conversation at Sassoon's encourages me to depend on your indulgent reception of it.

Sandhurst was away, and it was ten days before he replied, rather tersely: 'I regret the delay in answering your letter of the 8th inst . . . The letter has pursued me . . .' He then explained in simple terms that the fee had been returned because there was no reason to read the play again. This was picked up by Shaw in another brilliantly provocative letter of 20 October:

10 ADELPHI TERRACE

LONDON W.C.

20th October 1916

Dear Lord Sandhurst,

It is very kind of you to answer my letter. The reason you gave me for the return of the reading fee is exactly the reason I assumed. It happens that in order to write the preface to my last volume of plays I had to read the New Testament through very carefully. Of course I had read it before; and I thought myself – to use your phrase – 'thoroughly well acquainted with it' . . . I was amazed to find the number of things I had formerly read into it that were not there, and the number of things I had not noticed and that were there. In future I shall have to read it once a year to keep myself up to date; for though the New Testament will not change, my perception of it will change, just as the public perception of it will change. My contention is that 'Mrs Warren's Profession' should be read carefully through every year by your whole staff, including Col. Sir Douglas Dawson; and I repeat my offer to pay an annual reader's fee as an additional inducement to this exercise. My only fear is that it might end in the play being licensed, and my finding myself, as a respectable elderly gentleman over sixty, credited with the recent production of a play written with a brutality extremely unbecoming to my age and serenity.

The play, like the gospels, will never change; but the old rule of your department 'We dont [sic] object to vice, as long as you don't make it horrifying' is what I really want to have reconsidered. The stern moralist was muzzled while Mr Arthur Roberts was let loose; and I really think that this result was a reductio ad absurdum of the rule. However, Mrs Warren is having the time of her life with our men in training and on leave from the front; and as the older I grow the more inclined I am to believe that all plays whatsoever should be prohibited, I have nothing more to say, and am unaffectedly apologetic for having said so much.
Yours sincerely
G Bernard Shaw

Shaw's mockery had no immediate effect. In June 1917 his play was again submitted and returned unread, but a few months later the manager Edwin Heys sent it in again, this time accompanied by a petition with five pages of signatures of 'influential men and women' calling for the play to be licensed (see Plate 1). Heys also enclosed a letter Shaw had sent him which was obviously designed to irritate the Lord Chamberlain and goad him into debate:

Dear Mr Heys,

My play entitled 'Mrs Warren's Profession', was written more than twenty years ago ... I greatly doubt whether it will ever be licensed in this country, because it has against it the huge commercial interests in prostitution, which are not exposed by the plays of Brieux, or by the many other plays which deal with sexual vice in a frankly pornographic manner, and are licensed without demur ...

The reason for this special persecution of a play obviously much more innocent than the majority of those which are tolerated without question is that whereas these latter act as aphrodisiacs and actually stimulate the trade in women, my play makes it extremely repulsive, not in a sensational way – for all the sensational ways advertise what they pretend to condemn – but by simply exposing the venality of the transaction to which the prostitute is a party ... I think a really good performance of 'Mrs Warren's Profession' would keep its audience out of the hands of the women of the street for a fortnight at least. And that is precisely why it encounters an opposition unknown in the case of plays which stimulate the sex illusion to such an extent that the prostitute reaps a richer harvest from them than the actors.

My play ... strikes straight at prostitution by exposing its sordid economics ... How badly the play was needed was shown by the hysterical unpreparedness of the public for the White Slave agitation, and the useless and savage agitation which followed, and which had the effect of making Mrs Warren complete mistress of the situation by ridding her of her male competitors. Had 'Mrs Warren's Profession' been allowed to take its proper place on the stage when I wrote it, that blunder and all those hysterics might have been averted. But the Lord Chamberlain's Office would not allow Sir George Croft's business to be exposed; and I doubt if it will ever do so. It will allow the prostitute and the procuress and the brothel to supply the sensations of a hundred melodramas; but it will always ward off the one touch at which the attraction of these things withers like the garden of Klingsor.

I am no less convinced than I was in 1895 of the need for such a play as 'Mrs Warren's Profession'.

If England clings to the belief that her harlots are doing for love what they have been driven by poverty to do for money, let her cling to it; and much good may it do her.

I should let you have the play with pleasure if it were available. As it is, you must find some piece that will not threaten the profits of the Euston and Marylebone Roads.

Yours faithfully
(Signed) G. Bernard Shaw

Shaw's letter certainly succeeded in provoking Dawson, who accused Shaw of libelling the Office.

Even some who were neither admirers of *Mrs Warren's Profession* nor supporters of Shaw's right to state his argument in public thought that it might now be judicious for the Lord Chamberlain to concede. The distinguished poet and man of letters Edmund Gosse, who had been the first writer to introduce Ibsen to the British public, and had been central to the appointment of George Street as a reader, wrote to Sandhurst from the Marlborough Club in Pall Mall on 15 October:

> My dear Sandhurst,
>
> I had not heard – but I am not surprised to hear – that you are to be pressed to license 'Mrs Warren's Profession'. My own belief is that the best cure for it would be to let people see for themselves what an empty, ugly, essentially untrue and uninteresting affair it is. I take it to be the least amusing and the least skilful (or one of the least) of all Shaw's plays.
>
> The censorship is in this difficulty that no-one, not even the Bishop of London, could say that it is <u>immoral</u>. It is just its preposterous morality which makes it so offensive. It is like a priggish old clergyman preaching 'to men only' in a night shelter.
>
> I cannot help thinking that you might determine on the bold step of saying to the petitioners, 'Very well, then – there <u>is</u> your 'Mrs Warren's Profession'! Take the dull and dirty thing and make the most you can of it!' The result, I firmly believe, would be an ignominious fiasco for the play, and it would withdraw to appear no more.
>
> The difficulty seems to me to rest in the fact that you cannot by any stretch of terms call the nasty production <u>immoral</u>. It is as cold and uninviting as ditch-water or a tract. It is, in fact, a <u>tract</u> and a very tiresome one.
>
> Now, it seems to me very irksome to think of the Lord Chamberlain, on his high Throne, stooping to crush a <u>tract</u> between his thumb-nail and the floor. It is too small, and the value of the object not worth it.
>
> But I am sure you will act with wisdom. You have been by far the best Censor of Plays this country has ever had, and I think we may continue to trust you. But beware of the temptation of making a martyr of a flea.
> Sincerely
> Edmund Gosse

Sandhurst ignored the well-meant advice and stuck to his guns.

In the early 1920s the Duke of Atholl replaced Sandhurst and Dawson became State Chamberlain; yet the former comptroller maintained his close involvement with censorship as an ex-officio member of the Advisory Board. George Street had become the chief examiner of plays following Bendall's death, and in 1921 he took the plunge and gave his backing to *Mrs Warren's Profession*. Street pointed out that the play was now so widely known that it had become 'futile to prohibit its public performance' and that changing attitudes meant that 'An audience will no longer be shocked as it would have been.' No licence was granted, but three years later Street again recommended it to the new Lord Chamberlain, Lord Cromer:

> I think a Licence should be granted, because the Play contains nothing indecent and the frankness with which its painful subject is discussed no longer shocks an adult audience. Times have changed very much indeed in this respect since the Play was first refused a Licence. The Play has been performed all over Europe and America and has been produced many times by private societies in England, and in book form is

familiar to everyone interested in the stage or contemporary literature. It seems to me, therefore, to be a little absurd still to refuse a Licence for public performance unless on the strongest grounds and these, as I have explained, I think do not exist. It is an 'unpleasant' Play to be sure, as Mr Shaw calls it, and in my opinion a crude and poor one, greatly inferior to his best work, but I do not think its unpleasantness goes beyond the limits to which we are now accustomed.

In August 1924 Lord Cromer accepted that although the change in public attitudes might be 'regrettable' it would be 'absurd to go on refusing a Licence to this Play, ignoring the march of time'. *Mrs Warren's Profession* was finally licensed for Edinburgh's Lyceum Theatre the following month.

Damaged Goods and *Maternity*

During the First World War, some of those who defended Shaw's play had argued that it could be judged as useful propaganda. They were responding to the decision in early 1917 that the ban previously imposed on Brieux's *Damaged Goods* should be revoked on the grounds that the need to warn audiences about the dangers of venereal disease now outweighed the objections to airing the subject in public. In 1914 Bendall, while accepting the moral intentions of the playwright, had unhesitatingly recommended it should be turned down:

LORD CHAMBERLAIN'S OFFICE,
ST JAMES'S PALACE, S.W.

April 17th, 1914

'DAMAGED GOODS' – in three acts by M. Brieux, for production at the Court Theatre

This is a translation of 'Les Avaries', a play by M. Brieux originally condemned by the now-extinct French censorship, and recently much discussed on its pseudo-private London performance without the Lord Chamberlain's license [sic] . . .

Act I consists of a detailed interview between a Doctor and his patient Dupont, who as a sufferer from syphilis is warned against the probable consequences of his contemplated marriage unless he postpones it for at least three years.

Act II shows how Dupont, having disregarded his doctor's advice has married and is the father of a little girl, whose mysterious illness has caused this same doctor, when called in, to reproach the baby's father as a scoundrel. Further trouble comes through the wet nurse's suspicion of the danger for herself and her family, and through the failure of an attempt to purchase her silence and good will. The scene ends with the wife's hysterical rage when the nurse, before leaving, blurts out to her the horrible truth.

Act III winds up what is a medical tract rather than a drama with an argument at the Lock Hospital between the Doctor and Dupont's indignant father-in-law Deputy Loches, who wants to secure for his unhappy daughter a divorce. As to this the Deputy is philosophically pacified by the Doctor, who proceeds to see, in his presence, a series of syphilitic patients, in the hope that he will lay the matter before the Chamber, presumably with a view to legislation.

It is obvious that no modification of this passage nor elision of that, can alter the significance – doubtless well-intentioned – of this didactic drama, which must be taken or left as it stands. Venereal disease seems to me a subject essentially unfit for description or discussion on the public stage, no matter how good the motive for such discussion may be.

On this broad ground therefore – which will of course be regarded as a narrow one by advocates of the advanced pathological drama – DAMAGED GOODS is

NOT Recommended for Licence

(Sgd) Ernest A. Bendall.[23]

But desperate ills call for desperate remedies, and by 1917 the danger of syphilis to the British war effort was judged so significant that Sanderson was prepared to reconsider his ruling. He consulted the king and the Archbishop of Canterbury, and the latter indicated that he would no longer actively oppose Brieux's play being presented in public:

LAMBETH PALACE S.E.

20th Febry. 1917

My dear Lord Chamberlain,

I have read with care the Play you left with me last night. I could not go so far as to urge you to give sanction to its performance; but on the other hand I am inclined on the whole to believe that you would be taking a mistaken line if you were to veto it at a moment when the subject with which it deals is being freely discussed everywhere, the barriers which used to shut it off from the public gaze and talk being rudely broken down. All this I could expand to you in conversation, and I hope to have such a talk, as I could put it much more easily than I can in writing unless I were to inflict on you a lengthy essay.

I am

Yours very truly,

Randall Centaur

Damaged Goods was licensed, and statements were included in the programme excusing it as a practical addition to necessary propaganda, and promising that all proceeds would go to the National Council for Combating Venereal Disease. However, it had been a special case. In September 1918 the same playwright's *Maternity* was again refused a licence. Street was in two minds about it:

Mrs Shaw, in a 'Foreword' relates that in 1907 (apparently) the Censor accompanied a refusal to license the Play with the remark: 'inform whoever is responsible for this Play that it will never be licensed in England', but I am not absolutely certain that the Lord Chamberlain would be wise in adhering to this resolution of his predecessor. The Play

. . . is far less revolting than 'Damaged Goods' which also has been licensed. On the other hand I do not think this Play can be justified as useful propaganda. The difference in French social conditions makes much of the early part, with its moral, inapplicable here, and the last act is less a warning against abortion – as in the case of a Play recently refused – than a justification for it in the conditions of modern France . . . Since, therefore, the subject of abortion has not so far been allowed on our stage . . . I cannot advise its licensing.[24]

Bendall endorsed this conclusion:

I thoroughly agree with Street in not recommending this Play for License [sic]. It is only as propaganda that, like 'Damaged Goods' it could be passed: and I cannot see that propaganda concerning abortion serves any useful purpose. This subject was held to unfit Granville Barker's much better drama 'Waste' for performance on our stage: and I see no reason why its elaborate discussion, as in the last act here, should now be permitted.

Yet Brieux's work was strongly defended by Lord Buckmaster, a prominent and active member of the Lord Chamberlain's Advisory Board, and himself a former Liberal MP and Lord Chancellor in Asquith's government. Buckmaster was known as a social reformer with a particular commitment to the divorce law:

The Play itself is I think remarkable. It is true that it depends on three unpleasant facts, seduction, prevention of conception and abortion but from these three threads is spun a drama of unusual strength.

I find it difficult to know why this Play should not be produced. Each incident is one of the commonest facts in modern life. The cruelty and meanness of seduction and desertion has been frequently the subject of dramatic performance as for example in 'Faust', there can be no reason for its concealment and good rather than harm must result from its representation.

The artificial limitation of families is one of the familiar subjects at meetings and conferences of all classes of people who discuss social welfare and their proceedings are reported without any attempt at evasion in the daily press. The attempt of women to save themselves from disgrace or misery by illegal operations is again common and notorious. To point out that to this desperate remedy girls are driven by fear of shame and women by the harsh pressures of economic conditions is totally different from suggestions which other rejected plays have made, that there are well known and apparently respectable institutions where abortions are procured as a matter of course.

I would sanction the performance of this Play, it will be painful to witness but it cannot honestly shock anyone nor can it make vice familiar or lower the standard of conduct or morals.

But Buckmaster found himself isolated. For Dawson, it was a matter of principle that such subjects should be kept entirely off the stage (see Plate 2). And this time the Archbishop of Canterbury could see no sufficient reason to bend the rules:

I have read the Play carefully and with admiration of its force, its steady maintenance of high tone, and its avoidance, as it seems to me, of anything which can fairly be called coarse, or demoralising in tendency.

But I fail to see what good purpose, social or moral or intellectual or educational its production in England at present would promote. In this it differs wholly from 'Damaged Goods', the purpose of which was admirable, the moral clearly and effectively drawn, and the tale told with a minimum of mischief – except in so far as it might deter young women from facing the depicted risks of matrimony and lead them to remain single. Its production, and this is most important was supported by a weighty body of opinion on the part of men entitled to be listened to, and there is good evidence now as to the wholesome effect of its production on the stage, especially to male audiences. But in this case you have, as I understand, no body of opinion in favour of its production, and, at the very least you surely ought to have this, if the licensing of 'Damaged Goods' is to serve as a precedent.

I am not surprised that no such opinion has found voice. For, one asks, what is the object or the moral of this play? I don't think that it can be condemned as encouraging resort to abortionists[;] it does not do so [sic]. The girl who so resorts dies in consequence[;] so far as it goes therefore it discourages abortion. But that can hardly be described as its main motive or point.

What it does is to press the 'lesson', such as it is, that the production of many children is cruel to the wife, selfish on the husband's part and, in present economic conditions incapable of working well except among rich people. All these allegations are open to challenge and there is no real argument. But, anyhow, is that the lesson which wise people will say England needs to learn just now? Surely not . . .

In the absence therefore of any such appeal for its production as reached you, in reasonable form, in the case of 'Damaged Goods', I regard your decision against it as a wise and right one. For, presumably the performance, under Licence, of this kind of play needs to be justified by the powerfulness or point of the lesson it inculcates or the principles it asserts. No doubt this play does say severely just things against the cruelty of seduction and desertion, which are all to the good. And it advocates incidentally the raising of women's wages. But these are incidental, rather than to the purpose of the piece, and I confess to some difficulty in knowing what it is that Brieux desires, as his chief point, to inculcate.

It was 1932 before Cromer was ready to issue a licence for *Maternity*. Other playwrights who might have considered exploring similar areas would have known the score.

Treat it as a classic: Ibsen, Shelley, Pirandello, Cocteau and the unnatural minority

During the 1949 parliamentary debate on theatre censorship an MP declared:

> I am sure that in the Victorian days of hypocrisy and smug morality they were right not to allow 'Ghosts' and 'Mrs Warren's Profession' to be performed. It would have offended many people; it would have upset the thought of the time. People were not ready for those plays; they were ready only for 'The Second Mrs Tanqueray'.[25]

We have seen that plays sometimes received licences decades after they had first been submitted and only when they were judged safe and innocuous. To apologists for the system, such as the MP cited above, this process of delay made absolute sense; the duty of the Lord Chamberlain was to interpret and to follow public taste. But for writers such as Shaw and Granville Barker it was precisely the responsibility of serious playwrights to create work for which audiences were not yet 'ready'.

One of the legacies of theatre censorship with which the future must always live is the plays that were not written. Often it is relatively straightforward to recover texts which were refused licences, or to restore lines which were excised; what we cannot know are the 'unborn' plays, the ones which might have been written but weren't. Anticipating what would and would not be acceptable to the Lord Chamberlain, writers restricted their imaginations – consciously and unconsciously – by tailoring their ideas accordingly. It is no coincidence that so many significant conflicts occurred over the work of foreign playwrights, who had not written with an imaginary Lord Chamberlain peering over their shoulders and checking every word they put down.[26]

Having been written before the Theatres Act, the original text of *Oedipus Rex* would not have required licensing to be played in ancient Greek; but every translation was defined as a new play, and several versions had been turned down before Gilbert Murray's text was approved in 1910. Redford had opposed licensing this one, too, warning the producer and translator that the explicit references to incest had always put English versions beyond the pale. But despite fears that it would create a precedent for new plays on the same theme – 'Many writers will not I fear scruple to shelter themselves behind this licence' – the Advisory Board recommended approval on the grounds that the play 'deals with a purely classical story in a classical way and can make no appeal to the general public'.[27] This adoption of double standards, whereby 'classics' were eligible for special dispensation, became an increasingly visible feature of policy.

Ghosts and Peer Gynt

In May 1914 the Office agreed to reconsider its attitude towards Ibsen's 'melancholy study of heredity'; *Ghosts* had received a single private performance in London in

1891, given by the Independent Theatre Society, but it had been made clear that there was no chance of a licence being issued for public performance. Now Street was convinced that the time had come to overturn this decision:

> The violence of the attacks in this country on *Ghosts* twenty years ago seems almost incredible now, but I think may be explained by the play's having been made a sort of battle-ground for a general controversy about the theatre which drew its bitterness from the extremists in either camp, the rather pretentiously intellectual in the one and the rather brutally Philistine in the other. Except that its licensed performance would have insulted a public opinion worked up by its opponents I can see no reason why a licence should ever have been refused. At present that reason does not exist. The play is received with respect and with no attacks when it is performed in a technically private manner. Moreover its free performance everywhere else in Europe would make a refusal of a licence in London slightly ridiculous. It is an acknowledged masterpiece of the modern stage.
>
> What it exhibits morally – in perhaps rather a crude and unscientific fashion – is the effect on an offspring of a debauched life in one of the parents, and artistically the recurrence of the same unhappy moments to the consciousness of the wife and mother – 'ghosts'. There is no disgusting discussion or examination of syphilis specifically. As for the point about incest, that is extremely far-fetched and hardly needed Mr. Gosse's assurance in 'The Times' . . .
>
> I think the licensing of the play would be received everywhere as an inevitable and proper course.[28]

Lord Buckmaster agreed: 'No one can say it is coarse or immoral . . . I doubt if people who knew nothing of syphilis would know any more after reading or seeing the play while the irregular relations of a man and a woman necessarily form a common subject of serious dramatic art'. Another member of the Advisory Board – the Oxford professor Walter Raleigh – had more negative reasons for supporting Street's recommendation:

THE HANGINGS,
FERRY HINKSEY,
NEAR OXFORD

26 June 1914

Ghosts

One of the hardships that I suffer from the refusal of licences to plays like this, or like Mr. Shaw's *Mrs Warren*, is that they get a fictitious and enduring importance. They become heroic, the utterances of truths which a corrupt and self-indulgent age fears. This enrages me. *Ghosts* is almost hysterical. Syphilis in real life is bad enough, but the behaviour of humanity under the scourge is a model of dignity compared with the gibberings of this play. If it had been acted 20 years ago it would be dead now . . .

> If Ibsen tells a lie (and *Ghosts*, I think, is a lie) he ought not to be protected. Let him
> tell it right out, and pay for it.
>
> W. A. Raleigh

One of the reasons that 'classic' plays were sometimes treated more leniently was the assumption that, almost by definition, they would appeal only to a self-selecting 'highbrow' audience. This attitude is typified in Street's 1922 recommendation of *Peer Gynt*:

> Peer Gynt was written in 1867, but it is no marvel it should not have been produced in
> England before: it is altogether above the heads of any but an extremely select English
> audience . . .
>
> From the point of view of the censorship I think it would be absurd to interfere with
> the production of this European classic . . . I think it would be ridiculous to cut out
> anything from such a work and as a whole there is no reason for interference. There is
> not the faintest possibility of its appealing to 'popular' audiences.[29]

His superiors agreed – 'I would suggest treating this somewhat as one would treat Shakespeare – parts of which if written today would appear coarse. i.e. treat it as a classic' – and the licence was issued.

The Cenci

It was not only foreign plays which could be afforded the status of classics, but also older texts, and in the early twenties a licence was finally granted for *The Cenci*. Based on an Italian source, the plot of Shelley's play focuses on the incestuous desires of a debauched and elderly count for his daughter, his subsequent murder at the hands of his family, and their execution by the pope. Shelley himself had spoken of the need to 'increase the ideal, and diminish the actual horror' when creating a work of art out of such 'monstrous' events, so as to 'mitigate the pain of the contemplation of the moral deformity from which they spring'. But he had refused any notion that such a work should be made 'subservient to what is vulgarly termed a moral purpose', arguing rather that his play 'would be as a light to make apparent some of the most dark and secret caverns of the human heart'.[30] *The Cenci* had been published in 1819, and had received a single and private matinee performance by the Shelley Society in May 1886; however, several Lords Chamberlain vigorously declined to consider it for public performance; 'all the genius in the world cannot make a play of which incest is the central theme, proper to be licensed for public representation', commented the Examiner in 1873.[31]

In 1920 Street supported an application for licence:

LORD CHAMBERLAIN'S OFFICE,
ST JAMES'S PALACE

May 4th 1920

Memorandum on 'The Cenci'

The subject of the Play is of course distressing to the last degree. The gloomy and tragic study of Francesco's madness, culminating in his outrage of his daughter, Beatrice, done in mere devilry; his murder and the condemnation of Beatrice by the Pope – it is all one long horror. Nor as a matter of personal opinion do I think that Shelley's genius redeems the horror; there is little of his true poetry in the Play. But it is a famous Play by a great Poet; it is universally read; it is throughout on a level of high tragedy, and the subject of incest did not prevent the licensing of 'Oedipus Rex'. It is certainly, and strongly 'Recommended for Licence' so far as I am concerned.
(Sd). G. S. Street[32]

However, Buckmaster drew a distinction between Shelley and Sophocles: 'It differs from the 'Oedipus' for incest there was unintentional and here it is deliberate and designed'; he worried that Shelley's play 'can teach no lesson it can give no warning or instruction' but 'can only sicken and terrify and distress'. Nevertheless, Sandhurst seems to have intended to grant a licence, but as the planned production came to nothing it was never issued. When *The Cenci* was resubmitted in September 1922, the Duke of Atholl had replaced Sandhurst, and he felt bound to 'endorse the finding of my predecessor in office and pass this play'; for him, its saving grace was its age:

It is not as if a modern writer had invented the subject matter, which in such a case would be disgusting. On the contrary the whole thing is a drama of real life that was acted long ago and Shelley's version may be looked upon as a reproduction watered down to enable it to appear upon the modern dramatic stage, but written in the style of the date of the occurrence, which helps to put it amongst the classics.

The play will never be put upon the stage as an ordinary piece, but will only appear for the benefit of special audiences.

The Cenci opened at the New Theatre on 13 November 1922, and on the 27th the Westminster Catholic Federation expressed strong disapproval: 'it is, to say the least, surprising that an audience can be found to attend such a representation'. On 6 December the Public Morality Council complained to St James's Palace about 'the presentation of such a subject under ordinary conditions in a theatre open to the general public of any age'; it was, they insisted, 'one of those plays in which the atmosphere is likely to have an injurious effect upon the moral life and standards of the present day'. The Council itemized the dangers of the play, which it was convinced outweighed its potential merits. They also challenged the fundamental logic of applying different standards to different texts:

THE LONDON COUNCIL for the **PROMOTION OF PUBLIC MORALITY**

President & Chairman
RIGHT REV. THE LORD BISHOP OF LONDON

OFFICES:
37, NORFOLK STREET,
STRAND W.C.

6th December 1922

... The crime is an unnatural one, hence there can be no appeal to the argument that anything true to human nature is suitable for the stage. Even if the public welfare should require that the severity of the penalty the State inflicts for such a crime should be more generally known, to force such a subject upon public attention in time of recreation can only do harm.

A second objection lies in the presentation of the Cenci himself, who shows a combination of diabolical passion and cruel lust that has nothing human in it . . . it is degrading to Humanity to suggest that this animal is human.

Again very objectionable is the lust of cruelty that dominates the play, and that has been an element in several plays of late. Such scenes tend to leave a modern audience exhausted and demoralised. However strong the nerves of the Middle Ages, modern city dwellers cannot listen to screams from torture on the rack, or watch the partial throttling of a wife without an expenditure of nervous force wholly out of proportion to any artistic gain . . . Even in the character of Beatrice there is no redeeming feature, for she alienates sympathy by her efforts to save her life by false statements, and by her total absence of feeling for the man for whose horrible torture she is largely responsible.

With the critics' suggestion that the play is a Monument to Shelley's failure to understand life, the Council entirely agree, the play has no message, no purpose, reason or outcome; sin and crime result in tragedy and anguish, but there is behind this no scheme bound up with religious ideals or moral purpose. The play suggests simply the ravings of a genius obsessed by a grievance.

The Council are strongly of opinion that there is no justification for the view, that has grown up, that plays that are classics should not be controlled, neither do they believe that this is the desire of the thoughtful public of this country. They suggest that it is obvious that an <u>average audience, varying widely in experience and age, has not the background of</u> education which alone makes it possible to interpret wisely the different moral standards and outlook of an earlier age or of another country.

> I am, my Lord
> Your obedient Servant,
> Howard M. Tyrer
> Secretary

Sir George Crichton, who had now replaced Dawson as comptroller, explained why the Office was sticking to its decision:

while the subject matter of the play is from every point of view reprehensible, the view taken by the previous Lord Chamberlains and their advisors was that 'The Cenci' has been widely read ever since it was written, as a famous Play by a great poet, and that its style and the date of its occurrence entitle it to be considered as a classic. It can therefore hardly be considered in the same light as the work of a modern author.

A little over one hundred years since it had been published, Shelley's play was free to be performed on the London stage.

Six Characters in Search of an Author

As Crichton had explained, very different standards were required of new plays – which, by definition, could not be designated 'classics' – and it was primarily the taboo associated with incest which caused problems with Pirandello's most famous play. Barry Jackson had first planned to stage *Six Characters in Search of an Author* at Birmingham Repertory Theatre in the autumn of 1922, and the Lord Chamberlain's Office had received the script at almost the same time as *The Cenci*. Again, Street was favourably impressed – though he was unable to remember all the details about it:

CEREMONIAL DEPARTMENT
ST JAMES'S PALACE, S.W.1

October 23rd 1922

'SIX CHARACTERS IN SEARCH OF AN AUTHOR' a play in 3 acts.
To be produced at the Repertory Theatre, Birmingham, Oct. 30.

————

This extraordinary play was produced some time ago by the Stage or some other Society. I forget the author's name – it is not given here – and nationality. The play is a mixture of mysticism, comedy and horror, though the horror, as will be seen, is removed two degrees, so to speak. The idea is as follows. A manager is rehearsing a play when six characters enter – the Father, the Mother, the Step-Daughter, the Son, the Boy and the Little Girl. The Father explains that they are not living people in the ordinary sense but creations of an author. Having created them, he did not see his way to making a play of them and they seek an author to write the play so that, having entered the world of art they should continue to live. Their story so far is this: The Father and Mother were originally married and the Son is theirs. Then the Mother went off with another man and became the mother of the other three. The Father met the Step-Daughter in the pseudo-milliner's shop of one Madam Pace, with an evil intent, not knowing who she was, but before anything happened the Mother came in and declared the girl's identity. Then, the other man being dead, they all went to live with the Father. In Act II the manager tries to make a play of this; taking the incident of the shop, Madam Pace being 'evoked' or materialized. The real actors try to act this and are continually interrupted by the originals who are dissatisfied with their rendering. Act III is mainly taken up by metaphysics developed by the Father, but the play goes on with interruptions until the Boy shoots himself and all ends in confusion, the manager declaring he has wasted a day.

The only objection from the point of view of the censorship is the more or less revolting nature of the shop incident between the Father and his Step-Daughter. The Lord Chamberlain might like to consider this, and perhaps it ought to be modified. Act I, p. 16 and Act II, pp. 17 to end. It should be remembered, however, that the events are not supposed to have happened but to be a pseudo-play within a play, and the interest of the whole is not in the incidents but in the mystical or metaphysical theses. The performance also is of a special nature and there is no possibility of the play being put on for an ordinary run commercially. For these reasons I should not interfere.[33]

Recommended for Licence.
(sd.) G. S. STREET

However, largely on the recommendation of the Advisory Board, Atholl turned the play down. Lord Buckmaster had been particularly agin it:

To grant a licence for this play, would in my opinion to be to sanction the performance of a degrading spectacle . . . This is neither tragedy nor comedy it is plain filthiness . . . That the public taste will regret this play I do not doubt, it might interest the un-natural minority and vicious youth.

But Jackson was convinced of the play's importance and determined to stage it; and as a result, *Six Characters* . . . became the first serious problem to confront Lord Cromer when he took over as Lord Chamberlain after Atholl's brief period of duty. In December 1922 Cromer cautiously decided to maintain the ban:

I have gone very carefully into the play and no matter what may be said about its representing a new school of thought or acting, the fact remains that the theme of the play deals with a subject that is quite unnecessarily unpleasant. It is, moreover, the sort of thing to which the ecclesiastical and other authorities are taking exception.

In these circumstances, and even if Mr Street were to uphold his formerly expressed opinion, I should not consider myself justified in reversing the decision of my predecessor in Office, backed as it is by the Advisory Board, as I should be lending myself to allowing representation on the stage of exactly the sort of 'atmosphere' which I consider it my duty as far as possible to dispel.

Barry Jackson was not the only manager to recognize the theatrical significance of Pirandello's play. Lewis Casson submitted it from the New Theatre in January 1924, and in April of the same year Nigel Playfair wrote a personal letter to Street at his club:

LYRIC THEATRE, HAMMERSMITH, W.6.

April 28th, 1924

G. S. Street Esq
Savile Club
Piccadilly, W.1.

My dear Street,

I wonder whether you would consider that I were aking [sic] an indiscreet question, if I were to ask you to let me know what alterations would be considered necessary to obtain a favourable consideration for 'SIX CHARACTERS IN SEARCH OF AN AUTHOR'?

This is a play written by the greatest Italian dramatist, and considered to be his masterpiece; there is a very great demand on the part of a certain public to see it, and I should very much like to take an opportunity of putting it on for a few performances.

I know the general opinion is that it was refused on the grounds that it deals with the subject of incest, but this surely is not the case: even if the relationship between a step-father and step-daughter can be called incestuous, not only does no intercourse actually take place, but there is no question of its taking place when the relationship is established.

So sorry to bother you.

Yours sincerely
Nigel Playfair

Cromer held a private meeting with Playfair, but he was properly mindful of the fact that if it were to be licensed then Barry Jackson deserved the first option. In any case, the Advisory Board remained opposed to the play; Buckmaster acknowledged its 'dramatic merits' but objected not only to the incident between father and step-daughter but also to another reference he detected in the text: 'to base a scene on the horror of a boy seeing his Father and Mother in sexual relationship sickens and disgusts me and I therefore assume it would sicken and disgust a normal audience'. He was prepared to concede that he might have 'misunderstood this Play', but this was irrelevant since 'so also may the people who see it'. In effect, therefore, play-wrights were apparently obliged to guard even against possible 'misinterpretation' of their work by audiences.

In June 1925 a licence *was* issued for Pirandello's play – in its original Italian version, *Sei personaggi in cerca d'autore*:

The English translation of this play 'Six Characters in Search of an Author' has been banned. It has always been the custom, however, to extend greater freedom to Plays given in foreign languages. I think this is an occasion for such treatment . . . what was offensive in that Play in English is obviously not so to Italian audiences. People who speak Italian and are interested in Italian literature would be disappointed if they could not see this famous Play and the same can be said of the Italian colony.[34]

This was neither the first nor last occasion on which a play turned down in translation was licensed in its original language – the most famous example being Beckett's *Endgame* thirty years later.[35] Doubtless the class of audience the censorship was striving to protect (or control) was not thought likely to speak a foreign language. However, Barry (now Sir Barry) Jackson was prompted to submit a new English version. Street again supported it in principle, and used his report partly to refute some of the arguments previously raised by the Advisory Board:

Title:	*Six Characters in Search of an Author*
Place of Production:	Repertory Theatre, Birmingham
Date of Production:	November 8th
Author:	Put into English by H. K. Ayliff from the Italian of Luigi Pirandello

LORD CHAMBERLAIN'S OFFICE,

ST JAMES'S PALACE, S.W.1

July 23rd 1925

READER'S REPORT

This version is better than the one previously refused a licence and better than the English version which accompanied the Italian licensed recently. It reads more naturally and more vigorously. In one respect, of which later, I think it is also an improvement from the censorship point of view. Sir Barry Jackson assures us that it has been desired to eliminate anything likely to offend and is apparently ready to try to meet any further objections . . .

Comparing this version with the previous, I do not think that the first of the two objections made to the Play, the scene in the brothel, is in any way removed. This surely might be modified. The other, raised by Lord Buckmaster, that the Little Boy committed suicide because he saw his mother and stepfather in the sexual act, is certainly not sustained: I cannot find anything at all to that effect.

My original opinion, that the Play should be licensed, is to that extent strengthened. I append my reasons.

1. The events of the play within the play – the scene at the brothel – are not supposed to happen even in the theatrical sense. They are suggestions in the brains of the characters who are not even supposed to exist: reality is a further step removed.

2. The interest of the play is not in this story at all, but (a) in the metaphysics of created characters as compared with living people (rather hackneyed in their metaphysics, I admit), and (b) in the contrast of character as conceived by their creator and as interpreted by actors: the comedy of the play is all in this.

3. The play, when produced in English by the Stage Society and lately when produced in Italian, caused no remark, so far as I know, that it was unfit for public representation in English.

4. The play is the most famous of the most famous living Italian dramatist. Personally I think Pirandello's work is greatly overestimated, but the fact remains that among those interested in dramatic art there is a great desire to see it.

No single one of these reasons may be conclusive, but taken together I think they are so.

Recommended for Licence

(sd.) G. S. STREET.

However, the Board was not persuaded by Street's nice distinctions: 'When all is said and done about "fiction", "a play within a play", "morality", and so forth', opined Lord Ullswater, 'the chief theme of this play is the attempted seduction by a father of his daughter-in-law. However much this may appeal to the Italian mind, it appears to me unsuitable for the British.' Cromer's conclusions confirm the fact that he saw himself less as a judge with expert knowledge and more as a medium for interpreting and transmitting the will of people of influence: 'In Italian it was probably not fully understood by most English audiences, but when its full significance is brought home in English I cannot help feeling that most people wd. disapprove of its performance being permitted'. He informed Jackson of the situation, who 'expressed his determination to go on pressing for a Licence & said he wd. continue to pay Signor Pirandello his fees for the English rights until the play was produced.'

In 1926 Philip Ridgeway, the manager at the Gaiety Theatre in the Strand, wanted to discuss a possible production for London's Little Art Theatre at Barnes, under the direction of Fyodor Komisarjevsky: 'I am particularly anxious to do this play and to alter anything which you have objection to. On these lines it would seem a pity if England is not to have Pirandello's great masterpiece.' He was told there was no point even in having a meeting.

Finally, in May 1928, Lord Cromer was persuaded by Sir Barry Jackson to attend incognito a private performance of a modified version of the text at the Arts Theatre. Having done so, Cromer promptly did a U-turn and informed the members of the Board accordingly:

> You will recollect no doubt the controversy that has now dragged on since 1922 about Pirandello's play 'Six Characters in Search of an Author'. Sir Barry Jackson of the Birmingham Repertory Theatre and all the high-brow people have been very persistent over this play, as they consider it a stigma on our English theatre that a play which has been acted in every capital should be forbidden here.
>
> I consequently went to see a private performance of the revised version last Sunday night and, although to my mind it remains a disagreeable play, I felt bound to confess that it is quite inoffensively acted, and consequently I have agreed to issue a Licence.
>
> Apart from the fact that it has been banned for so long, I do not think it is likely to appeal to a wide audience, or to have a very long run. I may be wrong, but this is also the view taken by Sir Barry Jackson himself, and I think it only right to let you know of the step I have taken as you have been so kind in advising me at different times in the past when a play has had to be considered. It is certainly a case of a play difficult to

COPY OF PETITION TO THE
LORD CHAMBERLAIN

We, the undersigned, are of opinion that the ban hitherto placed upon the performance of George Bernard Shaw's play ''MRS. WARREN'S PROFESSION'' should now be withdrawn, and the play licensed for production in this country. We make this request on the grounds that:—

1. The problem with which the play so effectively deals is now recognised to be one of extreme gravity.

2. The stage is being more and more utilised as a much-needed educational factor in connection with this subject.

3. ''MRS. WARREN'S PROFESSION'' is a dramatic work of acknowledged excellence by one of our foremost British dramatists, and we would respectfully urge that facilities for its production should be accorded in the same way as has been done with other plays of similar tendency by foreign authors.

4. We believe there is a widespread desire amongst British playgoers to witness this play on the British stage. The play has been already performed many times in America and other countries.

*(Signed)

*Kindly sign and return in envelope herewith to
Edwin T. Heys, 17, Leicester Street, London, W.C. 2.

1. Petition submitted to the Lord Chamberlain in September 1917 supporting the licensing of *Mrs Warren's Profession*.

LORD CHAMBERLAIN'S OFFICE.

Sᴛ. JAMES'S PALACE. S.W. 1.

"MATERNITY"   310/18

I regret I have found it impossible to read through
this play, so I do not claim to be heard as regards this
piece individually.   But on the broad question I offer the
following remarks:-

I am wholly in favour of elasticity in our methods,
each case to be judged on its merits, no red tape and hard
and fast refusals.   But, as in every other problem, a
dividing line on which the policy is based seems to me to be
necessary.

Thus to my mind our policy is broadly speaking to
taboo indecency, blasphemy, and lese majeste.

Bernard Shaw may say what he likes with regard to the
stage license to portray any and every subject which are
universally known to be part of the daily life.   There are
certain subjects which in my opinion should only be dealt
with by the ecclesiastic or the medical profession.

I refer to Subjects on which we literally turn the key.   In a
civilised world we do not discuss openly the <u>details</u> of
sexual intercourse, of visits to the W.C., and I would add
to these such subjects as venereal disease and procuring
abortion.

I believe still in keeping such subjects for discussion
in privacy with the priest or the doctor.   I do not believe
in the value of the stage for propaganda purposes on such
subjects.   The class attracted by such plays is not that
which it is wished to convince, morbid and erotic natures
such as those who advocate the production of such plays
are drawn by them, natures that have already eaten the apple;
but <u>not</u> those to whom the lesson would be of value.

I believe that if a plebiscite could be taken of the
of such plays educated public, the proportion in favour of production on the
stage would be infinitesimal, while the enormous majority
would say what use to us is a Censor who allows such
uncleanliness to be discussed in public.

Douglas Dawson

2. Response by Sir Douglas Dawson (Comptroller of the Lord Chamberlain's Office) to the submission
of *Maternity* for licensing, October 1918.

STAGE PLAY SUBMITTED FOR LICENCE.

Title: "THE INFERNAL MACHINE"

No. of Scenes or Acts: 4 acts

Place of Production: Cambridge Arts Theatre

Date of Production: 10th May

Author: Jean Cocteau, translated by Carl Wildman

LORD CHAMBERLAIN'S OFFICE,
ST. JAMES'S PALACE, S.W. 1.

READER'S REPORT.   24th March 1943

As the Lord Chamberlain will see from the earlier file, this play met with some adverse criticism when submitted in 1936. My predecessor had a somewhat uncertain sense of the Theatre, which at times led him astray, and I consider this play a case in point. I am quite certain that if played reasonably (as it must be played to be in harmony with the other Acts) Act III will prove to be quite unobjectionable. Since 1936 one or more plays on the Byron-Augusta Leigh theme have been licenced and performed, with love scenes between the poet and his half-sister; and as far as I know nobody has turned a hair. I warmly support what Lord David Cecil wrote about this play, while perhaps not rating it quite so high as he does, as a work of art. The production is now sponsored by The Cambridge Arts Theatre Trust, of which the trustees, as the Lord Chamberlain will see from the list printed at the head of the covering letter, are a galaxy of Economic, Municipal, Musical and Scholastic eminence. The play will be performed before a cultured audience, and there is no fear of its later being performed before an un-cultured one: they would be bored to death and would never sit it out; the ordinary theatregoer shuns the high-brow Theatre like the plague-house. The Censorship therefore would make itself supremely ridiculous by refusing a licence, and so except for two words in Act II (page 57) I strongly recommend the Lord Chamberlain to grant a Licence for its performance.

(sd.) H C Game.

Cut here
I agree So do I.
26.3.43.

3. Reader's Report by Henry Game on *The Infernal Machine* when it was successfully resubmitted for licence, March 1943.

STAGE PLAY SUBMITTED FOR LICENCE.

Title :   "MISS JULIE"

No. of Scenes or Acts :   1 act

Place of Production :   Westminster Theatre

Date of Production :

Author :   August Strindberg

LORD CHAMBERLAIN'S OFFICE,
ST. JAMES'S PALACE, S.W. 1.

READER'S REPORT.

15th December 1938.

This is Strindberg's famous play "Miss Julie", which
was first submitted to this Office in 1913, and was refused a licence.
There have been several attempts since to get the ban lifted; but up
to now, just 50 years since it was written, they have been unsuccessful.

The play is a classic known to everybody who takes dramatic
art at all seriously, but so as to make my report a developed argument I
must briefly recount its theme.
There are only three characters, Julie, a young woman who
is the last of a noble but now degenerate stock; John, the footman, the
antithesis of Julie, of vigorous peasant stock, crude, virile, and ambitious;
and Christine, the cook, slothful, slavish and religious in a superficial
worldly way.
The scene is the kitchen of a country mansion on midsummer
night, while a dance of the tenantry is taking place in a barn nearby.
Julie is for various reasons in a morbid state physically and mentally.
She is attracted by John, makes tentative advances, overcomes any scruples
that the fundamentally servile minded John may have, and ultimately gives
herself to him. Remorse and self-loathing follow fast upon the act.
Flight from the scene of her shame is made impossible to Julie, first by
want of funds, then by the cook's jealousy and her father's return home.
The situation in which she finds herself finally destroys what little will
power Julie ever possessed, and it is from the virility of John that Julie
draws the needed strength to kill herself - an act comparative to the
hara-kiri of the Japanese Samurai.

The play was last submitted in 1935 and was again refused
a licence; but Lord Cromer always felt particularly antipathetic to this
theme, and I do not think that personal prejudices furnish sufficient reason
for banning a play.

In the old days such Societies as the Stage Society catered
adequately for those who took the drama seriously, but now the development
of the Cinema has resulted in a surprising revival of interest in dramatic
art, and the public who want to see and hear the classics is both numerous
and widespread.

The play is undoubtedly an ugly one, and belonging as it
does to Strindberg's realistic period, is lacking in the poetry which
suffuses such a play as "Desire Under the Elms".

But we have passed many plays in which seduction has taken
place, even the seduction of servant by mistress, and we cannot ban a play
with justice just because it is much more powerful than the work of lesser
men. The play may disgust some, but it can corrupt nobody. No footman
nor chauffeur need fear the more for his virtue for its passing, nor society
disintegrate in one glorious orgie in the servants hall.

There is a line on page 13 which is translated very crudely.
The "Anglo-Swedish Literary Foundation"version is much more discreet, and I

---

4. Reader's Report by Henry Game on *Miss Julie* when it was successfully resubmitted for licence, December 1938.

suggest the passage be altered to "Oh, she's not very well just now, and she always takes on so strange"; and "whore" (page 44) could with advantage be "filth" as in the A-S L.version. The word appears on the previous page and is necessary and justified; but is not justified here as "filth" is dramatically and artistically preferable – it's unimportant.

The play is of course *agreed to both. Have spoken to the producer who is looking into the better Swedish version*

Recommend for Licence

(sd.) H C Game.

Agree to both alteration.

"OUR BETTERS" a play in 3 acts by W.S.Maugham. To be produced at
the Globe Theatre.

This play is a fierce indictment of the ~~views~~ *wiles* of a
section of English society and primarily a satire on some
Americans who have made their way in it.   It is outspoken,
though not coarse in language, and extremely unpleasant and
painful, though in form a comedy, as the author calls it.
It will serve the purpose of a report to deal with the
characters and their relations and the principal event rather
than to give a detailed narrative of the plot.   The central
figure is Pearl, a rich American married to Sir George Grayston,
who never appears and is evidently a mari complaisant.   She is
an extraordinarily successful hostess (from the snob's point
of view) and is assisted by the money of Arthur Fenwick, a
very rich American, whose mistress she evidently is.   Another
rich American is the Duchesse de Surennes, who has divorced
her husband, and she is the mistress of a mercenary young
blackguard, Tony Paxton.   Another is married to and separated
from an Italian Prince: she is virtuous.   Thornton Clay is
a pushing American, a shameless snob.   The good element, apart
from the Princess, consists of Bessie, Pearl's sister, a
charming girl, newly arrived from America; Fleming Harvey, a
decent American boy, and Bleane, a pleasant young English peer
who wants to marry Bessie.   The great scene of the play is at
the end of Act II, at Pearl's country house.   Pearl and Tony
have conceived a passion for one another.   It is after dinner.
They make an appointment in the summer house.   The others play
poker.   The jealous Duchess (guessing the appointment) sends
Bleane to fetch her bag which she pretends to have left in the
summer house.   He returns and says it is not there.   She asks
Bessie to go.   Bleane, much embarrassed, interposes and says
she cannot - the door is locked.   Bessie, ~~sensing~~ the truth, *seeking*,
breaks down, humiliated.   Pearl and Tony reappear and Pearl,
realizing that the truth is out, turns to Tony: "You fool, I
told you it was too risky."   The last act in a series of
witty scenes, cynical to the last degree, shows Pearl
re-establishing herself, making Fenwick forgive her and also
the Duchesse by bringing down a famous dancing master for the
latter's delectation, so that the party is not broken up and
scandal prevented.   The vile Tony conciliates his Duchesse
who promises to marry him. But Bessie, fearing she may become
like her sister if she marries Bleane, goes home to America.

I believe there was some outcry over the play in
New York, probably over the end of Act II, for it is not an
attack on Americans in general, far from it, but only on some
who live here, and Mr.Maugham cannot of course mean that <u>all</u>
Americans who marry titled foreigners are bad.   From the
censorship point of view two main points arise.

1. The two people being caught <u>in flagrante delicto</u>
in Act II.   Originally, as I gather from alterations in the
text, Bessie discovered them, which would be much more
unpleasant. As it is, it seems to me merely a case of a thing
happening "off" which has so happened in other plays. With this I

join

5. Reader's Report by George Street recommending the licensing of *Our Betters*, April 1923.

CEREMONIAL DEPARTMENT,

St JAMES'S PALACE, S.W.1.

"OUR BETTERS."

join the general vi*ci*ousness, immorality and sordidness of several of the characters, and about it all I think the important point is that the effect is not sympathy with vice but intense scorn of it, not the less because it is made ridiculous as well as odious. If I am right in this it is the reverse of an immoral play.

2.   This seems far more difficult to me. Pearl will suggest to many people Lady Cunard. That is pointed by her country house being called "Feathers Nevill", as Lady Cunard used to live at Nevill Holt: ~~but~~ *that* I should think ~~it~~ is an accident.   How far the identification goes others will know better than I.   (The ringing up on p.41, Act I, suggests her "capturing" a statesman with musical tastes which may suggest somebody.)   If it were only a question of social ambitions and success there would not be much in it: Lady Cunard is not the only successful hostess: I am not of course implying that it would be fair to her at all. But Pearl is represented as a callously vicious and mercenary person, and if any real person were obviously meant and so painted it is another thing altogether.   I reserve this point as being less qualified than others, probably, to judge of it.   With regard to the play as a whole ~~while~~ I think it is clearly one which should be read by the Lord Chamberlain or the Advisory Board, and is certainly not a play for la jeune fille, as its effect is moral, a lashing of vice, though exaggerated in its presentation, and as there is nothing offensive ~~sexually~~ *verbally* it is tentatively and with the reserve indicated

Recommended for Licence.

(sd.) G.S.STREET.

Passed for Licence subject to the name of the country house being altered so as to give no hint of similarity with any existing names.

L. 8 May/23.

Licence endorsed. 11.5.23

BALMORAL CASTLE.

18th. September, 1923.

My dear Rowland,

Somebody has spoken to the King about a play
"Our Betters": and if the report is true His Majesty
thinks it must be decidedly objectionable and he is
inclined to wonder whether it was carefully considered
by the censor.   Apart from its immoral tendency it
apparently is not very favourable to the Americans.

His Majesty has also read the enclosed cutting
and concludes that its criticism upon the censor is in
connection with "Our Betters".

Yours ever,

Stamfordham

The
   Earl of Cromer,
      G.C.I.E., C.V.O.,
   Lord Chamberlain.

If you have not read the critique in the "Times" of the
13th., please look at it.

6. Letter from the King's Private Secretary to the Lord Chamberlain, September 1923, querying the decision
to license *Our Betters*.

Play "FALLEN ANGELS" by Noël Coward

GLOBE THEATRE, Shaftesbury Avenue, W.

Thursday Evening, 7th May, 1925.

392/25

We visited the above Theatre as indicated,
and the general impressions we gained from the play
were as under :-

1. That the effect of the play depends upon the
   ability of the two chief characters (Julia
   Sterroll and Jane Banbury) to work themselves
   up into a state of hysteria in anticipation
   of sexual intercourse with an man with whom
   they have had immoral relations before marriage, and hope to do so again during the
   absence of their respective husbands.

2. To arrive at this state of sexual exultation,
   Act II is entirely devoted to a representation of the two women drinking themselves
   into a condition of intoxication whilst waiting for the Frenchman with whom they desire
   to have indecent relations.

3. They confide in each other that as both in
   the past have misconducted themselves with
   this man, neither (being friends) shall

-1-

7. Report submitted to the Lord Chamberlain on behalf of the Public Morality Council, May 1925, detailing their
objections to *Fallen Angels* and to the decision to license it.

"cut out" the other but will indulge to-
gether : "We stand or fall together".
"That would be most embarrassing, Jane"
(Act I)

392/25

4. The most serious aspect is brought to a head
in Act III. This is a teaching of a single
moral standard for men and women (instead
of the present double one) but the standard
is to be a lower one, and, presuming that
most men are unchaste before marriage, unchastity in single women is to be condoned.
This is shown in the conversation between
the women and their husbands. When Frederick
Sterroll is asked about his conduct before
marriage, he replies "That is beside the
point" and this reply is the occasion for
the remark that if his conduct is to be passed
over, the woman's must be.

5. The husbands are depicted as being rather
stupid individuals, particularly for their
belief in their wives' chastity. The
Frenchman, Maurice Duclos, is shown to be
a frequent seducer of women, but, apparently,
no moral stigma attaches to such conduct, and
it is suggested that they arrange things much

-2-

392/25

better in France than in England and do not
pretend to be chaste.   No shame is shown on
the part of the wives when their conduct becomes known to their husbands and they allow
the Frenchman to argue them out of their difficulties by the most transparent lying,
which, however, is apparently effective in
deceiving the husbands.

6.   At the end of the play the wives rush off with
the Frenchman to his flat above and are heard
with him boisterously singing a love-song.
The finale shows vice triumphant, virtue non-
existent and the infaithful wives apparently
enjoying themselves in the company of their
paramour.

The whole is a revolting sex-play and has not
the redeeming feature of containing a moral lesson.   It
must have a demoralising tendency upon the minds particularly of young people who witness it and cause them to
reflect that if it represents real life, then moral re-
straints and marital fidelity are really boring and un-
natural and that to profess chastity before marriage and
fidelity afterwards is sheer hypocrisy.   The whole play
is full of innuendoes and suggestive remarks regarding
sexual relationships, in fact we felt that it would be

found difficult to select many examples of dialogue
of an elevating character.

A large section of the audience greeted these
sexual allusions with bursts of laughter and appeared
to be openly amused at suggestions of unchastity.

We feel that the effect of such a production
must be :-

1. To gratify unhealthy sexual imaginations.
2. To encourage women to be careless of their
   chastity.
3. To lower the conception of marital relationships and consequently have a degenerate
   influence upon home life.

We fell most emphatically that this play
should be immediately withdrawn in the interests of
public morality.

24th October 1928.

Dear Sir,

"The Hairy Ape"

With reference to your letter of the 15th instant regarding the above Play I am desired by the Lord Chamberlain to say that the alterations which you propose in the passages mentioned are approved, but that they do not go far enough to meet his Lordship's requirements.

In addition to those suggested the following other expressions must be modified:-
Page 3, "You're a bloody liar"
page 11, "bloody furnace" and "bloody apes"
Scene 3, page 33 "lousy"
scene 4, page 39, "bleedin' millionaire","Bloody capitalist"
          "bloody gold","bleedin' ship", "bloody
          boat" "bloody animals".
     page 40, "God" (three times).
     page 52, "lousey tart", "bloody cow" "Bloody
          stokehole".
     page 53, "wouldn't bloody well pay","bloody
          world"
     page 55,"bloody coppers"
     page 56, "tarts".

It would appear that the pages in the Script in this Office do not correspond with the script in your possession, and in order that the necessary alterations can be correctly made and the Licence endorsed it would be convenient if you could forward a copy of the play similar to the one you possess together with your proposals for alterations for the additional expressions mentioned above.

Yours faithfully,

(sd.) C. L. Gordon.

Assistant Comptroller.

Terence Gray Esq.

8. Letter of October 1928 from the Lord Chamberlain's Office to the Festival Theatre, Cambridge, demanding additional alterations to the language of *The Hairy Ape*.

25th October, 1928.

The Comptroller,
The Lord Chamberlain's Office,
St. James's Palace,
London S.W. 1.

Dear Sir,   The Hairy Ape

        I am in receipt of your letter of October 24th. Your further
requirements place me in a very difficult position. Your first
letter and my interview with you gave me no reason to suppose
that you intended such drastic alterations, which amount to performing the play as a polite social comedy. Indeed I understood
that you required merely a modification in the quantity of terms of
abuse, i.e. a removal of such forcible language as in my judgment,
subject to your concurrence, might reasonably be regarded as redundant and dramatically superfluous.

        You will readily see that these further requirements must com-
pletely change the character of the play, undermine the author's
intention, to some extent prejudice his reputation as a sincere
artist, and render his play feeble and dramatically ineffective,
since the force of this play largely depends upon its vivid and
brutal character. Had you made this clear to me in the first instance
I would have cancelled the production. As it is I risk a serious
failure and possibly unpleasant - even legal - consequences with the
author.

        I can merely protest formally, and suggest the substitution of
"bloomin" or "blinkin" for any "bloody" or "bleedin"; "verminous"
for "lousy", "harlot" for "tart".

        I need not tell you that I myself am profoundly opposed to this
form of censorship. I would most respectfully urge that you refuse
a license definitively to all plays which the Lord Chamberlain does
not find himself able to license without modifying their essential
character and their author's fundamental intentions.

        As requested I beg to enclose a copy of the play in the current
edition.

                Yours faithfully,

        Terence Gray -   The Festival Theatre (Cambridge) Ltd., 36 Newmarket Road, Cambridge

9. Gray's reply to the foregoing letter, October 1928.

STAGE PLAY SUBMITTED FOR LICENCE.

Title :	"ALONE"
No. of Scenes or Acts :	3 acts
Place of Production :	Kingsway
Date of Production :	17th December
Author :	Marion Norris.

LORD CHAMBERLAIN'S OFFICE,
ST. JAMES'S PALACE, S.W. 1.

READER'S REPORT.   December 13th 1930.

I have not read "The Well of Loneliness" but from what I remember of the reviews this seems to be an adaptation of it. At any rate it is a study of a sexually abnormal woman and a protest against women similarly affected being regaded as pariahs and outcasts - the extent to which this happens being surely exaggerated. Sir Geoffrey Seymour and his wife assumed that their child would be a boy and when a girl was born called her Paul. At the beginning of the play she is a girl in her teens and great at riding and fencing. A young man, John Brandt, tells her of his love and asks her to marry him. She is repelled and horrified. Her mother is annoyed but her father tells her he understands and proposes that she should go to Oxford and become a writer. Two years later he is dead. There is a scene between Paul and a young married woman, Fanchon, in which Paul advises her to leave a bullying husband who has shown jealousy of a lover, but her own attitude is not indicated precisely. A little later, however, her mother brings a letter from Fanchon's husband enclosing one of Paul's to Fanchon and intimating that their acquaintance must end. Paul's mother attacks her as unnatural, a monster. Paul replies eloquently, but her mother insists that they must part and Paul agrees to go away. She is comforted by the understanding of her old governess, Parkie, and then finds her name written by her father opposite a passage in Kruft-Ebing, showing that he perceived the nature of her abnormality. Seven years later Paul is living in Paris with the faithful Parkie. She is now a well known writer. She complains bitterly of her isolation. She then joins an ambulance service in the War and there is a scene between her and a young girl Pamela who wants to live with her after the war. Paul points out that if she does she too will be regarded as an outcast. Pamela insists and the arrangement has lasted for some time when John Brandt turns up in Paris. (I have omitted some unessential incidents.) He now understands Paul and merely wants to be friends. But he falls in love with Pam and gives Paul warning that he will try to take her away and marry her. Pam, by hypothesis, is normal and merely devoted to Paul. Paul at first says she will fight him on principle but later on gives in and sacrifices her own feelings to Pam by pretending to Pam that she is in the way of another female attraction. Pam goes to John and Paul utters a pitiful prayer to God about the exclusion of her kind.

The play is greatly exaggerated, I think people are indifferent to the abnormality in woman with which it deals until it becomes agressive - but it is sincerely and sensitively written and quite free from offence in detail. [I cannot, however, advise the Lord Chamberlain to set aside in its favour the exclusion of such themes] and it is

NOT recommended for Licence.

(sd.) G.S.Street.

P.S. I ought to add that one would not gather from the play that Paul's abnormality resulted in definite physical action, but I think that does not save the theme.

P. T. O.

2

10. Reader's Report by George Street recommending that *Alone* should be refused a licence, December 1930.

STAGE PLAY SUBMITTED FOR LICENCE.

Title : "JUDGMENT DAY"

No. of Scenes or Acts : 3 acts

Place of Production : Globe Theatre

Date of Production : Soon

Author : Elmer Rice

LORD CHAMBERLAIN'S OFFICE,
ST. JAMES'S PALACE, S.W. 1.

14DEC1934   **READER'S REPORT.**   December 11th 1934.

This is an unmistakable and bitter attack on the Hitler Regime and especially on General Goring, and, equally unmistakably a parody of the trial for the burning of the Reichstag. But it is all cleverly veiled. The scene is in "South Eastern Europe" and the names are Slavonic; also the trial is not for incendiarism but for attempted murder. I need not go through all the details of Acts I and II. Their gist is as follows. There is a National Government; everyone has to belong to the National Party; those who belong to the "People's Party" are under suspicion. One Alexander Kurman is in prison on this account, and the play consists of the trial of his wife Lydia, George Khitov, and Schneider (a German) for conspiring against the life of the President of the State Vesnic. Lydia was granted an interview by Vesnic about Alexander and Schneider who went with her, on a signal from her (according to the prosecution) fired at and wounded Vesnic with a pistol of George's. For the defence, partly conducted by Lydia's brother Conrad, a member of the American bar, it is urged that she had never seen Schneider before, that he was a tool of Rakovski's, the "Minister of Culture and Enlightenment" - a pretty ironical touch - and probably Vesnic was not hit at all, but only a mirror and that the pistol was stolen. The trial is conducted brutally and unfairly, only two of the several judges showing any decency. There is an incursion of Rakovsky, quite in Goring's style in the other trial - see p.129. An amusing touch is given by an Italian prima donna who proves Rakovsky's previous connection with Schneider. Act III begins with a conference of the judges. An old judge Slatarski, alone stands firmly for justice. Rakovski comes in and bullies them, insisting on the State being above trifles like justice. All give in except Slatarski. When the court resumes in scene 11 Alexander, who was stated by the prosecution to have committed suicide, but actually has escaped, is hidden disguised as a priest behind a curtain - various guards and police are anti-Vesnic - and when Vesnic himself appears to quench all opposition Alexander comes out and denounces him in a fiery passage (p.195) much as Hitler's enemies might denounce him. Vesnic, frightened, calls out for some one to kill Alexander, but is himself shot by the judge Slatarski, who then with a cry of "Down with tyranny" etc. shoots himself.

In spite of all differences there can be no doubt of the identification. In my opinion, however, the distinguished American author ought to "get away with it". It seems to me difficult to insist with an author that he **must** mean such an application and censor his play because it would offend Hitler or Goring. And would the German Embassy be foolish enough to fit on the caps? I should doubt it. Another point is that the numerous haters of the Nazi regime, as well as the exiled Jews, might make scenes of too noisy enthusiasm. Both these points deserve careful consideration and perhaps other advice. But so far as I am concerned the play is

Recommended for Licence.

(sd.) G S.Street

P.S.   I forgot to say that Schneider is represented as drugged and half-witted like the Dutchman in the Reichstag trial. The play was presented in New York in September.

Having been acted in America, I hardly think we can refuse its licence here on the grounds of similarity to German conditions.   13 December 1934.

13514

11. Reader's Report by George Street recommending the licensing of *Judgment Day*, December 1934.

visualise in production, and which reads much worse than it appears when actually staged.

Yours ever

(sd.) Cromer.

At least one member of the Advisory Board, Henry Higgins, the former chairman of the Grand Opera Syndicate, clearly thought the Lord Chamberlain had been duped:

7, BLOOMSBURY SQUARE,

LONDON

May 20 1928

Private

My dear Cromer,

I am in receipt of your letter of the 23rd. I have not got a copy of Pirandello's play and only recollect it vaguely, but my impression is that the most objectionable feature in it was the 'locus in quo' of one of the Acts.

Of course, the high brow group are very good at getting up an agitation and making copy for the papers, but I don't think that they really carry very much weight with the public, and I personally should be a little averse to yielding to their clamour.

In the days when I used to visit foreign musical centres to hear new operas and singers, I always found that the great difficulty was to resists [sic] local enthusiasm. An atmosphere is easily created and favourable opinions so dinned into ears that it becomes very difficult to resist them. I always found myself obliged to put them on one side and say to myself 'How will this sound at Covent Garden?' It is very much the same thing in the case of the members of these Stage Societies. They get up an agitation in favour of licensing a particular play, to which a licence has been refused by you, and having done so and induced you to go and see it, you are naturally affected, as I have often been, by the atmosphere thus artificially created.

Pray do not think however that I am in any way questioning the wisdom of your decision.

Yours very sincerely,

H. Higgins

The Earl of Cromer,

Lord Chamberlain's Office,

St James's Palace, S.W.

But Sir Barry Jackson had finally got his licence. If only Cromer had been willing to go and see the play six years earlier.

The Infernal Machine

Jean Cocteau's adaptation of the Oedipus story ran into trouble in the 1930s, when the innovative Group Theatre – which combined the artistic talents of, among others, Rupert Doone, Stephen Spender, John Piper and Benjamin Britten – sought a licence. Writing in October 1935, Street was ambivalent about this new adaptation of the myth:

> The Group Theatre seems destined to give the censorship more trouble than all the other theatres put together. I do not blame them. In the present instance, for example, they are offering an ingenious play of considerable artistic merit and naturally they wish to try if it can be passed. That is very doubtful . . .
>
> It is difficult to advise. The *Oedipus Rex* has been licensed in English in Gilbert Murray's translation. A translation of a great ancient classic is a different thing from a modern play, but still the incest of Oedipus and Jocasta has been admitted as a theme for our stage. There is this difference, however, in the treatment, that in Sophocles we are simply told of the marriage; here we see the couple in their bedroom and witness playful love making between them. There is a suggestion of Freud in Jocasta's remark about mother and son union – I, 26 – which is wholly unSophoclean. I have been told that the play was produced by the Stage Society but do not remember reading about it. What will, I think, horrify an ordinary audience is the love-making of Mother and son in Act III, passim. But the play is only meant for 'highbrows' who do not mind. In a way it is a brilliant play, though I think the irony of Sophocles is vulgarly emphasised in M. Cocteau. I do not wish the Lord Chamberlain to refuse a licence without reading the play or getting another opinion, but I cannot take the responsibility of advising him to grant one.[36]

Cromer consulted his Advisory Board, and the Oxford scholar David Cecil responded instantly to the brilliance of Cocteau's innovative approach. While the censorship often tended to reduce texts rather crudely to plot and content, Cecil stressed the significance of theatre and aesthetics:

MANOR HOUSE,

CRANBOURNE,

SALISBURY

1st November 1935

'The Infernal Machine'

I quite appreciate Mr Street's doubts on this play. But I must state emphatically that I think it should receive a licence. It seems to me a most distinguished and venerable work of the imagination – far above the ordinary run, even of 'good' drama, a successful attempt to restore the Theatre to a high poetical and tragic level. Of course it might be all this and yet involve scenes that would make it unsuitable for public representation. But I do not think that this is so. As Mr Street recalls, Sophocles's *Oedipus Rex* – and I would add Shelley's *Cenci* – deal with incest and have been passed for public representation without rousing adverse comment. In addition to their merits, they deal with the subject in a poetical and <u>un</u>realistic way. This is also true of M. Cocteau's play, with all its paraphernalia of phantoms,

Sphinxes, dreams, prophesies, its combined classical setting and direction, its sustained philosophic tone, it removes its subject to an unrealistic and symbolic state where it could give no real offence . . . I know when it was acted by the Stage Society it was warmly admired by reputable critics – I never heard a suggestion it was indecent. I must say I think it would be a pity if serious playgoers were deprived of the chance of seeing it.

The only cavil I should like to enter is over the bedroom scene. If the actors chose to play it in a very realistic manner making Jocasta a modern figure and emphasising her age, I think it might be a little disagreeable. Could not the Lord Chamberlain warn them not to do this – it might be possible to cut out one or two speeches in the scene that emphasise the incest relationship. If this were done I am sure people would not object. . . . this seems to me a most remarkable piece of work – an ornament to the stage.

(sd.) David Cecil

I also suggest that the blinded Oedipus should be bandaged or veiled in some way. Otherwise it would be inexcusably horrible.

However, another member of the Board, the author and former Conservative MP Sir Ian Malcolm, was more cynical about Cocteau's contribution:

'THE INFERNAL MACHINE'
By Jean Cocteau

Centuries ago Sophocles wrote a dignified and disgusting tragedy, the pivot of which was Incest. That drama has been studied in our public schools and acted in our Universities ever since we can remember – and long before then. Incest, therefore, has established a 'right of way' to pass across the British stage.

Why then cavil at the last of M. Cocteau's very 'french' fantasies? What has he done but borrow (without acknowledgement) the story of Oedipus, translated into an 'anglais de cuisine', give it a flavour of the servants' hall; throw in reminiscences of one or two characters from Wagner's operas, add a few pages from Edgar Wallace, and then offer the whole 'salade' for the acceptance of highbrows unacquainted with the original Greek.

If his Lordship's only business, as regards this play, were to protect our morals . . . the ground was cut from under his feet long ago by the licentious studies of the classics to which we (of both sexes) were subjected when at school. But if, as I hope, he is privileged by his functions to forbid the exhibition of so flashy and unscholarly an adaptation of a great and ancient drama upon the British stage, then I trust that he will exercise his aesthetic powers and influence in that direction.

The manager was informed that a licence could only be considered if the relationship between Oedipus and Jocasta was less explicit, causing Act III 'to be played in a formal and stylized manner and eliminating reality as much as possible.' But in the event, a licence was issued for Cocteau's script only in 1943 (see Plate 3).

The leer of the satyr: Coward, Maugham and Strindberg

Miss Julie

When Strindberg's play was first submitted to the Lord Chamberlain in December 1912 Brookfield described it as 'revolting'. He described the eponymous heroine as motivated by 'socialistic tendencies', and remarked disapprovingly that 'her mother had an intrigue with a brickmaker'. However, for once a member of the Advisory Board, Raleigh, seemed prepared to go to the barricades for it:

> I hope it will be licensed. A refusal to license would hand over (as it seems to me) some very heavy ammunition to the enemies of the Censorship . . . It really succeeds in doing what its English imitations try to do, and fail . . . I can quite understand the attitude of those who do not want to see the play. It is a grim ordeal. But surely it would be a disaster for the English public to be forbidden to see the best dramatic work of the best and most honoured names among foreign men of letters.[37]

Buckmaster was less generous; its basic narrative evidently failed to coincide with his own experience and observations: 'My view of the play is that it is painful and false to life. Women do stoop to servants now and again but not often and rarely, if they be knowledgeable people like Miss Julia, do they begin in the kitchen.' However, what did concern him was the possibility that rejecting the play might drive Raleigh to resign from the Advisory Board, undermining its essential credibility. Buckmaster admitted he was 'extremely anxious to retain Raleigh, whose name adds greatly to . . . our authority', and was even prepared to suppress as unimportant his own objections to Strindberg's play: 'If licensed it would probably die in a fortnight and no one be the worse except the performers'. However, Sandhurst was adamant that if the censorship passed a play like this one 'there would be good reason for saying such an institution was useless'. Unfortunately, there appears to be no record of the conversation which must have taken place between them, but Raleigh subsequently informed the Lord Chamberlain that he was ready to recant his heretical view of Strindberg's play: 'I don't want to see it myself, and I admit it might be terribly mishandled on the stage . . . I have bought it, and put it on my shelf; which closes this chapter.' It would be another twenty-six years before Miss Julie would receive a licence, and it is tempting to wonder what might have happened if Raleigh had had the courage to hold to his original convictions.

There is no record of Miss Julie being resubmitted until September 1925, when Frances Petersen sought permission for a special matinee performance at the Chelsea Palace; 'It is a very fine play and I should be grateful if you would allow me to produce it as Strindberg is not often played in this country.'[38] She told the Office that she had already censored the text herself and promised 'I can alter anything further that you would like'. Street was now prepared to recommend a licence, though his report showed little enthusiasm:

LORD CHAMBERLAIN'S OFFICE,
ST JAMES'S PALACE

September 10th 1925

READER'S REPORT

Like most of Strindberg's work this is a morbid and thoroughly disagreeable play. Julie, aged 25, is the daughter of a Count, in whose kitchen the scene is laid. John, a footman or valet, and Christine the cook are (it seems later) lovers. A servants' ball is in progress. Julie comes in and wants John to dance. She flirts with him and he at first discourages her. After much discursive talk Christine goes to bed. Other servants are heard approaching and Julie and John go to his bedroom, not to be seen. When they come out, the others being gone, he has seduced her, or she him. There is then a long colloquy between the two, in which John is as a rule contemptuous and brutal. She wants him to go away with her and he eventually consents. She goes to get ready. Then Christine appears again and vetoes John's going away. Julie returns, having stolen the Count's money. She wants to take a canary with her. John cuts off its head and this produced [sic] a wild outburst from Julie. Then the Count, who has been away, rings his bell. Julie resolves to cut her throat and tells John to order her to do it; he does so and she goes off to obey.

Strindberg is a coarse writer. I have marked passages on pp. 9, 43, 47, 55, 56 of words or actions. Other passages have been cut out already. But the thing remains coarse.

I am not sure if the offensiveness of this Play is enough to ban it. Two people misconducting themselves 'off' and reappearing have figured in other Plays passed. Here the whole sordid and beastly atmosphere makes the thing worse, however.

I am inclined to think there is <u>not</u> sufficient reason for banning the play, but I do not advise the Lord Chamberlain to license it without reading it.

Cromer hated the play, and although he sent it to the Advisory Board, his mind was effectively made up:

I have read this play, which I consider objectionable from two points of view.

In the first place there is the sordid and disgusting atmosphere, which makes the immorality of the play glaring + crude.

Then there is the very questionable theme in these days of the relations between masters + servants, which this play tends to undermine.

Even if the coarser passages were cut, this theme would remain objectionably prominent, so taken on the whole, I do not feel disposed to grant a Licence for this play, but would be glad of the views of the Advisory Committee before coming to a definite decision in the matter.

Dawson had no doubt that 'this beastly play is the very type which all public opinion that is worth consideration looks to the Censor to protect them from', and Lord Ullswater was similarly uncompromising:

In my opinion this is an objectionable play, to which great exception might and almost certainly would be taken by women – and with considerable justice.

The character of Julie, quite impossible in life, is represented as governed by an all conquering lust, for a man-servant . . . I should have no hesitation in refusing a licence.

In 1927, Terence Gray at the Festival Theatre in Cambridge and Milton Rosmer at the Everyman in Hampstead both sought permission to stage the play; the latter wrote to Cromer, playing the 'classic' card:

I am writing to ask if you would reconsider what I believe was your previous refusal to license a performance of Strindberg's *Miss Julia*? This to my mind is in the nature of a masterpiece which must eventually be recognised and accepted in this country as it is all over Europe. Many incidents have been performed in English plays which exceed in questionable suggestions those in the Strindberg work, and as a matter of fact the very passages to which exception might be taken, could, without affecting the psychological development which is the essence of the play, be omitted altogether or altered to meet your views, and this I should be only too happy to attend on you and discuss.

I shall be most grateful if I might have a reply saying you will consent to see me.

Though he was adamant that it would be a 'waste of time' and that 'no useful purpose would be served', Cromer agreed to meet Rosmer in October. Feeling himself 'pressed from various directions to re-consider the play', and with Rosmer willing to make any changes stipulated, the Lord Chamberlain consulted another member of the Advisory Board, the actor/manager Sir Johnston Forbes-Robertson; as so often, Cromer signalled his personal view in advance: 'My own opinion is that the whole atmosphere of the play, as well as its theme, is so objectionable that no amount of doctoring would really make it anything else'. Forbes-Robertson took the hint:

Dear Lord Cromer,

I have been at some trouble to wade through this filthy piece, *Miss Julie*, and am strongly of opinion that is should not be licensed.

I quite agree with you that no doctoring can do away with the loathsome atmosphere of this piece.

This was obviously the correct answer:

Dear Sir Johnston,

Thank you very much for returning me that horrible play <u>Miss Julie</u>. I felt sure you would agree with me that no amount of doctoring would warrant its licence.

I am so sorry that no envelope was sent with the play for its return, but you shall always have one in future.

In 1931 Terence Gray enquired once again but without success, and in 1935 the Arts Theatre Club invited Cromer to send a representative to a private performance. They were told that since it was not specific business or individual lines but rather 'the theme of this play to which objection was taken', this would be pointless. It was only in December 1938, when Lord Clarendon had replaced Cromer, that St James's Palace accepted the recommendation of its Reader, Henry Game, that to maintain the ban any longer would be absurd (see Plate 4).

Our Betters

On 17 September 1923 the *Daily Graphic* published an article under the headline 'IS A CENSOR NECESSARY?', accompanying it with a photograph of Cromer. He had been in office for less than a year, but under the guise of sympathizing with his difficulties and lamenting the immorality and decadence of the modern age, the article criticized his supposed leniency:

> Is the Censor of Plays nowadays necessary? The question arises not from a desire to accord unlimited licence to dramatists and theatrical producers, but from the nature of certain comedies now being staged in London, which seem to suggest that any Censor who endeavours to gratify modern requirements must have so little censoriousness in his composition that his title becomes a misnomer.
>
> It seems hardly fair to call an official a Censor and then expect him to give safe conduct to the sort of plays which are, at the moment, drawing crowded houses. One alternative title which suggests itself is the Non-Censor.
>
> In these days of sophistication the Censor of Plays must find himself in a tragic position.
>
> A Censor is supposed to guard the public morals. It will be a pity if he himself emphasises the fact that this priceless possession no longer exists.[39]

One of the plays the writer had specifically in mind was Somerset Maugham's *Our Betters*, which Cromer had licensed a few months earlier. Street had recommended approval (see Plate 5), and Buckmaster had agreed with him:

> I see no adequate reason for refusing a License to this play.
>
> There can be no sound objection to the introduction of vicious worthless people into drama; if they were used for the purpose of slandering a nation or an individual I should be most unwilling to license the performance but in the present case I cannot see that either the one thing or the other is attempted.
>
> Apart from the rather remote resemblance of the names of the country places I can certainly see no points of resemblance between Pearl and a well known London Hostess. If these names are sufficiently near to suggest resemblance they should be altered.
>
> Nor can I see any general attack upon Americans. No nation can afford to be too thin skinned in these matters.
>
> The end of the second Act is the only real dramatic incident in the Play and like many such incidents it depends upon an immoral act. But it is not told indecently, and I think the public will not be unduly shocked because a man and a woman are found

locked in a summer house. Indeed if my memory serves me well, precisely this incident occurs and is jested about in 'The Merry Widow'.
(Sd.) BUCKMASTER
21.4.23.[40]

Cromer agreed to the licence, but when Maugham's play opened it immediately provoked hostility. On 18 September the king's private secretary, Lord Stamfordham, sent a copy of the previous day's *Daily Graphic* article to Lord Cromer, with an accompanying letter passing on royal concern (see Plate 6). Cromer responded with a long and anguished reply to Balmoral:

Private

21st September 1923

Dear Lord Stamfordham,
The King is, I know, a regular reader of the 'Daily Graphic'. The 'Daily Graphic' is well known for the regularity of its attacks upon the Lord Chamberlain and his Department, and there is no novelty in my being the present victim as I am only inheriting from my predecessors a fruitful form of Press criticism. This being the case, I earnestly hope His Majesty will not be influenced by anything the 'Daily Graphic' may say regarding my Department.

Every Lord Chamberlain is apt at times to be the butt of Press criticism and while, at present, some papers are saying I am unduly lax, others have been saying that I am ridiculously strict. There is no pleasing everyone successfully, and my own line is that so long as I take what I consider to be the right and common sense view of things, I remain uninfluenced by newspaper blame or praise.

As to the Play 'Our Betters', this is a fierce satire on Americans who have made their way in European society through the influence of money. Before passing it I understood that it had already been acted in the United States where presumably American susceptibilities are more likely to be offended than in London.

The theme of the Play, which is admittedly objectionable, presented considerable difficulties to my mind and consequently I took the advice of the Advisory Board. Three members of this Board, namely Lord Buckmaster, Sir Squire Bancroft and Mr H. Higgins, all stated that they saw no sufficient reason to withhold a Licence from this Play. Owing to the shortness of time, and the fact that the State Chamberlain was at the moment pre-occupied with his own private affairs, I did not send the Play to him as I already had three votes out of four in favour of its performance.

I can quite understand that many Americans may not like the Play and that someone should have spoken to the King on the subject. At the same time, for me to have banned a Play which had been acted in America and which was recommended for performance by the Reader of Plays, as well as by three Members of my Advisory Board, would have been a somewhat strong order in view of the limited powers under which I act as Lord Chamberlain. In fact the 'Daily Graphic' and other papers would have hailed the opportunity of pointing a finger of scorn at the Censor for his squeamishness, and would have joined in the author's [sic] chorus for the abolition of censorship.

I make a point of reading Press criticism of all Plays, and in these one should be indulgent in the recollection that the critics have to earn their bread and butter by writing for or against everything. It is generally easier to be anti, rather than pro, in newspaper criticism, as it helps to sell the papers.

I could send all the documents as well as the script of the Play if it would interest His Majesty to see them, but they are rather lengthy. However, I would ask you to assure the King that the most careful consideration was given to this Play, as indeed it is given to all Plays that come before my Department before they are licensed, as the drama is a thing in which I take a great personal interest.

(sd.) Cromer

Probably Cromer was relieved and reassured by the reply from Balmoral Castle:

23rd September, 1923

My dear Rowland,

Although your letter of the 21st. instant was marked 'private', I showed it to the King, who desires me to say that he did not wish to find fault with what your department has done in the matter of the play 'Our Betters'; nor was His Majesty aware that the piece had been produced in America. which of course affects the King's adverse criticisms. Moreover, as three of the Advisory Committee, including a very important opinion like Lord Buckmaster's, recommended the sanctioning of the Play, you could not have insisted upon censoring it.

His Majesty, after reading the newspaper critiques, still thinks it must be an unsavoury play: but feels certain that the criticisms for and against it will be an excellent advertisement and no doubt everyone will take the earliest opportunity of seeing it! . . .

I return the cuttings: and you may rest assured that the notice in the 'Daily Graphic' will not be taken too seriously.

Yours ever,
Stamfordham.

The Earl of Cromer G.C.I.E., C.V.O.,
Lord Chamberlain

Still, as a letter from Colonel Stanley Bell at the Globe Theatre reveals, Cromer did unobtrusively persuade Maugham and the manager to amend the dialogue after Pearl is found in the summer house.

GLOBE THEATRE,
SHAFTESBURY AVENUE, W.1

PERSONAL

23rd September 1923

Dear Lord Cromer,

I have tried the new end to the second act of 'Our Betters', and after giving it consideration, am keeping it in.

95

Instead of saying: 'You damned fool, I told you it was too risky', Pearl now says: 'You damned fool, what did I tell you?'

Everyone seems to think it is much milder, and between ourselves I do not think it hurts the play.

I hope this will set your mind at rest.

With kind regards

Yours sincerely,

Stanley Bell.

The Earl of Cromer, G.C.I.E., C.V.O.
36 Wimpole Street W.

This change, trivial though it seems today, evidently made all the difference! Cromer replied to Bell: 'When next you see Mr Somerset Maugham I should like you to assure him of how much I appreciate the courteous and obliging manner in which he responded to the representations I made to him in our recent interview.'

The Vortex

Some of the official responses to *Our Betters* and *Miss Julie* betray a remarkable degree of political unease at the risk of depicting the wealthy as decadent and immoral, and it is hard now to believe just how seriously people took the possibility of a Soviet style revolution and the overthrow of the British economic and social order. The election of Ramsay Macdonald's first Labour government in 1924 made supporters of the status quo even more jumpy, as is evident in some of the anxiety over Noël Coward's depictions of the upper echelons of British society in such plays such as *The Vortex* and *Fallen Angels*. Though both of these received licences without delay – if not without misgivings – they again provoked vociferous criticism of the censorship for failing to stifle work which was at best unpleasant and at worst highly dangerous. In November 1924, Street's report on *The Vortex* had been fairly relaxed:

CEREMONIAL DEPARTMENT
ST JAMES'S PALACE, S.W.1

'THE VORTEX' a play in 3 acts by Noel Coward. To be produced at the Everyman Theatre, Nov. 24th

Mr Coward has been known so far as a writer of light comedy and revue, but the theme of this play is grimly serious – and painful in an extreme degree. Until the end, however, the atmosphere is that of frivolous people who speak in a tiresome jargon – everything it [sic] 'too divine', etc. – and attempt wit with rather poor results. Florence Lancaster is a middle-aged woman with a son, Nicky, in the early twenties. She is still a beautiful woman and insists on being still young and irresponsible, talking much of her temperament. She has a lover, Tom Veryan, a young man half her age in the Guards. Her husband, a negligible person, does not suspect this, looking on Tom as merely an admirer, as does Nicky until towards the end. Nicky is a wayward and nervy boy devoted to music. He becomes engaged to Bunty Mainwaring. She and Tom are old friends and of the same type – sporting and normal, as opposed to the artistic and neurotic type of Florence and Nicky. They are mutually attracted in a week-end party at the Lancasters, Florence's glamour for Tom wearing off and Bunty growing irritated with Nicky's nerviness. She breaks off with him and at the end of Act II Florence sees Tom, kissing her. Florence is madly jealous and abuses them both furiously. Then, as Tom is going away, she wants to call him back. This reveals the relations to Nicky. In Act III he goes to Florence in her room and forces her to admit the truth. He upbraids her with her life and points out that he himself is going to pieces – he is beginning to take drugs – and begs her to save herself and him by giving up her life of lovers and false youth and the rest and being a real mother to him. She, alarmed by the drug-taking, promises.

A scene in which a son upbraids a mother with her unchastity cannot be other than painful and in a way shocking, but I do not think is of a nature to make it necessary to ban the play. The author might plead 'Hamlet' as an example. The son is in deadly earnest to save them both and I think this tides one over the unpleasantness. The motive of the play is a good one and there are certainly people like Florence Lancaster whom it would do good to see how they look to an observer. The Lord Chamberlain might like to look at the third act, which is very short.

Apart from this more serious question there are a couple of trifles in the dialogue which I have marked. [1] Act 1. slip (pages not numbered) a sentence which suggests Lesbianism; it has nothing to do with play, [sic] however; and [2] Act II, page 13 'Byes' apparently means bed and the sentence, if so, is too frank.

Recommended for Licence

(sd) G. S. Street[41]

But Cromer, evidently mindful of the awkward situation with his employer over Maugham's play a year earlier, was inclined to adopt a stronger line:

CEREMONIAL DEPARTMENT

ST JAMES'S PALACE, S.W.

THE VORTEX

This sort of play is unfortunately the inevitable sequence to a play like 'Our Betters' by which it is evidently inspired.

This picture of a frivolous and degenerate set of people gives a wholly false impression of Society life and to my mind the time has come to put a stop to the harmful influence of such pictures on the stage.

The scene in Act III of the drug-taking son upbraiding his mother for the immoral conduct of her life is revolting in the last degree and it is no palliation to the story that the play ends with both mother and son making vows to give up their evil habits.

I cannot admit the principle that evil in any one play justifies its repetition in another, as I consider that each play should be judged solely on its own merits and not by comparison with others.

97

I am inclined to ban this play entirely, but before definite decision I should be grateful for the opinion of the Advisory Board.

Cromer 12 Nov 1924

Two months earlier, Dawson had expressed outrage at a farce which poked fun at a Colonel in the British army. Street's report had insisted that *Khaki* was 'so preposterously silly that the most ignorant audience could not think it represented reality in any way', but Dawson took a very different view: 'A l'heure qu' il est the agitator is at work with propaganda . . . winked at, if not supported, by the government in office. Is this the moment for a play to appear the moral of which is to cast ridicule on what may 'ere long be the only buffer left between us and revolution?'[42] It is hardly surprising, then, that Dawson now echoed Cromer's views on *The Vortex*:

> It is to be hoped that the scene between mother and son is but rarely true to life. But even if it is, is there any reason why such a loathsome situation should be shown on the Stage? I often discussed with Tree and Alexander the power of the stage for <u>useful</u> propaganda on the many thorny problems of life. Especially in these days the importance of this is intensified when class hatred is preached, not only to the adult at the street corners, but to the children in the Sunday Schools.
>
> For this reason I welcome the Lord Chamberlain's remark that the time has come to put a stop to such plays, and I hope he will ban *Vortex* for, in my opinion, it is a piece calculated to convey the worst possible impression of the social conditions under which we live today.

However, some of the Advisory Board questioned the assumptions underlying Dawson's attitude. Higgins was quick to identify the implicit ideological bias in the former comptroller's attitude. It was not that he liked the message of Coward's play:

> But I cannot help feeling that if its surroundings were those of squalid poverty & it were an 'East End' there would be no question of refusing it a licence. The same observation would apply if it were dated in the middle ages – The real objection is that it presents the prosperous of today in an odious light and to that extent partakes of the nature of socialist propaganda . . .
>
> But that is hardly I take it a sufficient reason for banning it altogether.

Buckmaster developed the argument further:

1 PORCHESTER TERRACE, W. 2.

19th November 1924

THE VORTEX

This is a weak and unpleasant play but I cannot agree with the view that a Licence should be refused for its performance. As opinions differ on this point I will explain in greater detail than is usual the reasons which influence my judgement. The censorship of plays is, apart from the criminal law, the last control that remains over the liberty of free publication. It is I think a valuable right but its exercise must be capable of justification on ascertained principles.

In my opinion a play is entitled to a Licence unless it is of a brutalising and degrading character, shocks or pains the moral or religious feelings of reasonable men and women, is likely to disturb international relations, subjects Members of the Royal Family to ridicule or contempt, or promotes public disorder, The present play does not come within any of these limitations.

The reason suggested against it is that it holds up to unfair opprobrium the vices of the idle and the rich. Now it is quite plain that wealthy people and those who constitute what is vaguely known as Society cannot claim immunity against publication of even extreme views of their conduct unless the same immunity is granted to all classes. No one has ever protested against plays disclosing brutalised behaviour on the part of the poor, such incidents were found in an excellent play called 'The Likes of 'er' while, in a play still running called 'The Fool', trades union leaders are represented as betraying their cause for money.

The imbecilities of a ballroom and the follies and vices of prosperous and irresponsible people are just as fit a subject for the stage as the coarser vices of poorer folk[;] as for its effect on public opinion[,] this play cannot encourage the repetition of the conduct it describes and so far as its moral effect is concerned it cannot be mischievous. 'Our Betters' to which reference is made is in its action and dialogue false and strained but again in its essence no one can deny that such things exist just as drunkenness and violence exist among the poor. It may be doubted if 'The Mariage de Figaro' would have had any effect – if indeed it did have any – had it not been suppressed in the first instance.

I agree as to certain modifications of the dialogue but they are quite small matters.

I dislike the play but I cannot advise against a Licence.

(sd) BUCKMASTER

The reference to Beaumarchais's play reveals that perhaps Buckmaster's position was informed not only by a liberal sense of fairness and justice, but also by the fear that excessive repression might actually be counter-productive and have the effect of stimulating a radical rebellion.

Another member of the Board, the nineteenth-century actor/manager Squire Bancroft, now in his eighties, was persuaded by the argument: 'This class of play is hateful to me. I am, however, so impressed by Lord Buckmaster's "Exposition" that I support the view he takes'. Dawson, on the other hand, was infuriated by the attack on his integrity, and fired off an angry riposte to Lord Cromer:

LORD CHAMBERLAIN'S OFFICE
BUCKINGHAM PALACE

<u>Private</u>

Lord Chamberlain

I have read carefully the opinions of Higgins and Buckmaster. They both start in my opinion on a false premise, and then argue on it.

I have been longer on the Board than anyone. It was created on my suggestion.

I have never known the 'wealthy' or 'society' classes to be given preferential consideration, and I maintain that no matter whether a scene is laid in Mayfair or Whitechapel, objection would, or certainly <u>should</u> be taken to (1) a son upbraiding his mother for her adulterous past, or (2) a step-daughter reciprocating the filthy advances of her step father. I regard the insinuation of favour to one class as a misleading opinion of the impartial way in which the Board has hitherto exercised its duties.

Further Lord B considers the Board entitled to recommend refusal of licence to a play calculated to 'promote public disorder'. – I hold that any play liable to foster class hatred comes within the scope of his contention.

23.XI. 24   Douglas Dawson

Despite Dawson's argument, Cromer had little choice other than to issue the licence against his own original wishes, and with only minor changes to the text.

Fallen Angels

A month later, Street found nothing to censor in Coward's new play, *Easy Virtue*, and was quite warm in some of his comments: 'If not a very good play this is at least an extremely intelligent one. For so young a man Noel Coward observes people for himself to a remarkable degree and understands certain sorts of temperament very well.' Cromer agreed, describing it as 'A very intelligently written play in the most modern style'; he warned that 'The title may arouse more criticism than is justifiable from the play itself', but concluded that 'it would be a mistake to insist on its alteration'.[43] However, Coward's next offering, *Fallen Angels*, looked more problematic, as Street reported in March 1925:

> There is not much amiss in the actual dialogue . . . and it is true that no adultery happens in the Play. But I think the whole atmosphere of lightness in that connection – both about the women's obvious willingness to go wrong and about their pre-nuptial going wrong – would cause too great a scandal. Adultery and unchastity are made light hearted jokes and even though the whole thing is unreal farcical comedy that will not do. I may be wrong, as it is a question of atmosphere more than concrete detail, but the Play is
> Not Recommended for Licence.[44]

Possibly as a deliberate tactic intended to create pressure on the Office, rehearsals for *Fallen Angels* had already begun and its performance advertised before the management had submitted the script. Coincidentally or not, it arrived at St James's Palace when Cromer was on holiday in Italy, and Crichton, the comptroller, turned to Buckmaster for advice. He recommended licensing – 'The humour of this Play makes no appeal to me but its utter unreality appears to me to take away its offence' – but was alive to the strategies employed by managers to create problems for the censorship: 'I should like to add that I respectfully suggest to the Lord Chamberlain that he should not permit his judgment to be rushed by Plays being thrown at his head when they have been advertised for production'.

To be on the safe side, Crichton sent the script to Cromer at his Italian address, taking the opportunity to update him on other matters:

> I am sorry to have to send you the attached. I understand that the Play is already in rehearsal to replace 'The Grand Duchess', so I have only sent it to Lord Buckmaster, as Harry Higgins is also abroad. To my mind it is a most unpleasant Play.
>
> The Archbishop has nothing against the Good Friday Play so I have sent a permit letter. The French Play has not yet come back from the Board.
>
> I am glad that you have found a peaceful spot, your first hotal [sic] does not sound too pleasant. I hope that by now you have got the good weather they seem to have further south. Here it is not at all too bad.

Cromer replied from his villa in Portofino. Perhaps the romance of the Mediterranean slightly seduced him:

> My Dear Crichton,
>
> Your letter of April 2nd reached me today + I am returning you 'Fallen Angels' by return of post. You were quite right to send it to me. Like most of that author's plays, it is unpleasant, but not half as much so, to my mind, as other plays of his. This has the redeeming feature of being light and unreal and humorous. If some of the allusions to 'sex' + 'illicit' + 'illegitimate' thrills [?] are taken out it will to some extent tone down the all too modern atmosphere of what I call 'naked speech', so dear to the modern author . . .
>
> The 'Sandringham' joke is quite good and I'm sorry to cut it out, but I dont think it wd do as it is sure to be repeated where it wont be appreciated. Besides it is not very respectful.
>
> I feel rather like Buckmaster in saying that a farce of this sort does not rouse any very strong feelings of antagonism in me, such as I felt over 'The Vortex' or some of these horrible sex problem plays.
>
> I can't conceive that a play like 'Fallen Angels' will do anyone any harm, while I do see that there is much in it to make people laugh.
>
> I may be back in England by the 10th or 11th so please forward nothing more abroad.
> Yours very sincerely
> Cromer

Commenting on Street's report, Cromer added:

I fully appreciate Mr Street's stand-point in not recommending this play for Licence. If seriously interpreted, it's [sic] licence could not of course be justified. But I take the view that the whole thing is so much unreal [?] farcical comedy, that subject to a few modifications in the dialogue it can pass.

The theme is immoral, but not more so than other farces of this kind. Besides the modifications mentioned by Mr Street, I shd require others to be made such as I have marked in the script. The object of these amendments, as shd be explained to the producer, is to tone down the atmosphere of offensiveness which some people will anyhow feel in a play of this sort. It is quite unnecessary to dot the i's to the extent the author has done, so that it will in no way injure his story to suppress some of the words I have struck out. It is not so much that I object to the actual words, as words on the stage, but their absence will help to render the atmosphere of the play less objectionable to some people who disapprove of quite unnecessary frankness of expression among women.

Subject to the alterations indicated, I agree to the play being Licensed. The producer shd be warned that he takes a great risk in putting a play of this sort into rehearsal <u>before</u> Licence, as I shd never accept the time and money spent in rehearsal as any justification, were I to consider that a play should not receive a licence on its own demerits.

Portofino

Italy   5th April 1925

Some relatively minor cuts were made, including the word 'illegitimate', the phrase 'rampant adultery', and the Sandringham joke,[45] and Cromer duly issued a licence: 'The fact of the two women in this play getting intoxicated on the stage will give rise to criticism in some quarters', he commented, 'but this is a risk I must take'.

Fallen Angels opened at the Globe on 21 April, and immediately provoked howls of protest; the very lightness and farcical nature of the action, which for the censorship had been its saving grace, was the basis of much of the condemnation. The *Stage* complained about the lack of any 'stern moral lesson' and suggested that 'the whole thing leaves a taste as nasty as that presumably clogging the mouths of Julia and Jane after their many, many drinks'. The *Sunday Express* also attacked the play: 'It is a pity that a desire to be original and daring should lead one into an artistic error as well as a sad lapse from good taste'; its reviewer found the 'stuffy, unhealthy atmosphere' to be 'essentially sickening', especially since there was 'no sign within the play of a protest against such an atmosphere'. The *Evening Standard* was particularly forthright in its condemnation:

The performance was, no doubt, extraordinarily clever. But it was also extraordinarily unpleasant, and the very ability with which it was presented made it more unpleasant still. It would be a depressing sign of the times if we could accept the enjoyment of the first night audience as typical of the theatrical taste of present-day England. Unfortunately, 'Fallen Angels' is only too typical of the fare which theatrical managements are now putting before our public. It is not at all the old question of frankness as against prudery which arises in connection with so many recent productions. We have no brief for those who declare that the stage should restrict itself to the production of 'Wholesome' plays suitable to the 'young person'. A play is for men and women, and in days when real men and women are much franker in the discussion of many subjects than they used to be, it is natural that dramatists should also be more outspoken.

But morality, while not concerned in preserving crudery, is interested in the attitude of those who put forward the pretension to give a fair picture of modern life. The smile of the satirist is one thing, the leer of the satyr quite another.

An author is doing a bad service to morality when, in presenting 'Fallen Angels' he fails to suggest, by introducing other types, that there are angels who have not fallen. He also sins against the canons of his art in populating his fancy world with only one, or at the most two, classes of people. Further, in making the great point of a play a business so painful and disgusting as female drunkenness, he is offending against mere good manners.

Such criticisms are important to our understanding of censorship, reminding us again that the Lord Chamberlain was not operating in a vacuum but with a weight of influential opponents repeatedly demanding a much tougher approach.

One of the quarters from which Cromer would correctly have anticipated criticism was the Public Morality Council, which bombarded St James's Palace with complaints and deputations on a regular basis. In this case the Council had begun its campaign four days after Coward's play had opened, and on 13 May they sent him a detailed criticism (see Plate 7). The following day the Bishop of London, who also happened to be the president of the Public Morality Council, wrote personally to Cromer, enclosing another copy of the Council's report:

I do not often write direct to you about plays, but if this account is a true one it seems to me an absolute disgrace that it should be allowed in London. I have not of course seen it myself, and, as you know, I often think that unnecessary fuss is made about some plays, for example: 'No, No Nanette', which many have complained of, but we see no harm in. But this seems to me sheer unmitigated filth and nothing else.

Cromer promised that he would give serious consideration to such complaints, and tentatively sought to justify – or at least to explain – his decision:

I have not yet personally had an opportunity of seeing this Play, but it has been witnessed by two Representatives of my Department, and I should mention that when the Play was under consideration it was held to be within the realms of farce. It was only after considerable modifications had been introduced into the script and that strict injunctions had been given as to the 'business' of production that a Licence was granted.

Five days later, on 20 May, Cromer wrote again to the bishop. He had now seen a performance of *Fallen Angels*, and was able to report that he had negotiated further modifications in both dialogue and stage business. However, the censors did not capitulate entirely to the moral watch committees, and were sometimes privately contemptuous of their attitudes. In 1934 one of the Lord Chamberlain's readers, Henry Game, commented that the members of the Public Morality Council were essentially confused 'between the functions of the Theatre and a Sunday School'.[46] In 1939, when the Council campaigned against the licensing of Coward's *Design for Living*, Lord Clarendon actually described its secretary as 'a curse', and the assistant comptroller, Brigadier Gwatkin, recounted his most recent encounter in rather dismissive terms:

> I have had a long and tedious interview with Mr Tyrer. As usual he was unconstructive except in the sense of complete destruction, and rebuilding on a standard of nursery rhymes and red flannel bloomers.
>
> He could quote no actual cases of either men or women who had slipped from the straight and narrow path by reason of attending or acting at the Windmill or other Theatres.
>
> I pointed out to him that one could not arrange entertainments designed only for those who are weak minded and impressionable at the expense of the larger majority which is reasonable in its outlook, and that we tried to keep plays on a level with current speech and thought at the same time to curb any undue licence . . .
>
> I really think he only comes here in order that his Committee may think him very active.[47]

From some perspectives, the Lord Chamberlain's Office could appear positively progressive.

The normal expletives:
Terence Gray, Eugene O'Neill, and the eating of dreams

The Lord Chamberlain's Office dealt not with playwrights but with managers, expecting that the latter would alter texts as necessary. This was one of the many areas of bitter dispute to emerge between the censorship and Terence Gray, who, as director of the pioneering Cambridge Festival Theatre in the late twenties and early thirties, clashed repeatedly with the Lord Chamberlain over the contemporary international repertoire to which he was committed.[48] In 1928, for example, he wanted to give the first public performance in Britain of Eugene O'Neill's *The Hairy Ape*; the play had been submitted for licence in 1923 and again in 1926, when Cromer had expressed his hope 'that this horrid play would never be brought up again for production on the Stage in this country'.[49] However, on 1 October 1928 Gray was officially informed that a licence for O'Neill's play could be issued, subject to a series of conditions:

1. The expression 'bleedin' Bible' to be omitted (page 11).
2. The killing by the gorilla to take place 'off'.

3. A reasonable compromise in the modification of language and terms of abuse throughout the play.

The assistant comptroller added: 'As regards this last condition, I should be glad if you could conveniently take an opportunity of coming to see me at this Office one day next week between the hours of 11 and 4.' Following that meeting, the Festival Theatre wrote to the Lord Chamberlain's Office on 15 October proposing the amendments they were willing to make:

festival theatre, Cambridge

15th October 1928

The Comptroller,
The Lord Chamberlain's Office,
St James's Palace,
London S.W.1

Dear Sir,

<u>The Hairy Ape</u>

Mr Gray asks me to submit the following list of abusive expressions which – in accordance with your request – he has prepared. This list comprises those terms of abuse, which in his opinion, can be omitted without seriously compromising the author's intentions or adversely affecting the atmosphere of the play. He suggests the substitution in each case of one of the following words: 'blinkin' ', 'bloomin' ', 'blarsted'.

Scene 1 page 7 line 9 bloody Dutchman
page 11 line 13 bleedin' bible
page 15 line 13 bloody engines
Scene 4 page 36 line 12 bloody engineers
line 16 you kin bloody well bet it ain't
line 21 he makes arf the bloody steel in the world
line 25 and she's 'is bloody daughter.
Scene 5 page 47 line 17 I wants to awaken your bloody class consciousness
page 48 line 23 They wouldn't bloody well pay that.

Yours faithfully

But Gray was informed that these proposals were insufficient to secure a licence and that further alterations were necessary. Other than abandoning the production altogether Gray had little option but to concede. However, he took the opportunity to vent his feelings in an angry but cogently argued letter, taking up the cudgels previously wielded by Shaw and Barker (see Plates 8 and 9).

In 1932, when the Lord Chamberlain imposed similar requirements on Rupke's *London Docks*, Gray told him: 'You will realise it is a little difficult when you insist that dock labourers shall use the language of the middle class, without the normal expletives of the latter.'[50] Even now, the word which had famously caused such upheaval in 1912 when first uttered on stage in Shaw's *Pygmalion* continued to be problematic: 'May I ask why, when the word "bloody" is to be heard in the majority of West-end theatres and music halls, you still insist upon its excision from our plays?' queried Gray. In this case, Cromer had been particularly provoked by the terms 'pisspots' and 'bumsucker', and Gray was warned that the text incorporated 'certain expressions which cannot possibly be allowed in any play, and it can only be regarded as impertinence to submit a play containing them'. Gray rarely backed down from his confrontations with the Lord Chamberlain:

> I take the strongest possible exception to the Lord Chamberlain's message. May I be informed by what ordinance I am required to step in between author and censor and make arbitrary alterations to authors' texts? In the first place I am concerned in the administration of several theatres and do not always find it possible, as in this case, even to read certain plays myself before they are put into rehearsal. In the second place I do not feel that I have any qualifications for the censorship of plays. Does the Lord Chamberlain realise that people who are not preoccupied with censorship do not so readily observe the expressions to which he refers: they might read such plays as London Docks without becoming conscious of any such expressions, for the reason that the examples in question come naturally from the mouths of the characters in that play. In fact, I do not think I should be required to understand the particular system of taboos which the Lord Chamberlain's Department endeavours to protect. I neither comprehend the system nor sympathise with it. I believe I understand the susceptibilities of my own audience and occasionally find it desirable to omit words from plays after they have passed through the Lord Chamberlain's Department.
>
> I only submit plays to the Lord Chamberlain because the law obliges me to do so and I cannot see that I should be under any further obligation in the matter.

Toller's *Hoppla!*, Wilde's *Salome*, Strindberg's *Miss Julie*, Tretiakov's *Roar China* and Lenormand's *Man and His Phantoms* were among the plays which Gray was prevented from staging in Cambridge. In the autumn of 1931 he was warned that there would be a delay in deciding whether a licence could be issued for Lenormand's *Eater of Dreams* which, according to Street, had been 'inspired by a study of Freud and his theory of the Oedipus complex'; Gray wrote to the Office in something like desperation:

festival theatre, Cambridge

26th October, 1931

The Comptroller,
Lord Chamberlain's Office,
St James's Palace,
S.W.1.

Dear Sir,
I am in receipt of a letter of October 23rd from the Chief Clerk, informing me that it will be some considerable time before a decision can be reached regarding THE EATER OF DREAMS.

I am anxious to put the case of a theatre such as this, a theatre whose whole circumstances differ so considerably from those of the established professional theatre that I feel an injustice exists in connection with the administration of the censorship. If you would be so kind as to bring this letter to the Lord Chamberlain's personal notice, I and those similarly placed, would be indebted to you.

Circumstances make it necessary for this theatre to produce three sets of eight plays, each set within a period of ten weeks, annually. This arduous work is not undertaken with personal profit in view, nor does it so result. In fact the articles of the company do not allow of the payment of dividends. The work in question is undertaken to assist the survival and re-establishment of that aspect of the Theatre which corresponds to the best literature, to the purest form of pictorial and sculptural art, to the best music. With the partial exception of a couple of 'rag' pantomimes by way of relief no play has ever been presented at this theatre under my management that did not in my view contribute definitely to that end. For this work I need literary material that has been composed by the best intellects, the most penetrating psychologists, the most gifted dramatic artists, and men of such a calibre are seldom bound by the narrow outlook as regards morality that circumscribes the censorship, nor are their works restricted as regards publication. Denied the proper material for my work I am not able to carry on that work, for the classics of bygone times and such modern works of standing as happen to avoid the subjects objected to by the censorship are insufficient.

Authors of this standing rarely if ever practise deliberate obscenity, but they treat of subjects that are of vital importance to human beings, and these subjects are objected to by the censorship. The entertainment trade is allowed to treat these subject in jest, a degree of pornography is deliberately employed to attract the public and that degree is allowed by the censorship, whereas such a theatre as this, which neither needs such pornography nor finds it in the works it seeks to perform, is deprived the use of its legitimate material in consequence.

... How, we may ask, can such a theatre as this be run? Must we always be prepared to close for a week and lose £300 because there exists no organisation whereby a theatre can know whether it may perform a play until some unknown circumstances enable the Lord Chamberlain to give a decision?

Both from the denial of its proper material, and from an apparently arbitrary withholding of censorship for an unstated and incalculable period a theatre such as this is effectively prevented from doing its work. We would be sorry to believe that this is the aim of the Lord Chamberlain's office, but at least I think it cannot be denied that a considerable injustice results, an injustice for which the courtesy of the department, which we heartily appreciate, cannot possibly compensate.

Yours faithfully,
Terence Gray
Director.

the festival theatre (Cambridge) ltd., 36 newmarket road, cambridge[51]

But St James's Palace was not prepared to concede an inch:

Dear Sir,

I write in reply to your letter of October 26th which I have duly brought to the personal notice of the Lord Chamberlain, who welcomes this frank expression of your feelings, if you are under the impression that you are receiving unjust treatment at the hands of censorship.

While the Lord Chamberlain is prepared to admit that the Festival Theatre at Cambridge in its annual programme is conducted upon lines which differ somewhat from those of the commercial theatre, he desires me to point out that this cannot in any way affect the examination of plays submitted for licence.

In the selection of these plays you are no doubt guided by your desire 'to assist the survival and re-establishment of that aspect of the theatre which corresponds to the best literature' . . .

According to your contention, therefore, censorship denies to you the only source from which adequate material can be found for fulfilling the aims of the Festival Theatre at Cambridge.

It is here that the Lord Chamberlain questions the justice of your contention as, although from time to time he has not seen his way to licensing certain plays you have submitted, Licences are granted for the majority.

As to the implication you make regarding delay in decisions from the Lord Chamberlain's Office, I should point out that, while every effort is invariably made to avoid such delays, certain of your plays are occasionally circulated by the Lord Chamberlain to the members of his Advisory Committee, a process which, while entailing the disadvantage of delay, has on several occasions spared you the refusal of a Licence had the reply been returned to you within seven days.

That this procedure is apt to cause dislocation in your plans and the possibility of financial loss, such as you indicate, is much to be regretted. At the same time it should be pointed out that the nature of the literature you submit, which you are anxious not to have mistaken for pornography, is open to other opinions as to its character . . .

By the time Gray was advised that Lenormand's play could in fact be licensed subject to amendments it was too late:

Dear Sir,

I am obliged for your letter of November 6th. The date of performance of 'THE EATER OF DREAMS' was November 9th, and unfortunately even this theatre cannot produce a play over the weekend, so there can be no advantage in my giving you the undertakings you ask for.

Gray resigned his post in 1932 and emigrated to France.

Hovering in the background:
Alone, Children in Uniform and *Love of Women*

Both Cromer and Clarendon (who took over as Lord Chamberlain in 1938) always claimed to operate as few absolute rules as possible, preferring the flexibility of treating each play on its merits, and drawing a distinction between theme and treatment of theme. In theory, it was the latter which was crucial. The ban on Christ and God was pretty well absolute (though exceptions were made for performances in religious buildings, which could be defined as 'acts of worship'), and Queen Victoria and her direct descendants were also proscribed until June 1937. One other subject which came close to being officially taboo was homosexuality, though drawing a definite line around the subject often proved difficult. In 1932, for example, a licence was issued for Mordaunt Shairp's *The Green Bay Tree*, the heart of which was the relationship between 'a rich dilettante' and a young man whom he has brought up after buying him at the age of eight for £500 from his father. Street chose to describe the subject as 'a struggle for a young man's soul', and was adamant that there was 'no suggestion whatever of anything pederastic in Dulcimer's relation to Julian'; however, he admitted that 'the former is and the other likely to be, a rather sinister and abnormal person.'[52] In fact, as most critics realized, even though there was no explicit reference to it, the play made little sense without acknowledging that homosexual attraction was the motor of the plot. The critical discussion of the play in the press led to recriminations within the Office, because of the precedent which had unwittingly been created. But the gap between what is stated or shown and what is only implied and can therefore be denied is perhaps the hardest area for any censorship to police – particularly one which wishes to be approved of and to define itself as 'fair'. One of the contentious areas for the censorship to negotiate was the recurring plot in which characters are *accused* or thought by others to be 'guilty' of homosexuality but where this is denied and remains unproven.

Alone and *Love of Women*

Just such a theme was at the heart of Lillian Hellman's *Children's Hour*, in which vindictive accusations are made against two female schoolteachers. Hellman's script was turned down for the first of several times in 1935 – it only received a licence three decades later – and Street's report on this 'horribly unpleasant play' insisted that 'Plays with not a tenth of the Lesbian element of this one have been banned'.[53] In explaining to a producer in the mid 1940s why Hellman's play could still not be licensed, Gwatkin was almost apologetic:

> There are, of course, degrees of the presentation of unnatural vice, and in this play 'Children's Hour', it could not be more delicately handled . . . The play does not centre round this attitude, which is anyhow shown as deplorable, nor indeed do the principals practice this vice – the reverse – but it is introduced into the play and therefore the Lord Chamberlain cannot give the play a licence.

To suggest that this forbidden subject should be exorcised from the play is, in my opinion, fruitless, because no other accepted social evil could be substituted and to attempt to do so would mean the ruin of a fine piece of work.

Certainly the censorship struggled with a number of plays in the early 1930s over similar issues. In December 1930 Street found himself unable to recommend *Alone* by Marion Norris, a play based on a recently banned novel (see Plate 10). His postscript, in which he noted the lack of any specific evidence of a physical dimension to the relationship, is particularly interesting; two years later, commenting on *The Green Bay Tree*, he seems to suggest that a similar absence renders it impossible to insist that homosexuality is present in the text. In the case of *Alone*, Cromer did not even invite the Advisory Board to comment:

> This is an exact adaptation of the story 'The Well Of Loneliness' the book of which has been officially banned in this country.
> Consequently it is impossible to Licence [sic] its production on the stage.
> Quite apart from this fact, I am not prepared to consider the theme of sexual abnormality in women or men as suitable for public performances in this country.
> Licence refused
> C 16 December 1930.[54]

Love of Women by Aimée and Philip Stuart was less straightforward:

CEREMONIAL DEPARTMENT
ST JAMES'S PALACE S.W.1

October 27th 1934

READER'S REPORT

This play came in yesterday with a request that a decision should be given before November 1st when the authors sail for America, so that they can make 'any slight alterations required'. Unfortunately the whole play is dubious, to say the least, and one of the most difficult to report on I have ever had. Homosexuality between two women is much of the theme: it does not exist but it is talked about.

Vere and Brigit, two young women, have been living together for some years. Vere is a little the elder and the stronger character, Brigit is the daughter of Wingate, the proprietor of a fashionable preparatory school. They live in a remote cottage and have for friend Jacqueline and Philip, children of a neighbouring peer. Vere and Brigit have written a successful play and so have come into 'the news', and comments and innuendos have been made about their relation to one another. These have alarmed Brigit's parents, who arrive to take her away. There is no truth in the suggestion. The young women are 'through with sex' and live only for their work. Brigit announces to her parents that she is engaged to be married, which is a shock to Vere. At the end of Act One, the parents having gone, Brigit's lover turns up, a self assured and virile doctor, John. The next day she is upset by hearing that her engagement is talked about as a joke and says she will not marry John. He has a long argument with Vere, telling her as a doctor and psychologist that her exclusion of sex is morbid and will ruin her work. Then he kisses her passionately and afterwards tells her her complacency provoked him but he loves only Brigit. Brigit by this time has reconsidered her decision. John tells her he won't stand having 'one eye on Vere' in their married life. They go off together. The girl Jacqueline makes a passionate advance to Vere, which is repulsed. Vere is left desolate. Lesbianism is never mentioned, but it is obvious that this is what the gossip implies and Brigit's parents fear. Mrs Wingate says 'it is worse than I feared', having seen the girls kiss. And though it is not supposed to exist, in Vere's case something like the feeling is suggested in her overwhelming sorrow at the loss of Brigit. The girl Jacqueline's advance <u>is</u> Lesbian, but that could easily be cut out. In fact there is no reason why the authors should not have written a play about the devotion of two women – like *The Ladies of Llangollen* – and the sorrow of one when the other marries without any suggestion of Lesbianism at all. But they <u>do</u> suggest it, not as a fact, but as an unfounded rumour, very prominently. They will perhaps plead the precedents of *Children in Uniform* or *The Green Bay Tree* as being occupied with homosexuality – wrongly in the latter case . . . But here the atmosphere of gossip implying it makes all the difference.

I may be wrong in this opinion and do not personally think that reference to homosexuality can always be kept from the stage, but in view of the rules and precedents I cannot possibly advise the Lord Chamberlain to license the play. I think, however, that if only the talk about gossip, Mrs Wingate's anxiety and so on were taken out the play might be passed.[55]

Cromer did send this script to his Advisory Board, where it found little support. Lord David Cecil commented:

This play is a border-line case: but on the whole I think it should not be licensed. It is true, as Mr. Street points out, that homosexuality is not ostensibly a motive of the action. But it hovers in the background of much of the dialogue, and would be more obtrusive in actual performance than in reading. Nor is the play a work of such serious value or written with such discretion and taste, as would justify its production, in spite of the implications of its theme.

Lord Ullswater was prepared to be generous and broad-minded, if only the crucial theme could be erased: 'I agree with Mr Street that if the suggestions about homosexuality could be suppressed there could be no objection to the play; but it is a big IF', he noted. Yet Ullswater suggested he would 'like to see the authors make the attempt to revise it in the sense indicated, as the play has many good points and some good characters'. But probably the most interesting and perceptive observations (not unusually) were those offered by Lady Violet Bonham-Carter, who, to the horror and chagrin of Douglas Dawson, had been the first woman invited to join the Advisory Board. She at least recognized the absurdity of trying to isolate and excise parts of a play which were integral to it, and recognized too that without less ambiguous definitions and guidelines, censorship must lack consistency and principle and finally come down to whim, taste and arbitrariness:

The question as to whether it should be licensed or not seems to me to hinge entirely on a technical question of principle, i.e. Are all plays in which the theme of homosexuality is discussed, or hinted at, to be automatically barred from performance on the English stage? If the answer is 'Yes' (just as the appearance of the Almighty on the stage is automatically banned) then this play most certainly comes within the scope of the ban.

You cannot – as is suggested – eliminate the parents' anxiety as to the situation, the references to 'gossip' etc., without robbing the play of its only point and completely puncturing its plot.

I am not competent to judge of this main principle, which no doubt rests upon tradition and precedent.

If the Lord Chamberlain wishes to discuss its justice or the advisability of its possible revision, I am of course ready to do so. I do not know whether our Committee exists to consider such questions or merely to apply hard and fast rules already made.

I may add that many of those who saw *The Green Bay Tree* (which was not circulated to the Committee and which I did not see myself) regarded the situation it depicted as frankly homosexual. I received many protests on the subject and I believe that Lord Buckmaster had the same experience.

I mention this only as illustrating the question of <u>precedent</u> – not as an argument on that of principle.

There is no record of the debate which Bonham-Carter sought to initiate taking place, and in November 1934 *Love of Women* was refused a licence. The following June Henry Game, who had joined the Office as an assistant examiner in 1930, attended a private performance of a slightly amended version by the Repertory Players at the Phoenix Theatre, as the representative of the Lord Chamberlain. His subsequent comments echoed those of Bonham-Carter:

The problem really boils down to one of policy. If any mention of perversion on the stage is taboo, then this play cannot be allowed.

If on the other hand perversion may be mentioned, then this play in which it exists merely as a rumour can be judged on its general intention , which is wholly moral, and could pass.

Cromer took further advice, before once again ruling that no licence could be issued for a public performance. The management were informed accordingly on 5 June:

It might possibly, as you say, be argued that the play is even a moral one, but the fact remains that it introduces a perversion as a factor in the plot, thus giving advertisement in the emotional atmosphere of a theatre to a fact in life, which appears undesirable.

Children in Uniform

Street's original report on *Love of Women* had raised the possibility that the management might cite as precedents in its defence not only *The Green Bay Tree* but also *Children in Uniform*, written by Christa Winsloe. This latter was a play which, like the former, had been somewhat surprisingly licensed in 1932. Street had reported more or less favourably in May of that year, six months before *The Green Bay Tree* burst into bloom:

CEREMONIAL DEPARTMENT
ST JAMES'S PALACE S.W.1

May 19th 1932

READER'S REPORT

This play has been sent in to see if there is any objection to the theme. It is said to be a literal translation from the German and that further adaptation will be necessary. The translation, however, is into idiomatic English.

I fancy that the chief intention of the original was to criticize the stupid and unimaginative discipline of a Prussian aristocratic girls' school, and that the unhappy passion of one of the girls for a mistress is subsidiary: it is no doubt, the latter, however, which is in question. The girl, Manuela, is a sensitive and affectionate child of nearly 15. A great part of the play is devoted to her experiences as a new girl in the school, with its various habits and customs. Fraulein von Bernburg is a popular mistress and the girls talk freely about falling in love with her. She herself is not at all a bad sort and is quite free from the sadism of a similarly worshipped schoolmistress in 'The Regiment of Women'. She is pleased by Manuela's devotion and seeing that the girl has been sent to school ill provided gives her a chemise of her own. The school does a play and Manuela performs (apparently) the part of Joan of Arc, or else some Knight. She is much applauded and at the supper afterwards other girls give her their portions of Swedish punch (which they don't like) and she drinks it excitedly, gets tipsy and makes a speech boasting of the chemise and her devotion to Fraulein von Bernburg. The Headmistress comes in and overhears it and is horrified. Manuela is to be ostracized but is respited during a visit from a Grandduchess Guardian of the school. F. von Bernburg talks to her kindly but says she cannot see any more of her. Manuela throws herself out of the window and the news is brought to the Headmistress while F. von Bernburg is criticizing the narrowness etc. of her methods.

Such an ordinary thing as the 'passion' of a schoolgirl for a mistress is not to be confused with adult Lesbianism, which has so far been ruled out as a subject for plays. It is unfortunate that the stupid Headmistress treats it as a grave perversion and even F. von Bernburg calls it a 'sin'. Personally I do not think the play should be banned. I have not noticed what was said about the film of the play recently produced. The Lord Chamberlain would no doubt be adversely criticised for allowing it, and though as I said the theme is not real Lesbianism it is still rather a morbid one for a long play. I suggest, therefore, that the Lord Chamberlain should consider it himself or take another opinion before admitting the theme as possible.

(sd.) G. S. Street[56]

Cromer's initial instinct was to run a mile:

Although there is no real parallel between this Prussian Girl's [sic] School and the usual run of Girl's Schools in this country, I think it would be unfortunate to have a play of this description on the English Stage . . .

It would be resented by Educational Authorities & many parents & comes within the category of unnecessarily doubtful themes.

Buckmaster, on the other hand, was all for licensing, provided certain modifications could be imposed:

I think too severe an opinion has been formed about this play.

A lonely and motherless child of 14½ years is sent to a school ruled by Prussian discipline. One of the teachers, represented as an honourable woman, kisses the child in bed and thus revives memories of her mother.

In the end the child becomes passionately devoted to the teacher, the affection is undoubtedly unhealthy but there is nothing whatever to suggest it is unclean and such a feeling is by no means uncommon between a young girl and a kind teacher nor does it produce mischief unless the teacher is an evil minded woman.

The fact that the child is allowed to become tipsy is not pleasant but it can afford no sound ground for banning the play.

When tipsy the child talks nonsense and the headmistress regards this as evidence of 'perversity', the child is cut off from all society and kills herself. The real point of the play is the inhumanity of a cast iron system that seeks to find evil where it does not exist. I can find no obvious suggestion that the child had any knowledge of what are euphemistically called 'the facts of life' nor was her passion consciously perverse.

I should excise the references to perversity and sin or modify them and let the play be passed.

Both Lord Ullswater and Sir Johnston Forbes-Robertson gave broad support to Buckmaster's position, and Lady Violet Bonham Carter took a favourable view of the play's message:

I have seen the film 'Madchen in Uniform' – which has extraordinary pathos and beauty. It follows the lines of the play very closely, except that the final tragedy of Manuela's suicide is averted through the action of the other children, who rescue her.

I am in favour of granting a licence to the play. As I understand it, its object is to show how the entirely innocent and romantic emotion of a lonely and motherless child, whose heart and imagination are being starved by a Robot regime, may be first driven into morbid and exaggerated channels, and then denounced and condemned in the name of a 'sin' – of which not the faintest apprehension exists in the mind of the child.

I do not think there is any intention to suggest more than this – or that the feelings Fraulein von Bernburg inspires in the other pupils is anything but a rather foolish, school-girlish 'schwarmerei'.

A condemnation of the system which produces these results is really the theme of the play, and the setting is so uncompromisingly German in every particular, that I should not have thought it could be taken as applying to, or reflecting on, educational methods in this country.

Only Professor Allardyce Nicoll was unconvinced. He admitted the play was 'a wholly worthy work of art, wherein the theme is handled skilfully and with serious purpose', but expressed concern about how it might come across on the stage, and, particularly, to whom it might appeal:

> I think it must be confessed that bad production could introduce a different atmosphere, so creating a less worthy impression, and that the theme itself would be likely to attract audiences because of its dangerous nature. While there is, certainly, a distinction to be made between Manuela's feelings for F. von Bernburg and adult Lesbianism, it still remains true that the former are clearly tending towards the latter and that Manuela, innocent though she may be, is in the grip of a potentially unnatural passion.

He concluded:

> After weighing these coincidences carefully, I should say that if *Children in Uniform* is likely to be brought out by a responsible and sympathetic producer, I should be in favour of licensing it.

Major Gordon, who was assistant comptroller between 1925 and 1936, warned that there was no such guarantee, even in the case of the first production for which a licence was being considered:

> Mr Gregory, who has submitted the play, is not a person I should recommend as being likely to produce the play either delicately or sympathetically. He has been concerned in the past with one or two rather risky productions, and is a person who does not mind 'spicing' a production if he can get away with it, and turn it into a commercial success.

Yet Gordon's main concern was whether audiences would realize that there was no connection between Britain and the world they saw on stage.

> If the play is presented as a study of German scholastic life and the scenes are kept in Germany, it might be comparatively harmless, with the excisions suggested. There is a vast difference to my mind, between a film presented in the German language, and a translation of a German play into English, as unless the scenes are definitely laid in Germany many people who see it will mistake it for a representation of life in an English school.

In mid-June, Cromer ruled that a licence could be considered if certain alterations were made and – unusually – 'subject to strict supervision in the production'. He even went so far as to specify that 'The setting will have to remain strictly GERMAN', noting: 'Before any definite decision is given, I must see the Producer and hear from him the lines on which he suggests production'. The meeting took place eight days later, and Cromer reported on the deal he had clinched:

Mr Gregory gave an undertaking that the German setting would be retained and that no attempt would be made to Anglicise the play. He further stated that it would be necessary for him to have a fresh version prepared, as the present one was really a literal translation from the German. He promised to take into consideration and incorporate the suggestions made to him by the Lord Chamberlain when preparing the new version, which would be submitted for approval in due course.

In the autumn, Street again recommended the revised version:

I do not think English educationalists will be offended, because the play is emphatically a criticism of the German system. Nor do I think it likely that people will go in a wrong spirit, the pathos of the child being almost unbearably moving. But it is a morbid sort of play

(sd) G. S. Street.

Cromer signed the licence on 23 September, 1932.

Vot iss all zis about?: *Robinson Crusoe*, W. H. Auden, Elmer Rice and the reasonable Germans

In 1924 Street responded to a complaint about a revue described as 'Communistic Propaganda' by stating that 'it is not in the province of the Censor to exclude the expression of political opinion from plays if kept within decent limits'.[57] Similarly, Cromer claimed in a letter to the Home Office in 1931 to be 'always anxious, as far as possible, to cut political censorship out of the theatre'.[58] And in 1949, an MP assured the House of Commons with supreme confidence: 'The Lord Chamberlain's office would not dream of imposing any restriction on a play because it was political. That factor would not come into the purview of that office.'[59]

But the devil lies in definitions, and whether we examine the portrayal of the monarchy, of war, of international and racial issues, of class and propaganda, or of a host of other issues, the political dimension to theatre censorship was pervasive.[60] It is true that the censors often took the view that the potential danger was not sufficiently serious to require banning, and that more publicity would be attracted by clamping down than by tolerating; no doubt the censors also believed that the limits they imposed were simply logical commonsense, which no one whose opinion was worth listening to would dispute. Yet perhaps in the political even more than in other fields, the effect of the censorship was that plays with genuinely radical tendencies were unlikely ever to be written and submitted for public performance. If putting a sycophantic celebration of Queen Victoria on the stage was beyond the pale, then not many playwrights were likely to waste their time on a play which criticized a more recent monarch or called for a republican coup d'état.

One of the most prominent features of political control was the policy of ensuring that international allies and the leaders of friendly nations were not subjected to criticism on the stage. A crucial factor driving this was the fact that because censorship was carried out by the head of the royal household, it was the king who ultimately licensed plays; this could be taken to indicate that the monarch not only sanctioned but actually endorsed the 'message' of every play publicly performed. This probably mattered more in relation to the international dimension of theatre censorship than elsewhere. As the novelist and playwright Hall Caine told the 1909 Joint Select Committee, every licensed play was in effect 'a national act, carrying a sort of national responsibility'.[61] So rather than relying on their own judgement or that of readers and advisers, Cromer and Clarendon regularly sent scripts and reports to the Foreign Office, and even to foreign embassies.

Through the 1930s the Lord Chamberlain was obliged to consider the wishes of the German embassy. 'It is not easy to go on shielding the Germans from their misdeeds being depicted on the stage in this country', wrote Cromer to the Foreign Office as early as November 1934.[62] But shield them he did – at least officially. In 1933 he commented in relation to a play which he refused to license:

> Whatever one may think of the Hitler regime, the prosecution of Jews etc. they are no direct concern of ours, so that the presentation of this picture of conditions on the British stage could not be regarded otherwise than unfriendly and lead to official complaint which would be difficult to answer. Besides which if we allow this in England, our authorities can hardly complain of retaliation by anti-British plays in Germany. At the present time it would be an unwise play to produce and will do no good, only possibly harm.
>
> I hardly think any alteration in the dialogue would remove the basic objection to the theme of the play.[63]

Even Street, recommending that another play be turned down in February 1934, advised: 'it would be unwise to allow a theatre to become a centre of anti-Nazi feeling and I cannot advise the Lord Chamberlain to take that risk'.[64]

Nevertheless, even if he had wanted to it would have been impossible for the Lord Chamberlain to prevent playwrights from finding ways to criticize Nazi ideology and practice. He could (and usually did) insist on removing references which explicitly and absolutely identified Germany or its leaders, but audiences were doubtless as adept as the censors at making the Brechtian leap which allowed them to realize that a distant or imaginary setting might still have a relationship to real events. A not untypical list of cuts and endorsements imposed on *Take Heed* in 1938, for example, included the following:

ACT I

Page	3	'health' for 'prosit' throughout
	6	'foreign' for 'Czecho-Slovakian
	12	Cut 'goose-stepping'
	13	'England' – alter to 'abroad'. 'Englishman' alter to 'people,' cut 'battleship
	14	Cut 'European' substitute 'our'. Cut Emperor, substitute King throughout
	22	Substitute 'Vann' for 'Berlin'

29 Substitute 'Marshal' for 'Leader' throughout. Cut 'Nordic' substitute 'Our'
30 Cut 'Herr' throughout
33 Substitute 'our Leaders' for 'the Leaders'. Cut 'National Socialism'
35 Substitute 'Military socialists' for 'National Socialist' throughout. Substitute song submitted in place of 'Judah Verrecke'
36 Substitute 'foreign' for 'Galician'
37 Substitute 'fled from persecution' for 'Poland'
40 Substitute 'millions' for 'two million'
41 No recognisable salute throughout . . . no recognisable uniform . . .

ACT II

Page 21 Cut 'brown shirts' substitute 'coloured shirts' throughout
24 Cut 'Basle' substitute 'Paris' throughout. Cut 'marks' substitute 'crowns'
33 cut 'Anti-Nordic' substitute 'Hebraic'
36 Cut '1933'
37 Any song outside to be unrecognisable

ACT III

Page 23 Cut 'Monster' substitute 'Terror'
27 for the first 'Hail' Substitute 'All Hail'
28 cut 'after the French' and substitute 'after we have dealt with others'
No sunlight to encircle the heads of Sophie and Opal.

Even so, a spokesman for the German Embassy told the Office 'it was a pity such plays had to be as "they did not help"'. Certainly, no one can have believed that even such extensive changes led to more than the most superficial veiling of the subject.

In March 1934 Street reported on *Whither Liberty* by Alan Peters, a doctor from Leeds, which was a rewritten version of a script which previously been banned:

This is the play which under the title 'Who Made the Iron Grow' was refused a licence on the advice of the Foreign Office. I gather . . . that the Lord Chamberlain hoped he would be able to license the play if an imaginary country replaced Germany, and other names were altered. This has been done. Germany becomes Nordia, Hitler Hacker, Nazi Nori, Brown Shirts Yellow Shirts, and so on. Otherwise the play is the same, with the outrages on Jews and the denunciation of the Nazi regime.

That Nordia means Germany and the other imaginary names those for which they stand will of course be obvious to everybody. But that was certain when the author was more or less encouraged to make the changes. That being the case, however, I should be inclined to cut out the accusation against Hacker, i.e. Hitler, of himself having the 'Senate House' "blown up" as being particularly offensive to the German government and as never having been proved, whereas for the outrages of the Jews there is a mass of evidence. But I think the play should be passed. The custom of allowing imaginary names when the real names would not be, even though everyone knows the identification, is open to objection in theory, but it has always existed and

25

(1.)

| METROPOLITAN POLICE DISTRICT) | The INFORMATION of the DIRECTOR OF PUBLIC |

METROPOLITAN POLICE DISTRICT)
      To Wit.

The INFORMATION of the DIRECTOR OF PUBLIC PROSECUTIONS and the DEPOSITION of GEORGE ALFRED TITMAN in support thereof, taken on oath this   day of January, 1937 before me, the undersigned, one of the Magistrates of the Police Courts of the Metropolis sitting at West London Police Court in the said Police District upon an application for a SUMMONS against AIMEE LOUISE MULHOLLAND of Milbrook, Upper Richmond Road, S.W.15., FOR THAT SHE on the 7th day of January 1937, did present a certain part of a stage play which had not been allowed by the Lord Chamberlain,

Contrary to Section 15 of the Theatres Act, 1843.

AND the said GEORGE ALFRED TITMAN upon oath saith as follows:-

1.   I am the Assistant Secretary to the Lord Chamberlain's Office. The facts hereinafter deposed to are true to my own knowledge and the necessary evidence and documents are available to prove them.

2.   In consequence of a telephone communication received at the Lord Chamberlain's Office from the Foreign Office on the evening of the 7th January, I visited the King's Theatre, Hammersmith, and having purchased a ticket, I witnessed the performance of the pantomime 'Robinson Crusoe'.

3.   The script of this pantomime was licensed by the Lord Chamberlain on the 21st day of December 1935 and the licensed copy of the said pantomime was retained

1.

12. Official police statement made by George Titman (Secretary in the Lord Chamberlain's Office) detailing the offence committed during a performance of *Robinson Crusoe*, January 1937.

in the Lord Chamberlain's Office.

4.   During the performance of this pantomime on the 7th
January, a scene was enacted in which white people were
defending themselves in a stockade against an assault
by black people. During this scene a gate of the stockade
is opened and a man appears who by his dress and facial
make-up was intended to represent and was taken by myself
and the rest of the audience to represent Herr Hitler.
He gave the German Nazi salute and said in broken English,
"Vot iss all zis about?", and the manner in which the
line was given was intended to be humorous and would give
offence to persons having patriotic German sympathies.

5.   This portion of the stage play was not and would not
be licensed by the Lord Chamberlain. It must be common
knowledge that this form of humour is highly undesirable
at the present time, and persons connected with the
Theatre should be especially aware of this fact.

6.   The King's Theatre Hammersmith is licensed for
stage plays by the London County Council to the said
Aimee Louise Mulholland, and by section 7 of the Theatres
Act 1843 the licensee of a theatre is the actually and
responsible manager for the time being of the theatre in
respect of which such license has been granted.

1959/6597

STAGE PLAY SUBMITTED FOR LICENCE.

Title :   "WAITING FOR GODOT"

No. of Scenes or Acts :   2 acts

Place of Production :

Date of Production :

Author :   Samuel Beckett

Submitted by :   Donald Albery

Title :   WAITING FOR GODOT.
No of Acts :   Two.
Place of Production :)   Not specified. Submitted by Donald
Date of Production :)   Albery.
Author :   Samuel Beckett.

     With many years on the Council of the old Stage Society,
I have had much experience of "advanced", "expressionist", and
and similar imaginative kinds of plays, but I find this one
extremely baffling. It is described as of " a surrealist
nature" by Donald Albery, and has run for two years in Paris.
It is written by a former Secretary of James Joyce, the Irish
author who finding it necessary to invent virtually a new
language to express himself, left his message to the world far
from clear in consequence. The Joyce influence and attitude
will be seen by a glance at Act I, pp 40-41.

     I can describe the simple happenings on the stage, and
indicate for elimination the words and lines of Joycean gross-
ness, but I can only offer the merest glimmer of a suggestion
of what the author intends it all to mean.

     Two elderly tramps, Estragon and Vladimir, are on a
desolate country road with a single tree (presumably in France)
towards sundown, waiting for a personage named Godot, who dis-
appoints them each day by his non-arrival. They hold prolonged
rambling discussions, including a contemplation of suicide.
Then a man named Pozzo appears, dragging on by a rope round
his neck another man named Lucky. Lucky is Pozzo's slave,
carrying all his impedimenta, urged on with whip and halter.
Pozzo for some reason is anxious to obtain the good opinion of
the tramps, and at their request compels Lucky to dance and to
make a speech for them. There is also much embittered conversation about Life. Then Pozzo and Lucky move on, and at
the end of Act I a small boy arrives to say that Godot will
not be coming that night but next.

     The Second Act is virtually a repetition of the First,
except that Pozzo is now blind and Lucky dumb; all four men
are much weaker and fall about a good deal. After the depart-
ure of Pozzo and Lucky in this Act, the tramps make a more
determined attempt at suicide, but they have no rope, and
Estragon's belt breaks on being tested. The small boy comes
with the same message from Godot, but the tramps decide that
when they return on the morrow to resume their vigil, they
will provide themselves with a stout piece of rope.

     The only clues through this interminable verbal labyrinth
are provided first when Estragon says of Pozzo "He's all man-
kind", and second when Pozzo, speaking of existence in general,
says "They give birth astride of a grave, the light gleams an

217   21

13. Reader's Report by St. Vincent Troubridge recommending the licensing of *Waiting for Godot*, March 1954.

instant, then it's night again."

So I will venture tentatively the following interpretation.

The play is a modern cry of despair, and Godot, for whom we human tramps are always waiting in expectation, is Death. Pozzo and Lucky are allegorical figures passing before our eyes of how men treat one another, by acts of enslavement that lead to blindness for the enslaver and dumbness for the slave. The best way out is a piece of rope - what Shakespeare called "the charity of a penny cord."

Why the shrewdest of our younger managers should contemplate the production of so bitter, dark and obscure an allegory is almost as mysterious as much of the play.

Act I , p 2. "You might button it up all the same." cut Cut

"   p 3. (his hand pressed to his pubis) cut..   Cut

"   pp 4-5. There is some conversation here between the   Leave
               tramps about the Crucifixion that seems all
               right to me, but as a precaution another eye   cut
               should run over it.

"   pp9-10. The lines as marked about unknown secodary effect Cut
               of hanging must come out.   to Cut

"   p 27. "kicking him out on his arse."   cut Cut

"   p 40. Mixed in the nonsense of the first 12 lines, I Allow
               detect distinct mockery of religion.   cut

"   "   "Fartov."   cut Cut

"   p 52. I don't like Estragon comparing himself to cut Cut
               Christ.

Act II, p 3. "You piss better...etc."   cut   Cut

"   p 16. (resumes his foetal posture)
               I conceive this to link with I,3. i.e. with his
               hand on his pubis, but I may be wrong. Cut

"   p 20. "Gonococcus! Spirochaete!
               (These are the microbes of gonorrhaea and Cut Cut
                syphilis)

"   p 30. "Who farted ?"
               (Though used in the plays of Ben Jonson, this Cut Cut

Act II, p 30. word is now out of favour.)

"   p 38. "give him a taste of his boot, in...the privates" Cut

"   p 45. The business of letting down Estragon's
               trousers, which may be all right.   better keep

Otherwise, in some bewilderment,   Leave provided keep
                                                   is well covered

    RECOMMENDED FOR LICENCE.

                                     Sr icent Trobidge
28/3/1954.   Assistant Examiner.

                                                              218

passages as proposed

Cut or alter all the texts referred to above.

The discussion on P.45 to be altered so as to eliminate the suggestion that there may have been a homosexual relationship.

CRITERION THEATRE

PICCADILLY CIRCUS, W.1

Licensed by the Lord Chamberlain to .. SIR BRONSON ALBERY
Lessees : THE WYNDHAM THEATRES LTD.
Managing Directors.. SIR BRONSON ALBERY & DONALD ALBERY

SAMUEL BECKETT'S

WAITING FOR GODOT

DIRECTED BY
PETER HALL

SETTING BY
PETER SNOW

6ᴰ

First produced at the Arts Theatre on Wednesday, 3rd August, 1955
Produced at Criterion Theatre, London, on Monday 12th September, 1955

Designed by IAN EMMERSON

14. Programme for *Waiting for Godot* at the Criterion Theatre, September 1955.

STAGE PLAY SUBMITTED FOR LICENCE.

Title :	LOOK BACK IN ANGER
No. of Scenes or Acts :	Three Acts
Place of Production :	Royal Court Theatre, London
Date of Production :	7.5.56
Author :	John Osborne
Submitted by :	

LORD CHAMBERLAIN'S OFFICE,
ST. JAMES'S PALACE, S.W.1.

READERS' REPORT.   1.3.56

This impressive and depressing play breaks new psychological ground, dealing
with a type of young man I believed had vanished twenty years ago, but which
must be generally recognisable enough to write plays about.   It is about
that kind of intellectual that threshed about passionately looking for a cause.
It usually married girls of good family, quarrelled with all their relations,
and bore them off to squalor in Pimlico or Poplar where they had babies and
spent all their spare time barracking Fascist meetings.   In this play the
venue is a large provincial town where Jimmy and Alison, his wife, share frowsty
digs with Cliff, Jimmy's friend.   The men run a sweet-stall in the market-place -
both having been at an university.   Cliff is platonically loving to Alison.   But
Jimmy, torn by his secret daemons - his sense of social and intellectual inferiority
his passionate 'feeling' that the old order is, in some way, responsible for the
general bloodiness of the world today, his determination to epater les bourgeois
at all costs and his unrealised mother-fixation for the kindly, charitable mother
of one of his friends (a charwoman who married an artist, completely uneducated
so that Jimmy can, quite unconsciously, patronise her while he praises her goodness)
- foams at Alison, insulting her parents, teasing her about her background in an
angry way and generally indulging in a grand display of tantrums that only differ
from those of the nursery in having an adult sexual flavour.   Alison has not yet
told Jimmy that she is pregnant, but she invites a friend (a correct girl of her own
class who has gone on the stage) to stay for a while.   Jimmy goes out of his
way to embroider his offensiveness to the two girls.   Helena xixxixxxixxxix wires
Alison's father to come and take her away.   He arrives just after Jimmy has rushed
off the London to the deathbed of the old lady, his friend's mother.   When he
returns, heavy with childish grief, he finds his wife gone and only Helena with

9170 11/55 H & S Ltd. Gp. 902

---

15. Reader's Report by C. D. Heriot recommending the licensing of *Look Back in Anger*, March 1956.

the courage to face him. It is a courage based on an unwilling-passion. They become lovers. Then Alison returns, the child having died, and Helena retires, leaving the two of them to begin all over again. It is characteristic that the unbreakable ties of their attraction should be garlanded with embarrassingly whimsical love-language. The play̦s interest, in fact, lies in its careful observation of an anteroom of hell.

Act i.	p.23.	Cut the lavatory reference.	*Cut*	*Leave*
	p.41	Cut the homsexual reference	*Cut*	*Leave*
	pp.43/44	The whole of this speech must be considerably toned down.	*toned down. last left*	*Yes especially*
ii, 2.p.15		Alter the reference to pubic hair	*Cut*	*Cut*
	16	ditto and reference to inversion	*Cut*	*Cut*
	19	Cut the marked speech	*Cut*	*Cut*
Act ii, 2.	p.14	Cut 'deep, loving bull!8	*Cut*	*Cut*
Act iii, 1.	p.14	Cut 'short-arsed'	*Cut*	*Cut*
	16	Alter reference to excessive lovemaking.	*? Leave*	

Otherwise

Mh

RECOMMENDED FOR LICENCE.

S   *C.D.Herot*

C.D.Heriot.

Footnote: The prototypes of Jimmy and Alison may be Giles Romilly and his
             wife. Romilly was killed in the war and his biography was
             sketched in a book called "Friends Apart" by Philip Toynbee,
             published in 1954.

STAGE PLAY SUBMITTED FOR LICENCE.

Title :   THE LESSON

No. of Scenes or Acts :   One Act

Place of Production :   Playhouse, Oxford

Date of Production :   29.1.57

Author :   Eugene Ionesco   Translated by Donald Watson

Submitted by :

LORD CHAMBERLAIN'S OFFICE,
ST. JAMES'S PALACE, S.W.1.

READERS' REPORT.

9.1.57

Another crazy effusion from the pen of the Franco-Rumanian avant garde writer
Eugene Ionesco.

A young girl comes to a professor for a lesson.   She is surprisingly ignorant of
the simpler aspects of the various subjects - mathematics, Geography, History,
Etymology - but appears to know a lot about the more advanced aspects.   The
professor gradually stifles her intelligence under a cloud of meaningless verbiage.
As her stupidity increases, so does his domination.   She appears to suffer from
an attack of toothache but the professor takes no notice.   He drones on until
at last he loses his temper with her lack of response and kills her.   His housekeeper
comes in to scold him, reminding him that this is the fortieth murder he has
committed in the same circumstances.   They remove the body and the curtain falls
as another pupil is announced.   The text is repetitive and meaningless.   All
'props' are imaginary and the action is, so to speak, mimed.

If this means anything at all, it is a clumsy allegory of the sexual act.   This
is, I think, born out by the business of the killing on pp.50/51.
And though it may kill the whole play I think the Lord Chamberlain will agree with
me that the body of the girl must not fall into an immodest position,   that the
professor must not stand (as he cannot fail to do if the stage directions are followed
between her legs to deliver the second blow, and that the second blow must not in
any circumstances resemble the male sexual act.   *Yes, this is pretty erotic symbolism or worse*

*I have read the play & must confess to a doubt whether it has any allegorical
meaning - or indeed any meaning at all. But in case it has I agree that the
knee directions should be given.*

Otherwise

RECOMMENDED FOR LICENCE
S

C.D.Heriot.

9795

14676 12/56 H & S Ltd. Gp. 902

Title : CAT ON A HOT TIN ROOF

No. of Scenes or Acts : Three Acts

Place of Production :

Date of Production :

Author : Tennessee Williams

Submitted by :

LORD CHAMBERLAIN'S OFFICE,
ST. JAMES'S PALACE, S.W.1.

READERS' REPORT.   2.11.55.

Once again, Mr. Williams vomits up the recurring theme of his not-too-subconscious. This is the fourth play (and there are sure to be others) where we are confronted by the gentlewoman debased, sunk in her private dreams as a remedy for her sexual frustration, and over all the author's horror, disgust and rage against the sexual act.

Big Daddy, a wealthy plantation owner in the Deep South, is dying of cancer, deceived by his family into believing that he has a spastic colon.   He is the coarsest possible type of tycoon whose favourite expletive is 'Crap!'   His elder son Gooper, is married to Mae, a vulgar heartless, utterly common woman, whose only claim to recognition is that she has five children and a sixth on the way. His 'Benjamin' is the younger son, Brick, married to Margaret who is several social strata his superior.   Their marriage is childless because Brick is repulsed by her, partly because of her too-ardent and too-obvious sexuality, and partly because his close friend and ball-game associate, Skipper, with whom he had a beautiful friendship, is dead after having been (according to her) Margaret's lover.   Brick tries to forget his disgust xxxxfxxxxx of treachery, sexuality and a possible guilt in alcohol.   The play, having established the relationships of this nest of vipers, is thereafter concerned with Brick's confession to his father that his wife Margaret and his brother and sister in law are hinting that Margaret's childlessness is due to his homosexuality, quoting Skipper as his real love.   He tries to explain to his father that his friendship with Skipper was not a perverse thing, and while doing so, inadvertently lets out the facts about his fathe 's real state of health.   I need hardly add that Big Daddy is himself revolted by his own wife Big Mamma and shares the materialist panic about death.

Two versions of the last acts are submitted.   In the first, and original, version, the family bicker and quarrel in the absence of the father, until Margaret suddenly announces the fact that she is pregnant – thus insuring that she and Brick will inherit the larger part (if not the whole) of the estate – and at th very end of the play, hiding all the bottles of drink from Brick and telling him that if he wants one, he must xxxxxxxxxxxxxxxxxxxxxxxxxxxxxxxxx impregnate her first.

The second version of the last act is the one in which the producer, Kazan, collaborated with the author for the New Yrok production.   It is sentimental and false.   Margaret's announcement is made in the presence of the father amid a symbolic thunderstorm, xxxxxxxxxxxxxxxxxxx the brother and sister in law are foiled of their share in the estate and Margaret dramatically splinters all the drink-bottles on the concrete below the verandah, while Brick sheepishly remembers his manhood.   There is an added and unneccessary indecent story about elephants.

The whole thing is pretentious, over-strained, over-emphasised and hysterical The author obviously believes that he is writing Literature with a big L.   (An example of his portentiousness can be seen on page 46 of Act II).   The language is repetitively coarse – and loses its effect in consequence.

As far as I can judge, the homosexual element is false – that is to say, we are to believe Brick when he says that his wife and relations 'dreamed it up'.   I think, therefore, that with a lot of cuts, listed below, the Lord Chamberlain might consider granting a license for this bogus play.

Act I.   p.6   Cut reference to 'boobs' and 'ass-aching' cut

27/28 Cut reference to sexual ability   cut

6131 G 3399 2/54 H & S Ltd. Gp. 902

(Contd.)

MINUTE BY THE LORD CHAMBERLAIN

I have decided to make a change in the policy of the censorship, and I think it desirable to place on record as clearly as possible the nature of the change so that all concerned may be fully aware of it.

First, the reason behind this change. For some time the subject of Homosexuality has been so widely debated, written about and talked about, that it is no longer justifiable to continue the strict exclusion of this subject from the Stage. I do not regret the policy of strict exclusion which has been continued up to now, and I think it has been to the public good. Nevertheless, now that it has become a topic of almost every-day conversation, its exclusion from the Stage can no longer be defended as a reasonable course, even when account is taken of the more effective persuasion which the living Stage can exercise as compared with the written word. I therefore propose to allow plays which make a serious and sincere attempt to deal with the subject. It will follow also that references in other plays will be allowed to the subject which appear necessary to the dialogue or the plot, and which are not salacious or offensive. Licences will continue to be refused for plays which are exploitations of the subject rather than contributions to the problem; and similarly references to the subject which are unnecessary or have merely an exploitation value will be disallowed.

I do not imagine that this change of policy will eliminate all difficulties with regard to this question. I have, in fact, little doubt that we shall continue to be faced with problems which it will be difficult to resolve. It may, however, help the Examiners of Plays if I answer a few questions which are likely to arise:-

(a) Every play will continue to be judged on its merits. The difference will be that plays will be passed which deal seriously with the subject.

(b) We would not pass a play that was violently pro-homo-sexuality.

(c) We would not allow a homosexual character to be included if there were no need for such inclusion.

(d) We would not allow any 'funny' innuendos or jokes on the subject.

(e) We will allow the word 'pansy', but not the word 'bugger'.

(f) We will not allow embraces between males or practical demonstrations of love.

(g) We will allow criticism of the present Homosexual Laws, though plays obviously written for propaganda purposes will fall to be judged on their merits.

(h) We will not allow embarrassing display by male prostitutes.

Lord Chamberlain's Office,
St. James's Palace, S.W.1.

31st October, 1958

18. Copy of the 'secret' memorandum on homosexuality, October 1958, kept with the papers relating to *A Patriot for Me*.

STAGE PLAY SUBMITTED FOR LICENCE.

Title :	THE BIRTHDAY PARTY
No. of Scenes or Acts :	Three Acts
Place of Production :	Arts Theatre, Cambridge
Date of Production :	28.4.58
Author :	Harold Pinter
Submitted by :	

x

LORD CHAMBERLAIN'S OFFICE,
ST. JAMES'S PALACE, S.W.1.

READERS' REPORT.

18.4.58

XXXXXXXXX

An insane, pointless play. Mr. Pinter has jumbled all the tricks of Beckett and Ionesco with a dash from all the recently produced plays at the Royal Court theatre, plus a fashionable flavouring of blasphemy. The result is still silly. The Emperor is wearing no clothes.

A deckchair attendant at a seaside resort lives with his imbecile wife and a lodger Stanley, who has no personality at all except a 'Look Back in Anger' rudeness to Meg the wife. Two lodgers arrive, Goldberg and MacCann who may be members of the I.R.A., but it doesn't matter. Meg decides that it is Stanley's birthday and insists on having a party. Stanley is forced by the visitors to remain. Lulu, a neighbour is the only other guest. During the 'festivities' Stanley attempts to strangle Meg. The lights go out for no particular reason and in the darkness Stanley is attacked by the two men. The morning after, the visitors depart having reduced Stanley (took-off-stage) to a state of idiocy by their violence. *Goldberg has spent the night with Lulu.* The deck-chair attendant lets them go with the inert body of Stanley. He and his wife continue their cliché-ridden existence without further comment.

Throughout the play everyone speaks in the same rhythm, in short Beckett-Ionesco sentences. There is never a motive implied or an explanation given for anyone's actions. Meg, by the way, is literally imbecile.

P.58.   Cut the marked line   *Cut also leave*

PP. 61 and 65. Cut the pointless pieces of blasphemy
I'd like two lots Cut too

Otherwise

14676 12/56 H & S Ltd. Gp.902   RECOMMENDED FOR LICENCE

C.D.Heriot

19. Reader's Report by C. D. Heriot recommending the licensing of *The Birthday Party*, April 1958.

As instructed I went last night to the Royal Court Theatre
and witnessed a performance of a stage play entitled SAVED.
I purchased a programme and a seat (K.17), programme and seat
counterfoil are attached.

At the box office I asked for a stall and was asked if I was
a member, I said 'yes' and was asked if I had a ticket: I again
said 'yes' and produced my wallet and started to produce the
ticket at which the box office lady did not look, so I did not
complete the manoeuvre.   The box office lady said 'I'm sorry we
have to ask you'.

I had previously read the MS of SAVED, and my general comment
is that the play was produced in accordance with this MS, including
all those parts which the Lord Chamberlain had disallowed.

Comments in particular are therefore few:

SCENE I

Pam lay on the couch and opened her legs quite wide, Len then
got on top of her and she received him in the position for intercourse.   It is true to say that the physical motions which
ordinarily next follow were not indulged in and that both
participants, except for shoes, were fully dressed.

Len then put his hands on Pam's breasts and later put his
hands inside her blouse so that when she got up off the couch (the
progress of their amour having been interrupted), her blouse was
open, showing a slip underneath.

(Scene I: Cuts included were those on pp. I-3.I-5,I-6,I-7,I-8,I-9)

SCENE II

The last line 'Right up. Like you darling', was accompanied
by Fred using his fore arm and clenched fist in simulation of a
penis and pushing it upwards.

(Scene II: pp. 2-14,2-19,2-20).

SCENE III

In this scene when Colin says 'What yer scratchin', one of the
actors is scratching his testicles through his trousers.

(Scene III: 3-21,3-23,3-24,3-26,3-27 (I am not sure about 'What
yer got at the top a your legs), 3-28).

SCENE IV

No additional comment.

SCENE V

No additional comment - Pam in Bed scene.

(Scene V: 5-40,5-41).

SCENE VI

In the Park
Barry held a long sausage shaped balloon in front of his trouser
flies to imitate a penis - the dialogue as in the MS.

The torture........../

20. Report on *Saved*, November 1965, by R. J. Hill of the Lord Chamberlain's Office, after an *incognito*
visit to the play.

SCENE VI (contd)

The torture and murder of the baby was enacted in full — the baby's knickers are drawn off so that the mob can 'case its ol' crutch', to see if its a girl, the mob spit in its crutch, rub its face in its own excrement and finally stone it to death.

(Scene VI: 6-46,6-49,6-50 (I am not sure about this), 6-51, 6-53,6-58,6-59,6-60,6-61(I am not sure about this), 6-62,6-63, all 6-64/73).

SCENE VII

Prison Scene
No special comment

(Scene VII: 7-74,7-76).

INTERVAL

SCENE VIII

Living room.

(Scene VIII: 8-82,8-84,8-88).

SCENE IX

Living room
The sexual by-play between the old mother, Mary and Len , although distasteful, was carried out within acceptable bounds — the double entendres about 'I'll jab yer', 'I'll juss give it a little stretch', 'Ow I'm stiff', did not come over as such.

(Scene IX: 9-95,9-96/98).

SCENE X

Cafe scene — including all cuts.

(Scene X: 10-101,10-107,10-108 (I am not sure), 10-109,10-110, 10-111,10-113).

SCENE XI

No special comment.

(Scene XI: 11-117 (I am not sure).

SCENE XII

No special comment.

(Scene XII: 12-125,12-127 (can't be sure of this).

SCENE XIII

All in silence.

The auditorium was two thirds full and without exception, so far as I could see — in their various styles, the audience looked well dressed and affluent: far removed from the characters on the stage.

The play itself was produced in the pinchbeck style of the Royal Court — that is essential props but no scenery, and personally I thought the piece generally mis-caste and unconvincingly acted.

In these circumstances..../

In these circumstances my reactions to the play were as follows:

1. There were two highlights (or should it be *nadirs*)

   (a) the seduction scene on the couch

   (b) Scene VI, the torture and murder of the baby.

After that the piece became more and more pedestrian, the last scene being played without dialogue and with very little action.   In fact I really wondered whether the author was endeavouring to see how ridiculous he could make the audience appear, without his intentions being evident.

2. Considered individually the indecencies of language and the degrading incidents related I found rather revolting; but by their sheer bulk they earned in the end bored acceptance.   Having accepted that such things were being uttered they became mere verbiage and their true meaning was not contemplated.

3. The three objectionable pieces of business have been detailed above.

4. This leaves the baby murder scene, which was quite horrible, even when so badly played that one could not really believe there was a live baby in the perambulator.

The addition to this play of what must be almost the ultimate in degradation had no point, since the author had already made abundantly clear that his characters were people without pity, scruple, or principles more lofty than those of hyenas.   At the Royal Court it is unlikely that anyone got more than a sadistic thrill from the scene, which was received in dead silence in an atmosphere of what I can only assess as tepid disgust.

It is my opinion however that this scene acted vividly by well cast characters, with all the appropriate props and business and before a different type of audience, which included a proportion of the gangs that now exist, could be a direct incentive to some of the sub-humans who now associate in gangs, to perpetrate a crime of this kind.   The whole play, whilst allegedly designed to illustrate the squalor of ugly lives has a secondary, perhaps unintentional theme, which is as strongly developed as the primary one.   That theme is the glorification of the teenage gangster and illustrative in detail of his utter callousness and immorality.

Since the Royal Court Theatre glories in the fact that its offerings are deductive *didactic* and not entertainment, this play is designed to teach, and to teach what may well be asked.

Only one woman walked out towards the end of the performance, which otherwise was received in dead silence except for a few sniggers at some of the more disgusting episodes, such as urinating in the parson's tea cup.   There was quite warm applause at the curtain call, intended I thought, for the actors rather than for the play.

During the interval I went to the bar and bought a bottle of light ale.   There was only one lady there, working like a demon. I was not asked to show my membership ticket and drinks were being bought quite indescriminately, that is unless everyone present was a member, a most unlikely circumstance.

5th November 1965.

PTO

I note on the last page of the programme an ironic
reference to the difficulty in becoming a member of the English
Stage Society.

I am an associate member of the English Stage Society.
I joined by the simple process of sending 5/- and a name from
an accommodation address and was made a member without any
formality, the membership ticket being sent almost by return
of post.

5th November 1965.

has saved many a situation. I recall that Guy Du Maurier's'play 'An Englishman at Home' in which the army of an imaginary country, recognised everywhere as Germany, invades England, was objected to by the German Ambassador, but the Lord Chamberlain of the time (before my Readership) did not interfere with it. That might be a precedent if the German Ambassador objects to the present play. My own opinion, for what it may be worth, and with the greatest respect to the Foreign Office, is that the stage should not be debarred from expressing an almost universal sentiment. I note that another anti-Nazi play refused here is being presented in France and America. Still more, do I think that this revised version with its imaginary names should be allowed.[65]

Cromer agreed, and admitted that the censorship was doing no more than playing a game. Yet the changes insisted on by the censors were not unimportant:

> Much as I regret resort to the subterfuge of a change from the real to an imaginary country, dictates of policy render this necessary. Although too transparent to hoodwink any audience, it is sufficient, or should be, to gainsay any official protests. The accusation about the Senate House being 'blown up' should come out, otherwise I suppose it can pass.

In one sense such attempts to keep the stage superficially free from negative depictions of the Nazis seems particularly pointless, especially when – as was often pointed out – newspapers and cartoonists were free to attack them. Nevertheless, what the stage policy did signal – above all, no doubt, to the Germans – was that the British state would not accept overt criticism of a 'friendly' nation in a medium over which it had control.

Robinson Crusoe

One rule which should in theory have been relatively easy to maintain was the absolute ban on any stage representation of Hitler. In January 1937, the Lord Chamberlain's secretary, George Titman, took a phone call from the British Foreign Office concerning complaints about a Christmas show playing in Hammersmith:

KING'S THEATRE, HAMMERSMITH
Pantomime 'Robinson Crusoe'

Mr Baxter telephoned to me yesterday that representations have been made to the Foreign Office by the German Embassy concerning the caricature of Herr Hitler in the above-named pantomime.

After perusing the script and being assured that no such representation of Herr Hitler, or a dictator, had been passed, I attended last evening's performance at the theatre.

I found that the German Embassy was fully justified in the protest made.

I also found that there were many other unauthorised interpolations which had crept in since the Pantomime was licensed in December, 1935.

After the performance, I interviewed the Manager and told him that the representation of Herr Hitler must come out immediately and he assured me this would be done. He said that it was not in the rehearsal and that the Comedian must have slipped it in later – (which is the old excuse).

I suggest that the Manager be asked for an explanation and a written assurance that there will be no recurrence of this unauthorised business, and that he will be warned that any dialogue or business added to a licensed stage play without permission is an offence against the Theatres Act. I will inform Baxter of the steps which have been taken.

It is significant that the offending Comedian is one of Mrs Henderson's regulars at the Windmill.[66]

A prosecution was duly brought under the Theatres Act, and Titman's deposition in court detailing the offending act resulted in both the manager and the comedian being fined (see Plate 2). Trivial and absurd, one might be inclined to think. Yet on 9 February the Berlin correspondent of the *Morning Post* reported not only that the case had been noticed in Germany, but that there was displeasure that the comedian had not received a heavier punishment:

Dissatisfaction is expressed at the smallness of the fine of £10 imposed on Mr Howell Bryan . . . The National Socialist 'Angriff' comments: 'Lenient punishment for impertinence' and 'England does her duty lackadaisically'.

In a country where only the other day an elderly Baroness was sent to prison for six months merely for speaking rudely about Herr Hitler, a £10 fine for impersonating him on the stage must indeed seem inadequate.

Most of the British press reached a somewhat different conclusion:

The mystery of what is or is not allowed on the stage in the matter of the representation of living celebrities cropped up again yesterday, when a fine was inflicted for a pantomime caricature of Hitler.

Counsel declared that 'the Lord Chamberlain does not permit "gags" about any foreign rulers or foreign personages or members of our Royal family or our ministers'.

Except in the case of the Royal family that ruling is certainly not always observed, for I cannot believe that in the innumerable instances I can recall the Lord Chamberlain has been ignored. Only last night, in Mr Cochran's new revue, was to be seen a pipe-smoking politician, whose country house was called 'Slackers'.

Mr Winston Churchill's hat was a stock music-hall joke for years . . .

The whole position surely needs clearing up.[67]

Judgment Day

In the summer of 1937, the German embassy complained to the British Foreign Office about Elmer Rice's *Judgment Day*. Again the narrative was outwardly fictional, but even though 'in no place is the Nazi regime or Hitler referred to by name', there was no doubting that its real subject was the manipulation of justice and the corruption of the Reichstag trial.[68] Rather surprisingly, Cromer had passed Rice's play in 1934, on Street's recommendation (see Plate 11), noting: 'Having been acted in America, I hardly think we can refuse its licence here on the grounds of similarity to German conditions'. That production was apparently cancelled, but when Rice's play ran at the Strand and Phoenix theatres in 1937, it soon came to the attention of the German authorities. Cromer had anticipated there would be problems when the production was mooted, but having once decided it could be licensed he was not inclined to turn back:

> It is usually an inopportune moment in our foreign relations to stage any play likely to offend the Germans, so that conditions in this respect differ little in April 1937 from those of December 1934 . . . I considered that this play had been produced in America and without any German protest, so far as I know – I did not think a licence could with justice be refused. This is also my opinion now.
>
> It is to be hoped that production may be postponed until the Autumn and of course there can be no 'make-up' of an offensive kind.

Gwatkin warned the Foreign Office to expect trouble:

> In the final scene the Dictator, Vesnic, is the victim of a plot, and is, very rightly, murdered. This fact, in itself, will not commend the play to the German Embassy, and, when taken in conjunction with the flagrant injustice of the trial itself, the characterisation of both Hitler and Goering, the obvious Nazi appeals to the stage audience, will probably call forth a protest from the German Embassy. As Mr Street points out there is a possibility that they will not be so foolish as to suggest that the cap fits the German people, but I do not think that the Germans at the moment are over-burdened with a sense of humour, or a vision of proportion.

The censorship had called it correctly. On 19 August 1937, C. W. Baxter at the Foreign Office received a phone call:

> Herr Fitz Randolph of the German Embassy told me this morning that they had instructions from Berlin to draw our attention to the play 'Judgment Day' which had now been running in London for some months. The play was clearly based on the Reichstag fire trial, and in German eyes was objectionable in that it was meant to cast discredit upon German judicial institutions. He appreciated that there was no direct allusion to Germany, and that it had been quite cleverly disguised, but at the same time it was perfectly obvious that it was intended as an attack on Germany; they had even brought in Van der Lubbe, though under a different name. He drew attention to the annexed article in today's 'Daily Telegraph', showing that the play had been banned by the Burgomaster of the Hague 'on the ground of its likeness to the Reichstag Trial'. He added that it was desired only to draw our attention to this matter, and not to enter a protest, and he particularly asked that, if we did find it possible to take any action, we should be careful that the fact of the German Embassy's intervention should not appear in the press, as this would only matters make worse.

However, with Anglo / German relations evidently at a low ebb, the Foreign Office had no intention of taking the hint:

> I replied that I could hold out no hope of our being able to take any action in this matter. As he would be aware, we had sometimes been able in the past to take action on the Embassy's complaints, for example, when some theatre was producing a skit on Herr Hitler; but this new matter to which he had drawn attention did not seem to be the sort of case on which we could possibly act.

It was convenient – and perhaps coincidental – that the production of *Judgment Day* was quietly withdrawn soon afterwards.

On the Frontier

Resisting pressure from the German embassy became more problematic the following year when the British government introduced its strategy of appeasement. However, after much agonizing a licence was issued for W. H. Auden and Christopher Isherwood's *On the Frontier*, thanks largely to the powerful advocacy of Geoffrey Dearmer, a published poet and playwright who had recently been appointed as reader. His report pointedly described the play as 'anti-war' rather than 'anti-German' and as an 'interesting poetic drama of conflict between the two ideologies' which was 'equally critical of both philosophies'.[69] Dearmer secured the support of his fellow-reader Henry Game, and they dutifully recommended not only that any references which pointed too closely at real people, countries and events should be altered but even that 'an undertaking should be required to alter all German-<u>sounding</u> names'. In case this was insufficient to persuade the comptroller and the Lord Chamberlain, Dearmer appended a separate note with a sting in its tail, which almost dared them to ban the play:

LORD CHAMBERLAIN'S OFFICE,

ST JAMES'S PALACE

'On the Frontier'

> As the case for the above Play may not have been fully stated in my report, I would like to put forward the significance of its claim as poetic drama.
>
> It is written by two of the leading young poets of their generation and could not have been written by anybody other than the authors of 'The Ascent of F6'.
>
> It has no reference to the recent crisis, nor is it directed solely against the Totalitarian states; the Democratic countries come off just as badly as advocates of the jargon of patriotic war fervour. The admirably conceived love interest between the son of one school of thought and the daughter of the other is supreme above the argument and gives the play its higher theme.
>
> A play that pleaded the cases for the democratic countries as opposed to the totalitarian would certainly be permissible, indeed to ban such would be to remove the right of free speech altogether, but this is over and above the anti-fascist question and is, therefore, all the more deserving of a licence.

Great care has been taken to create an impersonal Leader, but it is impossible to draw such a character without his resembling one of the two known living examples because they are to some extent mere advocates of a philosophy, a philosophy which it is the right, and duty, of modern English poets to attack.

To forbid this would be to subscribe to fascist ideology.

(sd.) G Dearmer

18th October 1938

Gwatkin's response was cautious. Or perhaps just cowardly:

At such a time as this the best interests of the country are served by avoiding any unnecessary exasperation to the leaders of the German people – even if this entails a certain muzzling of contemporary playwrights.

There can be no objection to criticisms of the principles and philosophy of Totalitarian states provided always that these criticisms are not directed, even by inference, at an individual state.

I agree that it is impossible to arrive at a description of 'a Dictator' which will not faintly bear resemblance to one of the many dictators in power at the moment, but care should be taken to avoid direct quotations or any pointers which must inevitably indicate a known dictator and consequently the country over which he rules.

I agree that the totalitarian principle is one which is abhorrent to the normal Englishman but I disagree that it is the duty of modern Poets to attack this principle.

19th October 1938

However, though the Office insisted on cuts which went beyond those suggested by Dearmer's report – even the word 'leader' was banned, as being linked too closely with Hitler – a licence was issued. Dearmer was less successful with Terence Rattigan's *Follow My Leader*, arguably one of the best plays to suffer from the refusal to allow the stage to criticize or mock the Nazis. Rattigan's sometimes brilliant (if politically naive) farce was first submitted in the summer of 1938; its target was more explicit than that of Auden and Isherwood, and it was repeatedly refused a licence until January 1940 – by which time, yet again, its theatrical and historical moment had surely passed.[70]

The Archangel Gabriel?

However it appears with hindsight, it was by no means obvious to anyone at the time that the Lord Chamberlain's role as censor of plays would survive anything like as long as it did. When Lord Cromer began his sixteen-year reign as Lord Chamberlain in 1922 he discussed with the king and the home secretary the possibility of transferring the responsibility to an alternative authority; it appears to have been they rather than he who insisted that the system should remain unchanged. Thereafter, a crucial influence on Cromer's (and his successors') strategy was the wish to ensure that the position of the Lord Chamberlain remained tenable; so far as possible, decisions and policies were influenced by the need to ensure that the system survived. Hence Cromer's insistence (against the wishes of the home secretary) that private theatre clubs should retain a degree of freedom to perform unlicensed (and sometimes unlicenseable) material for 'special' audiences, so as to buy off some of the strongest opposition to censorship. Hence, too, his awareness of the need to be broadly in tune with public opinion. In theory, Lords Chamberlain enjoyed absolute power beneath the monarch and had no obligation to please anyone else; in practice, they were by now working within a democracy and were well aware that plenty of people wanted to overthrow the system. Although its dealings with playwrights and others may sometimes smack of arrogance, St James's Palace saw itself less as all powerful and more as besieged and under fire – from all directions. It is a mistake to construct the Lord Chamberlain as a tyrannical oppressor, imposing by personal fiat a draconian regime. Inevitably, each holder of the post expressed some of his own prejudices and assumptions through his decisions, but during most of the period covered in this chapter there is more evidence of complaints from those who believed the censorship was too liberal than of calls for greater freedom.

And what if the Lord Chamberlain's responsibility as censor had been overthrown – would that have been the end of theatre censorship? Almost certainly not. The main reason managers fought to retain the existing system, with its centralized authority, was that they knew the alternative would be much worse. Without the visible security of the king's endorsement, they would have faced intensive campaigns of harassment and even local prosecutions by individuals and organizations whose instincts were considerably more repressive than those of the Lord Chamberlain's Office, and who would have been less amenable to gentlemanly agreements.

Touring, in particular, would have been all but impossible since different local authorities would have imposed different standards. During the 1949 parliamentary debate on the bill to end theatre censorship, the Conservative MP and theatre critic Beverley Baxter said he would be 'delighted to see . . . a civil war between one town supporting something and one town rejecting it'.[71] But to be charged with negotiating such a minefield on the ground would have been a nightmare for managers. The existing system, while not giving them carte blanche, was one they could live with, waving their proof of royal approval in the faces of those who complained.

In December 1944 Percy Smith, the playwright and MP who five years later would introduce to the Commons a bill aimed at repealing theatre censorship, raised a question in the House. He was concerned that because the Lord Chamberlain could not be required to explain his decisions or even to appear before MPs, Parliament could not ask questions about specific issues or principles of theatre censorship. One alternative – which had been discussed many times before and would be again – was that the power vested in him to license and censor plays should be transferred to another authority (such as the Home Office) which would be answerable to

Parliament. Technically, of course, this would have removed part of the royal prerogative; in 1924 the link between the Lord Chamberlain and the monarch had actually been strengthened when the appointment ceased to be in the hands of parliament, and Lords Chamberlain ceased to change as the government changed.

Nevertheless, the censorship was forced on to the defensive by Smith's question, and a lengthy document was prepared to assist the Home Office in justifying the present system. It included a résumé of some of the reasons rehearsed in 1924 in support of maintaining the existing system, and which were still seen as valid twenty years later:

1. Links with Crown much valued by theatrical profession.
2. Maximum continuity of policy as Lord Chamberlain would no longer change with the government.
3. No minister should be expected to take direct responsibility for decisions with regard to the censorship of individual plays.
4. Local Authority censorship would be cumbersome and vexatious to theatrical interests . . .
5. Censorship by a special Board would have little advantage over censorship by Lord Chamberlain.
6. The Lord Chamberlain works in close consultation with the Home Secretary on matters involving questions of law or policy or likely to be the subject of general controversy.

The document also insisted that the current system was 'probably better than any alternative likely to be generally acceptable'.

Meanwhile, Sir Alexander Maxwell, the permanent under-secretary of state at the Home Office, produced his own, perhaps complacent, response to Smith's attack:

> The broad defence for the present system is that though from time to time the Censor may give decisions which some people think are mistaken, this would happen whatever were the system of censorship. If the archangel Gabriel were Censor, he could not hope to avoid giving offence on some occasions. All that can be asked for is that broadly speaking the censorship shall be exercised in accordance with principles that are acceptable to public opinion in general. So far as the experience of the Home Office for the last twenty years goes, there has been no serious complaint against the general method by which the censorship has been exercised.[72]

No serious complaint? Even if we allow this barely credible comment to go unchallenged, it was not one that any defender of the status quo would be able to express for much longer. In May 1945 W. W. Blair Fish, who had been refused a licence because of perceived sexual innuendo in the line 'Nice, comfortable Chesterfield this' from his script of *Genius Limited*, launched the fiercest of attacks on the Lord Chamberlain and the censorship as 'a wholly arrogant, irrational, and arbitrary authority'. He claimed the censor was 'gratuitously abusing his already inherently abusive function', and that unless his Lordship holds himself bound to observe reasonable and consistent standards of judgement and to reply rationally to arguments against his judgement . . . he is functioning merely tyrannically in mutilating or suppressing their property in a manner which must be held to be intolerable in a supposedly free community which for more than five years believes that it has been waging a war for . . . freedom of expression.[73]

Clearly, the final period of the Lord Chamberlain's (and the monarch's) rule as censor of the stage was going to contain some bitter fights.

NOTES

1 See LCO CORR: 1938/1241: *The Farmer's Daughter*. The sketch was part of a revue entitled *Round The Dial*, and was licensed in February 1938 for performance at the Empire, Finsbury Park.

2 See Lord Chamberlain's Corresponndence Files: *Lorelei*, WB, 1938.

3 Steve Nicholson, *The Censorship of British Drama 1900–1968*, vol. 1: *1900–1932* (Exeter: University of Exeter Press, 2003); vol. 2: *1933–1952* (Exeter: University of Exeter Press, forthcoming).

4 The evidence and the report are published, along with certain other documents, as: *Report from the Joint Select Committee of the House of Lords and the House of Commons on the Stage Plays (Censorship) together with the Proceedings of the Committee, Minutes and Appendices* (London: HMSO, 1909).

5 Letter from Redford to Lord Althorp, June 1909. LCO Theatre Files, not catalogued.

6 Undated Office memorandum (November 1909?). LCO Theatre Files, not catalogued.

7 See *Report* 1909, p. 190.

8 Ibid., p. 11.

9 Confidential memorandum, 23 October 1911. LCO Theatre Files, not catalogued.

10 Letter from Dawson to Redford, 11 October 1911. LCO Theatre Files, not catalogued.

11 Letter from Dawson to Lord Stamfordham, 23 October 1911. LCO Theatre Files, not catalogued.

12 Brookfield made his views on theatre clear in an article, 'On plays and playwriting', *National Review*, November 1911, pp. 420–21. His comic play *Dear Old Charlie* had been denounced by a number of witnesses to the 1909 enquiry.

13 Barker was addressing the audience at a private performance of Housman's banned play *Pains and Penalties* on 26 November 1911. LCO Theatre Files, not catalogued.

14 Undated letter from Dawson to Vaughan Nash, the prime minister's private secretary (December 1912). LCO Theatre Files, not catalogued.

15 Letter from Dawson to Sir William Byrne, assistant under-secretary of state at the Home Office, 26 November 1911. LCO Theatre Files, not catalogued.

16 Letter from Dawson to Sir Edward Carson, 29 November 1911. LCO Theatre Files, not catalogued.

17 The question was asked by Arthur Lynch. Parliamentary Debates (Official Report), 5th ser., vol. 32, House of Commons, 27 November–16 December 1911 (London: HMSO, 1912), col. 582.

18 See *Report*, pp. 36–7.

19 Ibid., p. 37.

20 Letter written by Dawson, 25 January 1911 and sent with the script of *Waste* to members of the Advisory Board.

21 Dawson was writing on 12 November 1920. LCC CORR: 1920/3249: *Waste*.

22 Unless otherwise stated, for all correspondence and reports quoted here in relation to *Mrs Warren's Profession* see LCO CORR: 1924/5632: *Mrs Warren's Profession*. The play was licensed for the Edinburgh Lyceum Theatre in September 1924.

23 For this and all correspondence and reports cited in relation to *Damaged Goods* see LCO CORR: 1917/837: *Damaged Goods*. The play was licensed for St Martin's Theatre in March 1917. For further correspondence see also 1943/4669: *Damaged Goods*.

24 For this and all correspondence and reports cited in relation to *Maternity* see LCO CORR: *Maternity* LR (1924). See also 1932/11470. The play was licensed for the Regent Theatre in October 1932.

25 Captain Malcolm Bullock, speaking on 25 March 1949 against the Censorship of Plays (Repeal) Bill in the House of Commons. See Parliamentary Debates (Official Report), Session 1948–1949, 5th ser, vol. 463, 21/3/49–14/4/49, House of Commons (London: HMSO, 1949), col. 743.

26 See Steve Nicholson, ' "Unnecessary plays": European drama and the British censor', *Theatre Research International* 20.1 (Spring 1995), pp. 30–36. Also Nicholson, 'Foreign drama and the Lord Chamberlain in the 1950s', in Dominic Shellard (ed.), *British Theatre in the 1950s* (Sheffield: Sheffield Academic Press, 2000), pp. 41–52.

27 See LCO CORR: 1910/814: *Oedipus Rex*. The play was licensed for the Haymarket Theatre in November 1910.

28 For this and all correspondence and reports quoted in relation to *Ghosts* see LCO CORR: 1914/2853: *Ghosts*. The play was licensed for the Haymarket Theatre in July 1914.

29 See LCO CORR: 1922/4067: *Peer Gynt*. The play was licensed for the Royal Victoria Hall in February 1922.

30 See Shelley's original Preface to *The Cenci*; Percy Bysshe Shelley, *Poetical Works*, ed. Thomas Hutchinson (Oxford: Oxford University Press, 1971), pp. 275–8.

31 The private performance and nineteenth-century responses to the play are discussed in John Russell Stephens, *The Censorship of English Drama 1824–1901* (Cambridge: Cambridge University Press, 1980), pp. 140–42.

32 Unless otherwise stated, for all correspondence and reports quoted here in relation to *The Cenci* see LCO CORR: 1922/4437: *The Cenci*. The play was licensed for the New Theatre in October 1922.

33 Unless otherwise stated, for all correspondence and reports quoted here in relation to *Six Characters in Search of an Author* see LCO CORR: 1928/8393: *Six Characters in Search of an Author*. The play was licensed for the Globe theatre in May 1928.

34 See LCP CORR: 1925/6179: *Sei personaggi in cerca d'autore*. The play was licensed for the New Oxford Theatre in June 1925.

35 Samuel Beckett's play was licensed for the English Stage Company in its French version in March 1957, with a note specifying that the licence would not extend automatically to an English translation. When the same Company duly submitted an English version in December 1957 the licence was withheld on the grounds of unacceptable language and the statement by one character in relation to God: 'The bastard, he doesn't exist'. Only in August 1958, after extensive arguments and pressures, was a licence for the English version given – and this only when Beckett was apparently persuaded to substitute 'swine' for 'bastard'.

36 LCP CORR: 1943/4785: *The Infernal Machine*. The play was licensed for the Cambridge Arts Theatre in March 1943.

37 LCO Theatre Files, not catalogued.

38 For this and all subsequent correspondence and reports quoted in relation to *Miss Julie* see LCO CORR: *Miss Julie* LR (1925) and 1938/2153. The play was licensed for the Westminster Theatre in December 1938.

39 *Daily Graphic*, 17 September 1923.

40 For this and all correspondence and reports quoted in relation to *Our Betters* see LCO CORR: 1923/4877: *Our Betters*. The play was licensed for the Globe Theatre in May 1923.

41 For this and all correspondence and reports quoted in relation to *The Vortex* see LCO CORR: 1924/5762: *The Vortex*. The play was licensed in November 1924 for the Everyman Theatre.

42 LCP CORR: 1924/5673: *Khaki*. Dawson's comments were dated 2 September 1924, and Cromer agreed with him that the script could only be licensed after revisions and with the approval of the War Office. It was licensed for the Lewisham Hippodrome later that month.

43 LCP CORR: 1924/5854: *Easy Virtue*. Licensed for the Garrick Theatre in December 1934.

44 For this and all correspondence and reports quoted in relation to *Fallen Angels* see LCO CORR: 1925/6100: *Fallen Angels*. The play was licensed for the Globe Theatre in April 1925.

45 In Coward's original script, as the two women consume increasing quantities of champagne while waiting for their lover, Jane suddenly observes: 'Wouldn't it be awful if the King and Queen suddenly came in?' Julia replies: 'They won't, because they're at Sandhurst', and Jane corrects her: 'Not Sandhurst, dear, Sandown'. Coward managed to avoid losing the joke altogether, and after the Lord Chamberlain's refusal to approve these lines he altered the references to 'Mary Queen of Scots', 'Hollywood', and 'Hollyport'.

46 Game was writing in February 1934 in response to complaints made by the Public Morality Council against Terence Rattigan's play *First Episode*. See LCP CORR: 1934/12646: *First Episode*. The play was licensed for the Comedy Theatre in January 1934.

47 Gwatkin was writing on 19 April 1939. See LCP CORR: 1938/1778: *Design for Living*. The play was licensed for Theatre Royal, Brighton, December 1938.

48 Some of Gray's clashes with the establishment are discussed in Steve Nicholson, ' "Nobody was ready for that": the gross impertinence of Terence Gray and the degradation of drama', *Theatre Research International* 11.2 (Summer 1996), pp. 121–31. Also Steve Nicholson, *British Theatre and the Red Peril: The Portrayal of Communism 1917–1945* (Exeter: University of Exeter Press: 1999), pp. 21–5 details the censorship of Tretiakov's *Roar China*.

49 For this and all correspondence, reports and comments quoted here in relation to *The Hairy Ape* see LCO CORR: 1928/8601: *The Hairy Ape*. The play was licensed for Cambridge Festival Theatre, Cambridge in October 1928.

50 For this and all correspondence, reports and comments quoted in relation to *London Docks* see LCO CORR: 1932/11509: *London Docks*. The play was licensed for the Festival Theatre, Cambridge in November 1932.

51 For this and all correspondence, reports and comments quoted in relation to *The Eater of Dreams* see LCO CORR: 1932/11443: *The Eater of Dreams*. The play was licensed for the Festival Theatre, Cambridge in September 1932.

52 See LCP CORR: 1932/11621: *The Green Bay Tree*. The play was licensed for St Martin's Theatre in November 1932.

53 LCP CORR: 1964/4458: *The Children's Hour*. Although the ban was subsequently apparently lifted, the play was not performed publicly before 1968, so no licence was issued.

54 LCP CORR: *Alone* LR (1930)

55 Report by Street. For this and all correspondence, reports and comments quoted in relation to *Love of Women* see LCO CORR: *Love of Women* LR (1934).

56 For this and all correspondence, reports and comments quoted in relation to *Children in Uniform* see LCO CORR: 1932/11437: *Children in Uniform*. The play was licensed for the Duchess Theatre in September 1932.

57 Street was writing on 13 August 1924 in relation to a revue called *Rent Free*, following complaints which had been made to the War Office. See LCP CORR: 1924/5482: *Rent Free*.

58 Cromer was writing on 10 April 1931 in a letter to the Home Office about whether or not it was safe to license Tretiakov's *Roar China* for the Festival Theatre, Cambridge. See LCP CORR: *Roar China* LR (1931).

59 Mr K. Lindsay speaking on 25 March, 1949, in the debate on the Censorship of Plays (Repeal) Bill in the House of Commons. See Parliamentary Debates Session 1948–1949, vol. 463, col. 772.

60 One aspect of political censorship is discussed with examples in Steve Nicholson, *British Theatre and the Red Peril*, pp. 10–26.

61 *Report* 1909, p. 163.

62 Cromer to the Foreign Office, 9 November 1934. See LCP CORR: 1934/13372: *Crooked Cross*.

63 Cromer was commenting on 3 August 1933 on *Who Made the Iron Grow*. See LCP CORR: *Who Made the Iron Grow* LR (1933).

64 LCP CORR: *Take Heed* LR (1934). See also 1943/3106. The play was licensed for the Empire, Peterborough in March 1943.

65 LCP CORR: 1934/12916: *Whither Liberty*. The play was licensed for Bradford Civic Theatre in April 1934. The other anti-Nazi play referred to by Street was almost certainly *Heroes*, the English version of *Die Rassen*, a play written by the Austrian playwright Theodor Tagger under his pseudonym of Fredinand Brückner, which was also turned down by the Lord Chamberlain in March 1934. In fact, several international productions of this play were suppressed and cancelled – including one in New York.

66 For this and all correspondence, reports and comments quoted in relation to *Robinson Crusoe* see LCP CORR: 1935/14581: *Robinson Crusoe*. The play was licensed for the Wimbledon Theatre in December 1935.

67 *Evening Standard*, 3 February 1937.

68 For this and all correspondence, reports and comments quoted in relation to *Judgment Day* see LCP CORR: 1934/13514: *Judgment Day*. The play was licensed for the Globe Theatre in December 1934.

69 For this and all correspondence, reports and comments quoted in relation to *On the Frontier* see LCP CORR: 1938/1878: *On the Frontier*. The play was licensed for the Cambridge Arts Theatre in November 1938.

70 LCP CORR: 1940/3219: *Follow My Leader*.

71 Beverley Baxter speaking on 25 March 1949 in support of the Censorship of Plays (Repeal) Bill in the House of Commons. See Parliamentary Debates Session 1948–1949, vol. 463, col. 746.

72 Both these documents can be found in the Lord Chamberlain's papers currently held in the Royal Archive at Windsor Castle; see: RA LC/GEN/512/45: 'Issues raised in the House of Commons about the censorship'.

73 LCP CORR: 1945/6120: *Genius Limited*. The play was originally licensed for the Playhouse, Amersham in March 1945; however, the licence was sent back and withdrawn when the playwright refused to allow the theatre to make the cut required by the Lord Chamberlain. A fresh licence was issued to the same theatre in August 1945 following acrimonious discussions and a reluctant decision by the Lord Chamberlain to withdraw his objection.

PART III

Decline and Fall: 1945–1968

The post-war period

THE presidentships of the three post-war Lord Chamberlains – Lord Clarendon (1938–52), the Earl of Scarborough (1952–63) and Lord Cobbold (1963–8)[1] – spanned one of the most exciting and controversial periods of British theatre history. The immediate post-war years saw the foundation of the Arts Council and the establishment of the principle of state subsidy; the arrival of foreign productions, such as *Oklahoma!* (1947), *A Streetcar Named Desire* (1949) and *Antigone* (1949); and a concerted campaign against entertainment tax.

Entertainment tax had been introduced as a levy on tickets during the First World War to raise additional funds for the military campaign, but to prevent already straitened theatre producers from going bankrupt, a loophole was introduced to allow them to claim exemption if they could prove that their productions were 'educational'. The authors of the legislation had works by Shakespeare in mind but during the thirties and forties, producers such as Binkie Beaumont of H. M. Tennent Ltd chose to use an increasingly elastic definition of 'educational' to gain exemption. This ruse greatly enhanced Tennent's profits, since by 1948 the tax represented 25 per cent of the ticket price and *A Streetcar Named Desire* was their fortieth such 'educational' venture. Ivor Brown of the *Observer* led the campaign against this tax dodge and, following an investigation by a House of Commons Select Committee in 1950, provoked in part by the furore created by *A Streetcar Named Desire*, the practice was ended and, significantly, Tennent's became liable for income tax backdated to 1945.

All these developments began to shed some light on the parochialism and restrictive practices of the commercial West End stage and it was inevitable that if so powerful an institution as H. M. Tennent's was going to be attacked the institution of censorship would come under ever-increasing scrutiny.

'. . . but Diana knows too much about pansies and goes': 1945–1952

The last seven years of Lord Clarendon's tenure are characterized by a blithe unconcern that the theatrical world was demonstrating embryonic signs of change, coupled with indications of more serious trouble ahead. Although the number of licences refused outright had diminished since the thirties, the four examples of 1945 are a mixture of the quaint and the prejudiced.

With the benefit of hindsight they reveal how ill-prepared the readers would be for the change of theatrical fashion in the late fifties, when playwrights demanded the right to investigate whatever issues they chose.

To the category of the quaint belongs the faintly ridiculous *The Querulous Queens*, whose report was compiled by the senior examiner, Henry Game:

Title:	*The Querulous Queens*
No. of Scenes or Acts:	Play in 1 Act
Place of Production:	Lopping Hall, Loughton
Date of Production:	17th April 1945
Author:	Madge Pemberton

LORD CHAMBERLAIN'S OFFICE,

ST JAMES'S PALACE, S.W.1

12th April 1945

READER'S REPORT

This is a fantasy in which Agnes Strickland, a Victorian writer of popular history, dreams that she is arraigned before the Goddess Clio, who charges her with making fallacious statements in her books, and calls as witnesses certain of the Queens of England. Unfortunately amongst these Queens is Victoria! Quite apart from the fact that the dialogue in which the Queen is involved is at times distinctly unvictorian, to allow Queen Victoria to be a character in a fantasy would be to alter our present policy of limiting her use as a dramatic character to straight plays of an historical or biographical nature. Further, it would be a particularly unfortunate moment to alter our policy, recently re-affirmed in connection with Mr Monkton Hoffe's play, which gave rise to questions in the House of Commons a short time ago.

Our ban will inevitably cause dismay to the Women's Institute which is presenting the play at a Drama Festival, but I am afraid it cannot be helped under the circumstances. The promoters should be informed that a Licence cannot be granted unless the character of Queen Victoria is entirely removed from the play: pp. 11–13, 17–19, 21, 22, 23.

(sd) H. C. GAME

> I quite agree a licence cannot
> be granted for this play unless
> the character of Queen Victoria
> is entirely removed
>
> C

The Monkton Hoffe play in question was *Mr Lincoln Meets a Lady*, a fantasy piece in which the American president met Queen Victoria. It had been refused a licence after representations from Buckingham Palace in January 1944. *The Querulous Queens* was considered to be equally tendentious, not only because it breached the policy which decreed that a monarch could appear only in a serious work (however that was defined), but because it might bring unwelcome publicity for the Office of the Lord Chamberlain.

First Thing, 'a black-out sketch . . . implying an overindulgence of sexual intercourse', was also easily dismissed by Game, but more worrying for him were two plays which dealt with the theme that was increasingly to preoccupy the readers: homosexuality.

Game's response to Rose Franken's *Outrageous Fortune* is initially one of confusion at the complicated plot of love intrigue, until, that is, the playwright introduces a character not subject to 'normal emotions':

> . . . unfortunately the authoress has given Bert a brother, Julian, who is a pervert, and who is attracted by the young musician, Barry. Julian is about to make a loveless marriage with a sophisticated girl, Kitty; but Kitty's sophistication does not go so far as marriage to a pansy. When she realizes Julian's real nature, she tries to kill herself, and in one way and another the fat is in the fire and Bert learns the truth about his brother. Bert reacts violently on conventional lines, but calms down when Crystal counsels tolerance and understanding. Her words have an immediate effect on Bert's attitude to his wife and Barry, but what he does about his brother we never learn, as Crystal dies (off stage) from a heart attack, as the play ends.
>
> As plays including perverts are taboo, and wisely so, this one is
>
> NOT recommended for Licence.
>
> (sd.) H. C. Game[2]

Needless to say, the Lord Chamberlain endorsed this view on this intriguing work, with the comment that 'I entirely agree that as the pervert theme is introduced in this play it cannot be licensed, nor apparently can it be altered without destroying it.' The fact that *Outrageous Fortune* takes a sympathetic attitude to sexual difference made the work doubly unacceptable to the organs of censorship.

Even more robust was Game's attitude to *Surface*, the fourth work to have a licence refused in 1945, since it touched on the gravest fears of the establishment – the danger of young British men being 'encouraged' to become homosexual:

Title:	*Surface*
No. of Scenes or Acts:	3 acts
Place of Production:	Intimate Theatre, Palmer's Green
Date of Production:	September
Author:	Dail Ambler

LORD CHAMBERLAIN'S OFFICE,
ST JAMES'S PALACE, S.W.1

28th August 1945

READER'S REPORT

David and Peter share a flat, the same bedroom and there is every indication that they share the same bed! David is a writer, Peter is a musician, and both are pansies.

Their friend Ronnie, a Musical critic, introduces his sister Diana.

Diana falls in love with Peter and encourages him to compose. David is jealous.

Under the influence of Diana's sympathy and encouragement Peter writes an opus. He is playing it to Diana, when David enters! This brings David's jealousy to a head.

There is a tense scene, which ends in Diana at last grasping the full implications of the situation. She leaves in distress, Peter rushes out into the night and David sits up nursing his misery. Next morning Ronnie implores David not to carry on like an elderly pervert, and David sentimentalises about the hopeless future for his type of unfortunate. Peter returns to announce that he is leaving David, and Diana comes to say that she is returning to the country. Peter implores her not to desert him, and even begs her to marry him, but Diana knows too much about pansies and goes. David makes a last attempt to persuade Peter to stay, and fails. The curtain descends as he telephones to another pansy boyfriend to come round with his friends and throw a party. I might add that incidentally we hear a good deal about other perverts and their love affairs.

The play is comparable to Edward Bourdet's 'La Prisonnière' (frequently banned), and as far as possible, given the theme, is emotional rather than sordid; but sentimentalising about perverts is a most insidious method of encouragement, and I have not the slightest hesitation in advising that the play is

NOT recommended for Licence
(sd) H. C. GAME

Licence refused

C

If Game and Clarendon had hoped for a respite from what was often referred to as 'the forbidden subject' in 1946, they had reckoned without Oscar Wilde. The fiftieth anniversary of Wilde's disastrous libel trial fell in March 1945, and a ten-year-old play was optimistically resubmitted with a view to testing the water again. Game was distinctly unamused and signals how censorship in this area would be tightened even further:

Title:	*Oscar Wilde*
No. of Scenes or Acts:	3 acts
Place of Production:	[Playhouse][3]
Date of Production:	
Author:	Leslie and Sewell Stokes

LORD CHAMBERLAIN'S OFFICE,
ST JAMES'S PALACE, S.W.1

1st July 1946

READER'S REPORT

This is the Oscar Wilde play which was produced at the Gate Theatre in 1936. It was never submitted for Licence, I think, but I have a dim recollection that Norman Marshall made either verbal or epistolary enquiries at the time as to its chance of being licensed if submitted, and was told that they were nil.

Scenes in Act I tell enough of the well known story to make effective the adaptation of the evidence given at Wilde's libel action against Queensberry and the subsequent criminal indictment of Wilde by the Crown at the Old Bailey, which form the scenes in Act II. Act III shows an imaginary return of Wilde to his house in Tite Street on his release, and in a final scene his moral and physical dissolution during the last years in Paris is indicated.

This play is about perverts and perversion, and that its central character has been erected into a sort of literary martyr does not alter the fact. We do not license plays about pederasts and in my opinion, rightly so. During the period between the two World Wars a mistaken toleration gave a deplorable stimulus to the practice of abnormalities, and the Censorship is undoubtedly right in making perversion taboo as a dramatic theme. The Theatre is an emotional place in which ugly things easily take on false glamour. Wilde's story is tragic enough, but it is an ugly story. Wilde was the martyr of his own pride, not of British justice – and there is much to be said in this play's favour, that is plain. But the fact is, as I said above, this is a play about perverts and perversion and for that reason

I cannot recommend this play for Licence.

(sd) H. C. GAME

Licence refused

C

The matter did not end there, however. Eager to confirm that he was acting according to the consensus of establishment opinion, Clarendon wrote to a number of 'eminent members of the clerical, legal, scholastic and medical professions'[4] soliciting their views as to whether he should modify the absolute ban on homosexual themes. The majority were against any change of practice, but this did not prevent increasingly frequent attempts by the theatre profession to challenge the status quo. Two years later, *Oscar Wilde* was put on as a club performance at The Boltons, thereby avoiding the need for sanction by the Lord Chamberlain. Frank Pettingell took the lead role and was described by the *Daily Telegraph* in August 1948 as 'excellent', 'the subsequent dissolution [being] portrayed with true pathos and the most moving restraint'.[5] Emboldened by the favourable press reaction, Margery Vosper, the agent of the authors Leslie and Sewell Stokes, sent the Lord Chamberlain several cuttings, including one from the *Evening Standard* penned by the prominent theatre critic and Conservative MP Beverley Baxter, which demanded that the ban on the work for public performance be lifted. T. E. G. Nugent attempted to clarify the situation for her on 6 September 1948:

The Lord Chamberlain does not license plays in which perversion is the main theme. In the case of *Now Barabbas* perversion was a subsidiary theme, and as the play was a factual one about prison life it was allowed, but even on that occasion it was considerably toned down before being passed. In this particular play about Oscar Wilde, the trial scenes would be an added difficulty, with the representation of so many actual people.

The representation of living people on stage was a further barrier for the play to overcome, particularly as the Lord Chamberlain had insisted in 1945 that so prestigious a work as Terence Rattigan's *The Winslow Boy*, which was based on a father's attempt to clear his son's name that began in 1908, include the following programme note if a licence were to be issued: 'This play was inspired by the facts of a well-known case but the characters attributed to the individuals represented are based on the author's imagination and are not necessarily factual'.

But following a further request[6] to reconsider from one of *Oscar Wilde*'s playwrights, Leslie Stokes, – and mindful of the press's keen interest in the matter – Nugent wrote back to say that the Lord Chamberlain would send a further representative to The Boltons to review the play.[7] C. D. Heriot visited the show on 23 September and submitted a clear-cut opinion to the Lord Chamberlain. The production was still beyond the pale since:

> there was little or no indication of the psychological disintegration which is symptomatic of the last stages of most homosexuals. Now this implicit condonation of the vice is precisely what I presume the Lord Chamberlain tries to prevent in stage presentations . . . The authors claim that their treatment is not offensive, and this is so; but the text, when well acted as it was last night, seemed to skate perilously on the thinnest of ice, so that what was <u>not</u> mentioned loomed with a reality larger than if it had been dragged into the open. What would happen to this play in the hands of bad actors or those themselves perverse, makes one shudder.
>
> Sir Cedric Hardwicke has recently stated in a press interview that he does not believe that very many masterpieces have been lost to the public through the action of the censor. *Oscar Wilde* is not a masterpiece . . . the Lord Chamberlain should continue to ban this play.

Clarendon, having read Heriot's report two days later, reaffirmed the earlier verdict: 'I agree that the ban on plays about perversion and perverts must be maintained. Accordingly I have refused to grant a licence.'[8]

The highbrows and the lowbrows: 1945–1952

It was rare for the Lord Chamberlain to disagree with his readers, but one such case occurred in 1947 with the play *Hinkemann*,[9] and the episode gave an insight into the class snobbery that bedevilled St James's Palace:

Title:	*Hinkemann*
No. of Scenes or Acts:	3 acts
Place of Production:	Rudolf Steiner Hall
Date of Production:	
Author:	Ernst Toller, translated by Vera Mendel

LORD CHAMBERLAIN'S OFFICE,

ST JAMES'S PALACE, S.W.1

18th April 1947

READER'S REPORT

This play was submitted in 1935 and was refused a licence, no doubt inevitably in those days. But public opinion has since then become very much more sophisticated, and what would have shocked many people in 1935, in 1947 is accepted as a legitimate subject for the dramatist's pen. But even in 1935 I do not think I should have agreed with Mr Street in describing Toller's play 'a mixture of obscenity and raving', though I would certainly agree that Toller was an 'over-rated German', and I might add, a bore!

Certainly the dramatist's theme is an embarrassing one, but his subject is obviously not obscenity. What the play is about is the mental torture suffered by a hefty working class type, who has been sexually mutilated in the war and who believes that in his fellows' eyes he has in consequence become an object of ridicule, and the psychological effects of that mental distress. Given the theme, I do not think the treatment – European Expressionism of the early twenties – can be considered extravagant or unjustifiable. The play is now a museum piece of a bad and rather bogus period of dramatic art; but apart from the likely embarrassment of those who still believe in reticence, I personally see little against the play except the meanness of the tragedy. One may not care for this sort of thing, I do not myself; but I don't think one can argue that anybody is going to suffer moral degradation by seeing it acted.

The Rudolph Steiner Hall has by this time, I expect, the reputation of housing high-brow plays, and it is the high-brow (or pseudo-high-brow) that this sort of play will attract. It would bore a low-brow, or even a middle-brow, to tears, so if licensed for a production by the Centaur Theatre I cannot think that the play is likely to be produced elsewhere except by Repertory and similar uncommercial intellectual theatres.

To sum up, if the highbrows want to see the play, I really don't see why we should prevent them.

But I do think a little editing of Teutonic coarseness will do no harm and I have accordingly indicated the passages which could be cut, and which will not be missed, on pages 13, 22, 27, 42, 45, 46, 53, 54, 57, 63, 67, 68 and 79.

There are also rather a lot of 'bloodies' (6, 8, 21, 32, 49, 65), one or two might go.

If cut as indicated the play is

Recommended for Licence

(sd) H. C. GAME

> This play is I agree a most unpleasant one and I agree it should be banned
> Licence refused
> C

Clarendon's handwritten comment indicating his agreement to a ban seems curious, since Game had, albeit tortuously, reluctantly conceded a licence. It is almost as if the Lord Chamberlain, preoccupied with his other royal duties, had only had time to have a cursory read of the report. But subsequent correspondence proves that this was not the case. The assistant controller, Norman Gwatkin, noted that the disagreement between the Lord Chamberlain and his reader was 'a bone of contention', and he requested a second opinion from a long-running member of the advisory panel, Lord David Cecil.[10] A month later Cecil offered his advice:

> I can't see that anything so dull and so highbrow could demoralize anybody. On the other hand, it is a sordid piece and not good enough to justify one in making a special exception in its favour on literary grounds alone. Still, on the whole, I wouldn't be against licensing it.[11]

Two-one to Game, but the report was obviously doing the rounds of St James's Palace as another reader, Heriot, weighed in with the opinion that a ban would 'help relegate [*Hinkemann*] to the limbo of repulsive errors'. Clarendon stayed steadfast and insisted on a ban, and this remained the case even when the work was resubmitted seven years later in 1954, with the observation that the play could not receive a licence on account of its 'coarseness' and its 'embarrassing theme'.[12]

Public scrutiny: the British Theatre Conference of 1948, the Censorship of Plays (Repeal Act) bill and *A Streetcar Named Desire*

The censors thoroughly disliked the spotlight of publicity, preferring to get quietly on with their work with little need to explain their decisions, but three events at the end of the 1940s foreshadowed the increasingly sceptical attitude towards theatre censorship that would develop in the late 1950s. In March 1948 the British Theatre Conference, chaired by J. B. Priestley, passed a motion denouncing stage censorship by 447 votes to 3. Pressed to respond to this near-unanimous verdict, the home secretary, James Chuter Ede, stated that there were no plans to amend the Theatres Act. The Attlee government had rather greater difficulties to face.

Encouraged by this show of defiance, however, the Conservative MP E. P. Smith then introduced into the House of Commons his Censorship of Plays (Repeal Act) bill which aimed 'to exempt the theatre from restrictions upon freedom of expression in excess of those applicable to other forms of literature'.[13] It passed its second reading in 1949 by 76 votes to 37, but the calling of the general election in 1950 destroyed its chances of reaching the statute book. One can only speculate how the course of British theatre might have changed if Attlee's government had been re-elected with a working majority. What the bill did expose, however, was the faultline that lay between playwrights, who, with the notable exceptions of William Douglas Home (brother of the future Conservative prime minister Sir Alec Douglas-Home) and A. P. Herbert (who was also an MP),[14] generally supported repeal, and theatre managers, such as Binkie Beaumont, who were vigorously against, because they benefited from the legal protection that the Lord Chamberlain afforded them.

Just how skilled Beaumont was in dealing with Clarendon is illustrated by his quiet negotiations over a licence for the theatrical event of 1949, the London premiere of Tennessee Williams's *A Streetcar Named Desire*, which would see Laurence Olivier direct his wife, Vivien Leigh. Public anticipation for this latest example of American writing (against which British new plays seemed so pallid and staid) was enormous. The Aldwych Theatre received over 10,000 applications for tickets, but few people were aware of how close they had come to being deprived of the experience by the censor.

Binkie Beaumont submitted the script for licence in June 1948, and H. C. Game's report initially gives a characteristically sniffy response to this American blockbuster. The play was

> a mixture of the lurid and the high-brow, which has, I believe, been having a very long run in New York . . . Although the central character is, if I understand the author's intentions rightly, a tragic nymphomaniac, or something of the sort anyway, there is nothing in the story which could justify a ban . . . I have an idea that Professor Nicoll may have seen the American production and have written to ask him.[15]

There was one serious problem, however: Blanche had 'a boy husband who turned out to be a pervert', and this in a production that starred theatrical royalty and would be talked about by thousands. Game found the play confusing – 'one is left in the dark by much of the business on the stage, which is perhaps why the impression the play makes on one is blurred' – so this was why he had quickly decided to appeal to another authority:

> . . . We shall see what Allardyce Nicoll has to say; but I have an idea that a general warning to Tennents that they must see that reasonable restraint is exercised in production to suit the (still) milder taste of an English audience compared to the American, might be salutary.

Nugent knew what was stake when he wrote to Gwatkin at the end of June that the 'forbidden subject' theme – merely a verbal reference by Blanche to her entering her husband's room several years previously to discover him in bed with another man – was 'strong stuff'.[16] There now began a detailed period of negotiation with Beaumont. His eventual suggestion that the controversial passage – 'By coming suddenly into a room that I thought was empty – which wasn't empty but had two people in it . . . the boy I had married *and an older man who had been his friend for years*' (author's italics) – be amended to '. . . *and another*' was rejected out of hand by Gwatkin, who conveyed the news to Beaumont in April 1949 that Clarendon was not budging: 'I am afraid that "and another" did not reach the starting post'.[17] This may have been because Clarendon, demonstrating the censorship's incipient racism, had initially requested that 'the passage should be altered, making the young man found with a negress, instead of another man'![18] Two days later Beaumont replied with a fascinating letter, showing how the censor was now shaping the artistic effect of the work:

> Tennessee Williams feels that the speech under discussion is the entire basis of 'Blanche's' character and, as I think I have already explained, Sir Laurence and Lady Olivier, who will direct and play in this production, feel strongly that unless the discovery is, for the sophisticated audience, plausible, it does entirely change the character of *A Streetcar Named Desire*, and removes its artistic tragedy to a purely commercial play and turns Blanche into a character which Vivien Leigh does not really feel would be an artistically satisfactory one, or necessarily a very pleasant part on the English stage.
>
> After long talks with the author he has made the following suggestion, which I hope will be acceptable to you because it seems to remove any difficulties. When you have had an opportunity of considering the following I shall be most grateful for your views:
>
>> 'Then I found out. In the worst of all possible ways. By coming suddenly into a room that I thought was empty – which wasn't empty but had two people in it . . . the boy I had married and . . . Afterwards we pretended that nothing had been discovered. Yes, the three of us drove out to Lake Casino.'
>
> You will see from the above suggestion that Tennessee Williams has offered to cut 'and an older man who had been his friend for years'.[19]

The play was due to be premiered on 10 October 1949 and negotiations continued right up until the wire. Only four days before the first night, the director, Laurence Olivier, confirmed the eventual compromise, which was that only 'an older man who had been his friend for years' would be omitted and there would be no further changes.[20] It had been an uncomfortable process for all parties, and a note on the file left the day after the first night reveals that the censors felt that they may have been duped: 'There have been so many letters and telephone messages about this that something may have been missed. It appears that not all of our requested deletions have not been made.'[21] It was a feeling that they would increasingly experience with high-profile productions.

Clarendon's last hurrah – 1951

Clarendon retired from office in 1952 and his final year saw licences refused for familiar reasons. *My Good Brown* was a work about Queen Victoria's manservant which interestingly made no allusion to the possibility of a relationship between the pair, but did not treat the royal family with the necessary deference. Heriot was clear – 'I have said that this comedy is innocuous. So it is; but if we do not allow musical comedies about Victoria and Albert I do not think we should allow comedies that present the Queen as a silly conventionalized 'Victorian' and her son, later King Edward VII as a frivolous ass'.[22]

Ceremony of Innocence was banned for being disrespectful to Christianity, and the Lord Chamberlain commented that 'the play would offend a large number of people. It cannot be passed.'[23] He may have had in mind the furore surrounding *A Streetcar Named Desire*, since this new work had also been submitted by Laurence Olivier. Judith Warden's *The Lonely Heart* was equally clear-cut:

Title:	*The Lonely Heart*
No. of Scenes or Acts:	Three acts
Place of Production:	
Date of Production:	
Author:	Judith Warden

LORD CHAMBERLAIN'S OFFICE,
ST JAMES'S PALACE, S.W.1

30.5.51

READER'S REPORT

Lindsay is a Lesbian living with fluffy but normal Suzanne. When the latter falls in love with a man, Lindsay is upset; and when the engagement is announced she gets tight, assaults Suzanne (off-stage) and then tries to commit suicide. The faithful charwoman comes in time to turn off the gas, after which Suzanne's mother has a sympathetic talk with Lindsay, then her own mother visits her and reveals a total lack of understanding of her daughter's case. Finally the family doctor talks a lot of pseudo-medical nonsense and the play ends with Lindsay agreeing to try a psychiatrist or hormone injections. The play is not even a serious attempt to cope with the subject of abnormality. Lindsay's mannishness is supposed to be because her mother wanted a boy and brought her up in a boyish manner. Suzanne is quite unreal because she is made out to be a simple little thing with not an idea in her head about the real quality of Lindsay's affection for her. The whole thing is on the intellectual level of an article on popular psychology in the 'Daily Mirror'

NOT RECOMMENDED FOR LICENCE

C. D. Heriot

Obviously a play which cannot be allowed

Licence refused

C

Andrew Rosenthal's *The Third Person* left no room for doubt, either:

Title:	*Third Person*
No. of Scenes or Acts:	Three acts
Place of Production:	Arts Theatre, London
Date of Production:	
Author:	Andrew Rosenthal

LORD CHAMBERLAIN'S OFFICE,

ST JAMES'S PALACE, S.W.1

19.9.51

READER'S REPORT

Hank and Jean are happily married and have a small daughter. Hank returns from the war, after active service in the Pacific, with a young man, Kip, for whom he has formed a deep friendship. Kip has no visible attachments and comes to stay with Hank and his wife indefinitely. He is adored by the little girl and everyone is happy. Then Hank's pre-war friend Felix and his wife Pauline return to their home to settle down after the war. Felix takes an instant dislike to Kip and gradually reveals that he, Kip, is a neurotic homosexual who has had a most unhappy childhood and who has three times tried to commit suicide. At one period of his life he was taken up by a notorious homo., a patron of the arts – Kip is an artist in so far as he paints one good portrait a year. Under the constant whisperings of Felix, Jean begins to feel that her marriage is threatened. In the end there is a showdown; Hank throws Kip out of his house and is reconciled with Jean. Kip, we are led to believe will probably commit suicide successfully this time. The only change is that Hank and Jean have broken their friendship with Felix and his wife.

The play is tense and interesting, with only occasional lapses into bathos – a fault that most American plays seem to suffer from. The homosexual element is very delicately handled. I must stress that. The play is, in fact, an attempt to explain the male friendships that exist which are intensified by the atmosphere of war.

I found it so difficult to decide about this play that I asked for Mr Game's opinion of it. His letter to me is attached. His opinion tipped the balance for me. The play is, therefore,

NOT RECOMMENDED FOR LICENCE
C. D. Heriot

Licence refused

C

But this is another example of the Lord Chamberlain being forced to reconsider under pressure from public opinion. Following the refusal of a licence, there begins the interesting process of the playwright and the theatre manager (Brian Maller) altering certain scenes that were found to be inappropriate. Letters from the public, support from the drama director of the British Arts Council, John Moody, threats of a petition to change the Lord Chamberlain's mind and articles in the *Observer* (Ivor

Brown) and *Evening News* all added to the pressure and the play was eventually granted a licence on 31 December 1951, probably because the dismal experience of Kip is seen as a warning (albeit a crude and inhumane one) against leading a life of 'perversion'. Nevertheless, it was still felt necessary to issue a warning that the character of Kip should not 'be played in an effeminate manner'.

There is an interesting footnote to this. Following the granting of a licence to *Third Person*, Judith Warden wrote in January 1952 to the Lord Chamberlain querying why *The Lonely Heart* (which was premiered at the New Lindsey Theatre Club in May 1951) was not equally acceptable.[24] Gwatkin sent her a confidential reply which pointed out that *Third Person* had been 'severely pruned of the homosexuality inherent in the original script' and unnecessarily adding that 'even as now produced, [it] will in some minds reek of perversion, but I don't think it need do, nor – in fact – does'.[25] In the face of this provocation, Warden's response was immaculately dignified. In that case, she replied, 'I shall put [my play] away and take it out when I'm a white-haired old lady!'[26]

In an era where the Lord Chamberlain had a strong relationship with theatre producers who had a monopoly on the type of drama that could be produced in London, this process of negotiation enhanced his power. When the London stage began to open up five years later, however, this shifting of the goalposts would ultimately contribute to censorship's demise.[27]

Signs of change: 1952–1955

The Earl of Scarborough, the former Conservative MP Roger Lumley (1922–37) and an ex-governor of Bombay (1937–43), succeeded Lord Clarendon as Lord Chamberlain in 1952. He was to oversee the British stage until 1963, at a time when British theatre underwent a revolution of attitudes and practices. What becomes interesting now is not simply the readers' responses to plays that contravened accepted policy, but their views on the new wave of work that flooded the British stage from 1955 onwards. The old certainties swept away, they often found it difficult to hold the line, accepting that there was never any decisive sense of where that line should be.

An early test of Scarborough's attitudes occurred when Oscar Lewenstein submitted Jean Genet's *The Maids* for licensing for production at the Royal Court, three years before it became the home of the ground-breaking English Stage Company. The assistant examiner, St Vincent Troubridge, was clear in his recommendation: 'Though written with a certain hysterical power, this is a horrible, deeply decadent and morbid play, quite unsuited I should have thought, to public performance before mixed audiences',[28] and it was not recommended for licence. Scarborough, in one of his earliest pronouncements, concurred – the work was 'unwholesome and macabre' with a 'suggestion of Lesbianism'[29] and a licence was consequently refused. If the play had proved critical of sexual difference, however, it would have stood a better chance of being approved, as the experience of *Third Person* had hinted at and Philip King's *Serious Charge* demonstrated.

Heriot penned the initial report on this work and offered an interesting conclusion: 'The play is strong and sensible. We are in no doubt at any time that the vicar is innocent of the "serious charge". Therefore, though the forbidden topic of homosexuality shadows this play, it does so in an inoffensive manner'.[30] Scarborough was called in to arbitrate, because Gwatkin disagreed with Heriot's line. His judgement was finely balanced:

> I am not convinced by the report that because the accusation was untrue no question of propriety can arise. But neither am I convinced that the relevant part of the play should be cut or altered. It is a straight play and though it is conceivable that some embarrassment might be caused, I think on the whole no great harm will be done and that the play should be licensed. S.[31]

Gwatkin quickly penned a short, irritable note to Heriot: 'CH. There you are. The judgement of Solomon has been given! "And may God have mercy on your soul".' He still disagreed about the innocuous nature of *Serious Charge*, since they had, after all, cut *Third Person*, with 'far less obvious homosexuality' and they were not being 'consistent'. On the same-dated note, Heriot defended himself: 'But I am being consistent. Here there is no real suggestion of homosexuality – it is all lies. *Third Person* dealt with an accusation of one doubtful pervert by another certain one.'[32]

But this was becoming an increasingly difficult line to tread, not least because of the scrutiny of a new, irreverent and brilliant theatre critic, Kenneth Tynan, who from the moment he became the chief reviewer of the *Observer* in September 1954 chose to campaign against the suffocating nature of censorship. When *Serious Charge* was finally produced in February 1955, Tynan was swift to point out that the work's deficiencies were an inevitable consequence of the Lord Chamberlain's control:

> Its subject is small town gossip, aimed at that most vulnerable target, the English male virgin – in this case a young clergyman living with his mother (Miss Olga Lindo). The first act hedges and dallies: Mr King loves suspense, and sixty minutes pass before he tells us where his play is going, during which time we have the sensation of flying blind through a heavy mist. Are we to focus on the frumpish spinster (avidly played by Miss Victoria Hopper) who seeks the vicar's heart? Or on the pregnant village girl who gets run over? Mr King says nothing, and says it in English small-talk, which, being so much smaller than the talk of other nations, has effectively aborted the emergence of many a fine English dramatist.
>
> The second act lifts us into the world of cause and effect. The vicar denounces the girl's seducer, a repulsive blonde spiv, who responds by crying for help and alleging indecent assault: the village, already predisposed to think the vicar a homosexual, credits the accusation: and so ends an admirable act, bitterly exciting and extremely well-played by Messrs Anthony Wager and Patrick McGoohan. But English censorship will not bear so perfect a trap. To avoid a miscarriage of justice, the villain must confess, which involves a scene of melodramatic falsification wherein he behaves like a certifiable lunatic. The promise of the middle act is dissolved in untruth. A master dramatist, rewriting *Serious Charge*, would have given the hero suppressed

homosexual tendencies of which he is made suddenly and poignantly aware; that would have been the forging of a tragedy as honest as Miss Lillian Hellman's *The Children's Hour*. But Miss Hellman's play is banned in this country, and so would Mr King's have been had he ventured so far. Perhaps the idea occurred to him; and with it the certain knowledge that the Lord Chamberlain would have crushed it on sight. One cannot blame him for playing safe.[33]

Playing safe was the worst thing that a playwright could do, in Tynan's eyes, although he was fully aware that the Lord Chamberlain often left dramatists little choice. Tynan's famous review of Rattigan's brilliant *Separate Tables* in November 1954 took the form of a pastiche of the work which simultaneously praised its construction, whilst lamenting its circumscription:

(The scene is the dining-room of a Kensington hotel, not unlike the Bournemouth hotel in which *Separate Tables*, Terence Rattigan's new double bill, takes place. A Young Perfectionist is dining; beside him, Aunt Edna, whom Mr Rattigan has described as the 'universal and immortal' middle-class playgoer.)

AUNT EDNA: Excuse me, young man, but have you seen Mr Rattigan's latest?

YOUNG PERFECTIONIST: I have indeed.

A.E.: And what is it about?

Y.P.: It is two plays about four people who are driven by loneliness into a state of desperation.

A.E. (*sighing*): Is there not enough morbidity in the world . . . ?

Y.P.: One of them is a drunken Left-wing journalist who has been imprisoned for wife-beating. Another is his ex-wife, who takes drugs to palliate the loss of her looks. She revives his masochistic love for her, and by the curtain-fall they are gingerly reunited.

A.E. (*quailing*): Does Mr Rattigan analyse these creatures?

Y.P.: He does, in great detail.

A.E.: How very unwholesome! Pray go on.

Y.P.: In the second play the central character is a bogus major who has lately been convicted of assaulting women in a cinema.

A.E.: Ouf!

Y.P.: His fellow guests hold conclave to decide whether he should be expelled from the hotel. Each contributes to a symposium on sexual deviation . . .

A.E.: In pity's name, stop.

Y.P.: The major reveals that his foible is the result of fear, which has made him a hermit, a liar and a pervert. This revelation kindles sympathy in the heart of the fourth misfit, a broken spinster, who befriends him in his despair.

A.E. (*aghast*): I *knew* I was wrong when I applauded *The Deep Blue Sea*. And what conclusion does Mr Rattigan draw from these squalid anecdotes?

Y.P.: From the first, that love unbridled is a destroyer. From the second, that love bridled is a destroyer. You will enjoy yourself.

A.E.: But I go to the theatre to be taken out of myself!

Y.P.: Mr Rattigan will take you into an intricately charted world of suspense. By withholding vital information, he will tantalise you; by disclosing it unexpectedly, he will astound you.

A.E.: But what information! Sex and frustration.

Y.P.: I agree that the principal characters, especially the journalist and the major, are original and disturbing characters. But there is also a tactful omniscient *hoteliére*, beautifully played by Beryl Measor. And what do you say to a comic Cockney maid?

A.E.: Ah!

Y.P.: Or to Aubrey Mather as a whimsical dominie? Or to a pair of opinionated medical students? Or to a tyrannical matriarch – no less than Phyllis Neilson-Terry?

A.E.: *That* sounds more like it. You console me.

Y.P.: I thought you would feel at home. And Peter Glenville, the director, has craftily engaged for these parts actors subtle enough to disguise their flatness.

A.E. (*clouding over*): But what about those difficult leading roles?

Y.P.: Margaret Leighton plays two of them, rather externally. Her beauty annihilates the pathos of the ex-wife, who should be oppressed with crow's-feet. And her mousy spinster, dim and pink-knuckled, verges on caricature. It is Eric Portman who commands the stage, volcanic as the journalist, but even better as the major, speaking in nervous spasms and walking stiff-legged with his shoulders protectively hunched. He has the mask of the true mime, the *comédien* as opposed to the *acteur*.

A.E.: Yet you sound a trifle peaky. Is something biting you?

Y.P.: Since you ask, I regretted that the major's crime was not something more cathartic than mere cinema flirtation. Yet I suppose the play is as good a handling of sexual abnormality as English playgoers will tolerate.

A.E.: For my part, I am glad it is no better.

Y.P.: I guessed you would be; and so did Mr Rattigan. Will you accompany me on a second visit tomorrow?

A.E.: With great pleasure. Clearly, there is something here for both of us.

Y.P.: Yes. But not quite enough for either of us.[34]

Indeed, Rattigan's treatment of the homosexuality of Major Pollock in the second play had been so necessarily reticent that Dearmer had spotted nothing problematic at all in his reader's report. *Table by the Window*, the first play of the two-hander, was 'a familiar dramatic mise-en-scène but Rattigan can be expected to handle it better than anyone else . . . Rattigan's characters, even when "impossible", are never sordid . . . Rattigan makes plausible this unlikely situation. His wonderful sense of theatre can make the incredible seem inevitable. His taste in dialogue is, as ever, impeccable. There is little action as the play consists of a resurrection of the past.' In *Table by the Door* 'Major Pollock has been bound over for molesting women in a cinema [and] this is much the better of the two plays, I think being in no way far-fetched in plot. It is a little masterpiece.'[35]

There had been no such reticence in the treatment of homosexuality in the adaptation of Gide's *The Immoralist* in November 1954, even if it was still a long way from an honest, open depiction of the issues. No embarrassment on the part of the author though, meant no possibility of the Lord Chamberlain issuing a licence. The price for public exposure was relegation to the tiny Arts Theatre, to which one had to belong as a member to see the show. It was a situation that Tynan found ridiculous, particularly given the play's recent exposure on Broadway:

... *The Immoralist* is the frankest, most detached play about homosexuality our theatre has yet seen, as free from sentimentality as it is from sensationalism ... Plays like this are always accused of naïveté: we scoff nervously, forgetting that censorship has so brusquely retarded the theatrical treatment of sex that it is still, to our shame, in its infancy. *The Immoralist* is a stumble towards maturity ... In America *The Immoralist* ran for ninety-six performances; here the ex-Governor of Bombay has celebrated his second anniversary as Lord Chamberlain by refusing it a licence. The rules governing his curious office lay down the following reasons for suppressing a play: profanity, improper language, indecency of dress, offensive representation of living persons, and anything likely to provoke a riot.[36] Nothing in *The Immoralist* comes under any of these headings. As when *Oedipus* was banned forty-five years ago, the Lord Chamberlain seems to have overstepped his brief. The granting of a conditional licence, forbidding twice-nightly exploitation while permitting serious managements to stage the play, would be an excellent face-saver.[37]

But there was no chance of that, since Heriot had suggested in his confidential report that the work would be liable to corrupt:

This ... is a dramatisation of a well-known French novel by a doyen of French modern literature. The plot will be familiar to anyone with the slightest knowledge of Gide's work. But the play is riddled with its subject, which, in my opinion is not treated detachedly enough (not be wondered at, when one considers that Gide himself was a homosexual) and no amount of 'payment' for Michel's pleasures conceals the fact that it would, in my opinion, have a corrupting effect on any person not conversant with the subject. It is therefore not recommended for licence.[38]

Scarborough endorsed this view a week later: 'I have read through this play. The theme is predominantly homosexual. However skilfully or powerfully it may be written, it will arouse curiosity in the theme and for that reason a licence is refused.'[39]

Waiting for Godot and Look Back in Anger

How did the readers deal with these two totemic plays, which helped usher in a new wave of British theatre? With some insight, it has to be said. *Waiting for Godot* was submitted for consideration by the producer, Donald Albery on 23 March 1954, and he indicated that at this stage he had Ralph Richardson in mind as one of the tramps. St Vincent Troubridge was charged with producing the report (see Plate 13) and he foreshadowed the general incomprehension that was to greet the work's first British appearance in 1955:

With many years on the Council of the old Stage Society, I have had much experience of 'advanced', 'expressionist', and similar imaginative kinds of plays, but I find this one extremely baffling ... [the author has found it] necessary to invent virtually a new language to express himself ... I can only offer the merest glimmer of a suggestion of what the author intends it all to mean ... [it is an] interminable verbal labyrinth.

Nevertheless, he makes an interesting attempt to interpret the work:

> The play is a modern cry of despair, and Godot, for whom we human tramps are always waiting in expectation, is Death. Pozzo and Lucky are allegorical figures passing before our eyes of how men treat one another, by acts of enslavement that lead to blindness for the enslaver and dumbness for the slave. The best way out is a piece of rope – what Shakespeare called 'the charity of a penny cord'. Why the shrewdest of our younger managers should contemplate the production of so bitter, dark and obscure an allegory is almost as mysterious as much of the play.[40]

St Vincent Troubridge recommended that a licence be granted if twelve cuts were made. On 14 April Albery wrote back reporting that Beckett had agreed to ten of these ('this is a big concession and I make it with the greatest reluctance') but had refused to concede points 5 and 6 ('Act I, page 52, omit from "But you can't go barefoot" down to "and they crucified quick" + Act II, page 3, omit "you see you piss better when I'm not there" '). Several letters were then exchanged on the nature of the alterations suggested and by 21 June 1954 matters had boiled down to one line, with Gwatkin suggesting to Albery that 'Who farted' on page 30 of the submitted script (which can be viewed today at the British Library) be changed to 'Who did that?'. Albery wrote back on 28 June to inform Gwatkin that Beckett wanted to suggest 'belched' instead of 'farted', and Gwatkin replied on 1 July that the Lord Chamberlain was content with this. Here the dispute ends in the correspondence file, and it is hard to see from the paper trail alone why it was necessary for the work to be premiered in a club theatre, the Arts, in August 1955 (see Plate 18). Indeed, a licence was granted for the West End transfer to the Criterion Theatre on 25 August 1955, although the matter did not end there. An audience member, Lady Howitt, complained to the Lord Chamberlain on 16 November that the work was 'sordid, bestial and brutal' since 'one of the main themes running through the play is the desire of two old tramps continually to relieve themselves'. Such a dramatization of lavatory necessities, she felt was offensive and 'against all sense of British decency'. She urged him to intervene. Consequently, Heriot was despatched to the theatre to produce a new report on the production and he set down his thoughts on 30 November 1955:

> I visited this play last night and endured two hours of angry boredom. Peter Hall's production seems to emphasise the slapstick elements, while the entire cast act like mad to inject drama and meaning into a piece quite without drama and with very little meaning. Lady Hewitt's [sic] case is not proved . . . no useful purpose could be served by pruning – and the Lord Chamberlain might endanger the dignity of his office if he rescinded his licence at this point in the play's run . . . There is only one interval. At the fall of the first curtain, the man next to me cried 'Brother, let me out of this!' and fled, never to return. He was not alone, many empty seats gaped during the second act. In the bar, several women were apologising to their escorts for having suggested a visit to such a piece. The general feeling seemed, like mine, to be one of acute boredom –

except for a sprinkling of young persons in slacks and Marlon Brando pullovers with (according to sex) horsetails or fringes, who applauded pointedly.

One of the many fascinating dimensions of the Lord Chamberlain's papers is the inclusion of spy reports such as these, which give an intriguing insight into the atmosphere of significant first runs, no matter how jaundiced the testimony.

Look Back in Anger was much less contentious for the censors, even if Heriot concluded his report by stating that 'The play's interest, in fact, lies in its careful observation of the anteroom of hell'[41] (see Plate 15).

Title:	*Look Back in Anger*
No. of Scenes or Acts:	Three Acts
Place of Production:	Royal Court Theatre, London
Date of Production:	7.5.56
Author:	John Osborne

LORD CHAMBERLAIN'S OFFICE,
ST JAMES'S PALACE, S.W.1

1.3.56

READER'S REPORT

This impressive and depressing play breaks new psychological ground, dealing with a type of young man I believed had vanished twenty years ago, but which must be generally recognisable enough to write plays about. It is about that kind of intellectual that thrashed about passionately looking for a cause. It usually married girls of good family, quarrelled with all their relations, and bore them off to squalor in Pimlico or Poplar where they had babies and spent all their spare time barracking Fascist meetings. In this play the venue is a large provincial town where Jimmy and Alison, his wife, share frowsty digs with Cliff, Jimmy's friend. The men run a sweet-stall in the market-place both having been at university. Cliff is platonically loving to Alison. But Jimmy, torn by his secret demons – his sense of social and intellectual inferiority, his passionate 'feeling' that the old order is, in some way, responsible for the general bloodiness of the world today, his determination to epater les bourgeois at all costs and his unrealised mother-fixation for the kindly, charitable mother of one of his friends (a charwoman who married an artist, completely uneducated so that Jimmy can, quite unconsciously, patronise her while he praises her goodness) – foams at Alison, insulting her parents, teasing her about her background in an angry way and generally indulging in a grand display of tantrums that only differ from those of the nursery in having an adult sexual flavour. Alison has not yet told Jimmy that she is pregnant, but she invites a friend (a correct girl of her own class who has gone on the stage) to stay for a while. Jimmy goes out of his way to embroider his offensiveness to the two girls. Helena wires Alison's father to come and take her away. He arrives just after Jimmy has rushed off to London to the deathbed of the old lady, his friend's mother. When he returns, heavy with childish grief, he finds his wife gone and only Helena with the courage to face him. It is a courage based on an unwilling passion. They become lovers. Then Alison returns, the child having died, and Helena retires, leaving the two of them to begin all over again. It is characteristic that the unbreakable ties of their attraction should be garlanded with embarrassing whimsical love-language. The play's interest, in fact, lies in its careful observation of the anteroom of hell.

Act i.	p. 23 Cut the lavatory reference	leave
	p. 41 Cut the homosexual reference	leave
	pp. 43/44 The whole of this speech must be considerably toned down	yes, especially last half
ii	p. 15 Alter the reference to pubic hair	cut
	p. 16 ditto and reference to inversion	cut
	p. 19 cut the marked speech	cut
Act ii, 2	p. 14 Cut 'deep, loving bull!'	cut
Act iii, 1	p. 14 Cut 'short-arsed'	cut
	p. 16 Alter reference to excessive love-making	leave

Otherwise

RECOMMENDED FOR LICENCE

C. D. Heriot

Footnote: The prototypes of Jimmy and Alison may be Giles Romilly and his wife. Romilly was killed in the war and his biography was sketched in a book called 'Friends Apart' by Philip Toynbee, published in 1954.

The trouble with religion

Sometimes the most innocuous plays caused the censors the greatest difficulty. In the same month that *Look Back in Anger* was premiered (May 1956), a gentle Christian drama was submitted for licence, but ran up against one of censorship's firmest unwritten rules.

Title:	*The Life of Christ*
No. of Scenes or Acts:	
Place of Production:	Odsal Stadium, Bradford
Date of Production:	
Author:	J. W. Brannigan

LORD CHAMBERLAIN'S OFFICE,

ST JAMES'S PALACE, S.W.1

15th May 1956

READER'S REPORT

In this play which is a perfectly reverent, dignified and accurate life of Our Lord, Jesus himself speaks, and appears throughout. There are even scenes of the Last Supper and (stylised) a scene of Jesus on the Cross. Jesus says nothing that is not in the Gospels, and no fault can be found in the taste and decorum of the presentation.

Nevertheless, the play cannot, of course, be allowed. And quite apart from the law on the subject, it would be grossly unfair to make an exception on account of the play's quite proper and accurate representation, when far better dramatists have necessarily been prevented from attempting it.

(sd.) G .Dearmer

Saw LC and explained
28 June 56

> Then why are the Mystery Plays in York
> Continually played – under my Presidentship – and
> to the satisfaction of the two Archbishops? Is it because
> they date originally from the Middle Ages – even though
> the version now played has been edited and translated in the
> last few years? Christ is impersonated and speaks throughout, the Almighty also
> appears, to say nothing of Satan

Scarborough's discomfort was reflected in the letter of rejection sent to H. J. White, the producer of the Bradford Charity Players: 'As, I am afraid, there is a rule that Our Lord must not be impersonated on stage, a Licence cannot be granted for the public presentation of your play, *The Life of Christ*. This is the rule and must apply to your play, in which no fault can be found in either the taste or decorum of the presentation.'[42] Under no obligation to explain the reason for any rejection, the final sentence was a rare deviation from imperturbability, and a clear sign of unease.

The new wave

The English Stage Company, established at the Royal Court and Theatre Workshop, based at the Theatre Royal, Stratford, played a key role in bringing about the reorientation of British theatre over the next five years. The readers often struggled to reconcile the proliferation of this new type of work with their previous certain conviction about what public taste would permit, and this is reflected in many of their comments on the notable plays of this period. This is not to say, however, that all their observations were anachronistic or foolish. St Vincent Troubridge was surprisingly benevolent towards Brecht's *Mother Courage*, submitted by Theatre Workshop for a performance at Barnstaple in 1955 in which Joan Littlewood was to play the lead:

Bertolt Brecht is the leading Communist dramatist outside Soviet Russia and he writes exceedingly well . . . Thus, in a generally acceptable denunciation of the horrors of war, he is able to slip in a good deal of the Communist party line . . . There are many fine strokes of irony, such as the death of her son Eilif, who, earlier congratulated and feted for obtaining twenty bullocks by theft for a starving battalion, is shot for looting a peasant's cow during what turns out to be a very brief interval of peace . . . we have just to consider the verbal coarseness, all appropriate to the Thirty Years War, but less well admissible in Devon.[43]

With some earthy language cut, including 'bollocks', 'sod' and 'wet my pants', a licence was readily agreed to. He was less impressed by another Theatre Workshop play, *The Quare Fellow* (1956), however, describing it as a 'horrid play', which, although possessing 'a slice of life power', employs crude language which 'will cause no offence whatever in Stratford East', a working-class area of London.[44] And Ionesco's *The Lesson* received the familiar expression of incredulity which generally greeted most Absurdist work: 'Another crazy effusion from the pen of the Franco-Rumanian avant garde writer'[45] (see Plate 20).

By 1957, though, the tone of the reports on the flood of new British writing had become much sharper and, at times, bitter. It was as if the readers sensed that theatrical taste was changing so quickly that their autocratic control was likely to be threatened. They were also disturbed by the contemporaneous nature of the subject matter. This is most apparent in the response by St Vincent Troubridge to the script of Osborne's follow-up to *Look Back in Anger*, *The Entertainer*:

> This is the eagerly awaited second play by John Osborne, whose *Look Back in Anger* was the main sensation of 1956, and who is the acknowledged head of the Angry Young Man school (or racket) of dramatists. In the modern fashion, it has scarcely any story at all, the merest and flimsiest scaffolding, the characters, their circumstances and emotions representing the true content of the play. While the whining self-pity of Jimmy Porter in the earlier play is not here concentrated in a single character, the vitriolic negativism is now dispersed over an entire family of tatty, broken down music-hall pros . . . Just as samples of how Angry Young Mannery is coming along, I have flagged three passages in brown; these are Archie's view of life (1, 29–30), his view of the family (2, 17) and his son Frank's view of life (2, 36) . . . the author has come under the influence of Brecht's 'epic' technique' . . . the whole play is impregnated with sex, sexy references and half references and general lavatorial dirt . . . with aversion and disgust, as an angry middle-aged man, recommended for licence.[46]

The secret memorandum of 31 October 1958

That the readers' grip on the stage was loosening was confirmed by the first significant change to the practice of stage censorship since the Second World War: the relaxing of the absolute ban on homosexuality in 1958.

It was, ironically, the man who had perhaps benefited most from a compliant relationship with the censor, Binkie Beaumont, who contributed to the concession that began the process that was to lead to the removal of the stage from the clutch of the censor in 1968. A few weeks before the Suez hostilities broke out in October 1956, a surprising conflagration erupted in the West End, initiated by some of the keenest adherents of conservatism. Binkie Beaumont, his fellow producer Donald Albery,

Stephen Arlen (a director of Covent Garden) and Ian Hunter (an ex-director of the Edinburgh Festival) announced their intention of reviving the New Watergate Theatre Club. By taking advantage of the loophole in the law which permitted private performances of unlicensed plays to paid-up members of a theatre club, they wanted to present three banned works – *A View from the Bridge*, *Cat on a Hot Tin Roof* and *Tea and Sympathy*. They stated that all three had been deprived of licences by the Lord Chamberlain for touching on homosexuality, but this was not quite true. *Cat on a Hot Tin Roof* had attracted Heriot's ire (see Plate 21), but he had actually recommended a licence be granted.[47]

A View from the Bridge was also reluctantly passed by Heriot, as long as cuts – unacceptable to the playwright – were made:

> Miller's work is always objective, and his themes treated with better craftsmanship and sense of the theatre [than Williams's] . . . The implication of homosexuality is clear, though it is always oblique, but Eddie kissing Rodolpho has to go. Licence recommended.[48]

It subsequently annoyed Heriot that Beaumont claimed that the play had been banned. Beaumont had simply decided not to re-present the amended script, which was the producer's fault in the eyes of the myopic censor. Only *Tea and Sympathy* had been refused a licence in 1954, even though Deborah Kerr's performance on Broadway had been a huge hit.

Although the producers stated that their intention was not to circumvent the law, but to offer 'interesting plays to minority audiences', this was seen as a flimsy ruse. For a start, every one of the plays had been huge Broadway successes, and there was little commercial risk. Instead of going to the usual little theatre, the Arts Theatre, they intended to transform the much larger Comedy Theatre into a club venue (the New Watergate) to maximize their profits. Gwatkin, the assistant comptroller, met Beaumont and Albery to discuss their already announced plans on 25 October 1956. Following their discussions, he starkly warned the Lord Chamberlain that such a stratagem would either mean the end of censorship or the demise of the club system: 'They both, honestly, deplored either possibility . . . [but on] the general principle of Homosexual plays they produced the usual arguments: That it is no longer a hidden subject but mentioned in practically every newspaper, frequently by the BBC, in literature, quite a number of drawing rooms, and quite unconcerned by the young.'

At the producers' suggestion, Scarborough, the comptroller and Heriot went to a private showing of the film version of *Tea and Sympathy* arranged by Beaumont, but Heriot made clear in a memo of 31 October that the film had deleted all the references to homosexuality and it had been 'a very tedious two hours'.

The following day the stakes were raised when Heriot told Albery that the filmscript version would gain a licence, but that the ban on the play version remained. He added darkly that if the New Watergate arrangement proceeded the Lord Chamberlain would 'feel obliged to reconsider the position of such theatres'. The producers went ahead with *A View from the Bridge* but held back on *Tea and Sympathy*.

Kenneth Tynan, unaware of the behind-the-scenes negotiations, was riled by the necessary chicanery required to get the works staged at all, and made his views clear in his theatre column in September:

> I am in little doubt that the true creator of the new venture, the catalyst to whom our thanks are due, is that anachronistic bogey, the Lord Chamberlain.
>
> Forbear, if you can, to smile at the mighty machinery of evasion that had to be constructed before London might see, properly produced, three plays which have been staged with no trouble at all on Broadway and almost everywhere in Western Europe. Do not mistake me: I applaud the new enterprise: but I wish it had taken a firmer stand against the mischievous anomaly of a censorship which Walpole invented for his own political use, which licensed Ibsen only because it thought his characters 'too absurd to do any harm', and which is implicitly to blame for the fact that the whole panorama of British theatre contains only a handful of plays dealing at all controversially with sex, politics, the law, the Church, the Armed Forces, and the Crown . . .

He quite correctly pointed out that it was the theatre profession's acquiescence in this state of affairs which was as much to blame as the censor:

> The obstacle to reform can be simply stated: most theatre managers approve of the Lord Chamberlain. He is their guarantee of safety: once blessed with his licence, they are immune from legal action. This attitude is likely to persist as long as our theatre skulks inside the nursery, irresponsibly refusing to claim the right which, long ago, the film industry demanded and won: that of censoring itself. The Lord Chamberlain should be replaced by an advisory panel, drawn from and elected by the theatre itself. To this body all scripts would be submitted; but its veto (unlike that of the film censors) would not be absolute; the management concerned would retain the right to go ahead and run the risk of prosecution under the existing laws relating to blasphemy, sedition and obscenity.[49]

People flocked to *A View from the Bridge* in October 1956, encouraged by the whiff of controversy, the Broadway pedigree and a clutch of admiring notices. Tynan felt that Eddie Carbone's lack of self-knowledge led to the play falling 'just short of being a masterpiece' but he counselled that the Lord Chamberlain should be made an honorary member of the club to be confronted by 'a spectacle that he has pronounced unfit for human consumption'.[50] His exasperation was exacerbated by the presentation of Lillian Hellman's *The Children's Hour* at the Arts Theatre. This time he argued that the work, banned over twenty years previously for its reference to lesbianism, was being performed to a liberal audience which least needed to be confronted by the work's progressiveness. Utilizing Nancy Mitford's social sub-division of people into Us and Them, he wryly observed that 'to present it to Arts theatre audiences who are predominantly Us, is like sending oil to Texas. And to present it to Them, for whom it was originally written and to whom it would still appeal, is legally prohibited'.[51] How limited a victory the New Watergate exercise proved to be was revealed when Beaumont and Albery, emboldened by the commercial success of *A View from the Bridge*, went to Lord Scarborough to explain that they intended to open a second club theatre to stage *Tea and Sympathy*. This was swiftly met with the threat of legal action and they immediately backed down, but a chink in the armour of censorship had been found, and by not preventing the club production of *A View from the Bridge*, the censor had appeared less than all powerful.

Public interest in the 'forbidden subject' grew over the next two years. In April 1954, following the Montagu and Wildeblood court cases, the home secretary and the secretary of state for Scotland had agreed to the appointment of a Departmental Committee to examine and report on the law on homosexual offences and also on the law relating to prostitution. The composition of the Wolfenden Committee was officially announced in August. It was chaired by John Wolfenden (1906–85), who had previously been headmaster of Uppingham and Shrewsbury schools, and had become the vice-chancellor of Reading University in 1950. Other members of the Committee included a consultant psychiatrist, the chairman of Uxbridge magistrates court, the vice-president of the City of Glasgow Girl Guides, a Scottish Presbyterian minister, a professor of moral theology, a high court judge, a Foreign Office minister, and the Conservative MP for Putney. There were all in all fifteen men and one woman.

The Committee met for the first time on 15 September 1954, in a room provided by the Home Office – room 101. They deliberated over a period of three years during which time they met in private on sixty-two days, thirty-two of these being spent interviewing witnesses. The Home Office civil servants, reflecting the repressive nature of the time, were concerned about the sensibilities of the secretarial staff when dealing with the material and in internal memoranda they referred to homosexuals and prostitutes as 'huntleys' and 'palmers'. (Huntley and Palmer's were a well-known firm of biscuit makers.)

Whilst the Committee was sitting, further events highlighted the inequities of the current repressive law. In November 1955 Peter Wildeblood published his autobiography, explaining both the horror of his arrest and imprisonment, and his emergence from the ordeal as a stronger and more honest person who was not ashamed to announce to the world that 'I am homosexual'. He later gave the following evidence to the Wolfenden Committee: 'The right which I claim for myself, and for all those like me, is the right to choose the person whom I love.' Nevertheless, the persecution continued: the 1955 annual figure for 'indecency between males' offences peaked at 2,322, with 1,065 men gaoled.

On 4 September 1957 the Wolfenden *Report on Homosexual Offences and Prostitution* was published and it made the startling (and welcome) recommendation that homosexual behaviour in private between consenting adults (defined as those over 21) should be decriminalized, but that curbs on prostitution should be tightened. Of the thirteen members of the Committee who had served for the full three years, twelve recommended that homosexual behaviour between consenting adults in private should no longer be a criminal offence. The definition of the words 'consent' and 'in private' were not defined but were to be interpreted as they would in the case for heterosexual conduct. Contrary to the evidence provided by nearly all the psychiatric and psychoanalytic witnesses the Committee found that 'homosexuality cannot legitimately be regarded as a disease, because in many cases it is the only symptom and is compatible with full mental health in other respects'.

The publication of the report produced a storm of debate in the press and filled the front pages of the newspapers. The lumping together of the issues relating to homosexuality and prostitution in general allowed some newspapers to refer to it in headlines as the 'VICE REPORT'. Beaverbrook's *Daily Express* was particularly virulent, wondering in its editorial column why the government had ever sponsored 'this cumbersome nonsense' and expressing relief that Tory MPs, nervous about an electoral backlash, were likely to scupper plans for legislation.[52] However, in October 1957 the Archbishop of Canterbury, Dr Fisher, surprisingly voiced his support for the Wolfenden Report, arguing that there was 'a sacred realm of privacy . . . into which the law, generally speaking, must not intrude' and the recommendations were also endorsed by the British Medical Association, the Howard League for Penal Reform and the National Association of Probation Officers.

The first parliamentary debate on the matter was initiated on 4 December 1957 by Frank Pakenham (later Lord Longford). He had already become known as a social reformer and prison visitor, and as a result of the Montagu case came to know Peter Wildeblood and C. H. Rolph, who was to become the chair of the Homosexual Reform Society. Of the seventeen speakers in the debate, eight broadly supported the recommendations in the Wolfenden Report.

The home secretary, Sir David Maxwell-Fyfe, spoke for the government. He expressed doubt that the general population would support the recommendations and stated that further research was required. The report was, quite simply, 'ahead of its time'. This seemed to the liberal sections of the press to be prevarication of the worst kind. After the Home Office asked the sociologist Richard Hauser in 1958 to undertake another survey of homosexuality in Great Britain, there was an outcry. A. E. Dyson and the Revd Hallidie-Smith founded the Homosexual Reform Society in May 1958, as a pressure group dedicated to persuading Parliament of the strength of support for law reform by public figures, and to refuting the claim that the recommendations were 'in advance of public opinion'. Also, in June 1958, the *Daily Telegraph*, *Observer* and *Daily Mirror* all called for an end to the home secretary's shameful prevarication in implementing the Wolfenden recommendations – but it would be another ten years before homosexuality was decriminalized in Britain.[53]

It was against this background that Scarborough, ever mindful of public opinion – and rather more enlightened than perhaps his critics were prepared to concede – began to consider the place of censorship in modern society. On 24 May 1957 he sought the Queen's permission to examine the whole matter of censorship and then went to visit the home secretary, R. A. Butler to discuss the possibility of issuing 'adult-only' licences in the light of the controversy surrounding homosexuality. At a second meeting on 28 February 1958 with a lukewarm Butler, who was fearful of increased criticism from his party about any signs of incipient liberalism in the run-up to a general election, Scarborough stated that it might be better if the Lord Chamberlain ceased to act as the censor to protect the position of the Queen. A letter from the home secretary on 11 August brought some resolution to the question as to whether there should be any amendment to the practice of stage censorship. Butler was against any loosening of control, since it 'would inevitably lead to a debate on censorship generally and might result in a demand for the substitution of some method of control less acceptable than the present arrangement'. It was the classic fudge, but Butler tried to offer a sop by observing that 'my colleagues marvel at your success'. Nevertheless, Scarborough felt that some change was necessary and he issued his symbolic secret memorandum to his readers on 31 October 1956 on the 'forbidden subject' as a sign of his desire for reform (see Plate 22).

The first practical change that this relaxation of the rules created was the allowance of the character of Geof in the Theatre Workshop production of Shelagh Delaney's *A Taste of Honey*. Heriot's initial report of the work in May 1958 was equivocal:

> Helen is a freelance tart and Josephine is her teenage daughter . . . Geof has the reputation of being a pervert – and he confesses that there is a little flame to the immense amount of smoke; but he explains that he is really quite a normal young man, only not very strongly sexed, and with a very real desire to marry and settle down and have a family . . . This is a surprisingly good play – though God knows it is not to my personal taste . . . this play is balanced on a knife-edge: it is the perfect border-line case, since it is concerned with the forbidden subject in a way that no one, I believe, could take exception to . . . but I think that the Comptroller and the Lord Chamberlain should both read the play carefully themselves.[54]

Gwatkin felt that there was nothing borderline about the work at all: 'I've read it and think it revolting, quite apart from the homosexual buts. To me it has no saving grace whatsoever. If we pass muck like this, it <u>does</u> give our critics something to go on.' The view of Scarborough was sought and he demanded that the suggestion of homosexuality be eliminated. On 6 June 1958 Heriot commented on the revised manuscript that the 'the character of Geof has been toned down in accordance with the Lord Chamberlain's instructions', and a licence was subsequently granted, but it seems fair to conclude that the play could only really have been produced after the memorandum had been issued, since it was evident to the audiences at the Theatre Royal, Stratford East, that Geof was not only a homosexual but an empathetic (although not necessarily positive) character. Whilst an air of melancholy did cling to him, he did not specifically see himself as the 1950s type of unfortunate.

A more direct result of the memorandum was the reconsideration of plays for licence which had previously been banned. Thus, *The Immoralist* was reviewed on 25 November 1958 after being submitted by Christopher Mann Ltd on 7 November, the very day that the change of policy was announced to the public. The Lord

Chamberlain himself commented that 'Having re-read the play in the light of our change of policy I have no doubt that it can be rightly be termed a serious play on the theme of homosexuality and can now receive a licence. There are no obscenities to be cut'. Similarly, the formerly controversial *Oscar Wilde* by Leslie and Sewell Stokes was deemed by Heriot to pose no difficulty in 1961:

> Time has dealt harshly with this play, which I saw in 1936 and then considered good. Now it seems like an outline drawing after the two elaborate films on the subject and Michael MacLiammor's astonishing one-man presentation of Wilde (all of which I have seen) . . . There is nothing in the piece that has not already been dealt with in the films, and the subject of Wilde's perversion is handled tactfully (though truthfully) with stress laid on his overweening pride and the impossibility of ever changing his character. I see no reason why this play should not now be recommended for licence.[55]

The slippery slope

The readers were not alone in struggling to keep pace with the rapid change in theatrical sentiment by the late 1950s. Heriot believed Harold Pinter's second production, *The Birthday Party* (1958), to be pointless and futile (see Plate 23). In this dismissive opinion, Heriot was in agreement with nearly all the theatre critics other than Harold Hobson of the *Sunday Times*, whose crusading review single-handedly rescued Pinter's career from being stifled at birth. St Vincent Troubridge's report of Pinter's next play, *The Caretaker* (1960), whilst expressing similar distaste, interestingly acknowledges the role that Hobson was playing in sustaining Pinter's career:

Title:	*The Caretaker*
No. of Scenes or Acts:	Three acts
Place of Production:	Duchess Theatre, London
Date of Production:	30th May 1960
Author:	Harold Pinter

LORD CHAMBERLAIN'S OFFICE,
ST JAMES'S PALACE, S.W.1

18th May 1960

READER'S REPORT

This is a piece of incoherence in the manner of Samuel Beckett, though it has not that author's vein of nihilistic pessimism, and each individual sentence is comprehensible if irrelevant. Produced a fortnight ago by the Arts, and received with enthusiasm by the high-brow critics, it is now to be transferred to the Duchess for public performance.

Two brothers, Aston and Mick, live in a single room, piled with junk and with a leaking roof in a dilapidated house owned by the latter. Aston rescues a garrulous tramp named Davies from a fracas in a cafe, and allows him for the present to use Mick's bed in the room, as Mick is sleeping elsewhere. Davies believes at first that the house belongs to Aston, who makes him an offer to act as caretaker in return for a roof over his head. Davies later discovers that the house is Mick's, and Mick makes him a similar offer to act as caretaker. The tramp tries to play the brothers off against each other, but has no success as the brothers, though they bicker among themselves, resent criticism from an outsider. Finally Aston turns Davies out, mainly because the tramp groans in the night and keeps his host awake.

That is the story, such as it is, but each of the three characters has one more leit-motif obsession to which he returns continually in conversation and in soliloquy. With Aston it is his experiences in an asylum and, more understandably, Davies's nocturnal noises; with Mick it is fantasies of the modernistic interior decoration he will apply to the ruined house; with Davies it is to obtain free a good pair of shoes, to get to Sidcup, where a man he has not seen for 15 years is supposed to have his documents of identity, and, more locally, to adjust his bed so that the rain does not come through a broken window onto his head.

It is one of those plays of which I can report drearily that if the Lord Chamberlain glances through any page, he will receive a correct impression of the play as a whole. In case it may be of interest, I also enclose the review of this play in *The Sunday Times*

1, 7.	'piss off'	cut
8.	'piss off'	cut
21	'Would you like me to have a look at your body?' (An invitation to indecent exposure)	alter
24	'Bugger it'	cut
II, 4.	'up your arse'	cut
15	'buggered'	
III, 17.	'from arsehole to breakfast time'	cut

Otherwise

RECOMMENDED FOR LICENCE

18/5/50
St Vincent Troubridge
Assistant Examiner

But the era of quiet compliance with the whims of the censor on the part of the theatre sector was coming to an end, and as the 1960s began, there was ever more vigorous questioning from playwrights and critics alike as to whether a system of censorship was compatible with a Western democracy. As Scarborough expressly feared, the rise of satire led to a new focus on whether the censor was more concerned with defending royal sensibility than anything else and the case of Glendon Alvine's banned *The Knights of Song* (1961) bore this out. St Vincent Troubridge recommended that this work – about the Victorian musical duo Gilbert and Sullivan – be refused a licence because of references to the lascivious Prince of Wales,[56] even though the events had occurred over sixty years earlier. The new assistant comptroller clarified the issue for Scarborough: 'We have not allowed King Edward VII to be represented in a play' – presumably because of the embarrassment that his sexual liaisons might cause the royal family – and this 'play shows up King Edward VII in a tiresome light as regards girls'.[57] The Lord Chamberlain needed no persuading, replying a week later that it might have been fifty years since the king's death, but 'this is not the kind of play on which to begin the relaxation of the ban on the representation on the stage of King Edward VII'.[58] The prospective producer, F. Benson of Joseph Weinberger Ltd, sought to appeal and requested to know which sections of the work in particular were deemed offensive, but this request – one which many felt was a perfectly reasonable one to make when a play had been turned down – was bound to fail. Penn simply offered that the work had been disallowed 'on account of the representation of Queen Victoria, King Edward VII and King Edward VIII . . . The Lord Chamberlain would be prepared to consider the representation of King Edward VII on the stage only in a semi-historical play.'[59]

This lack of accountability on the part of the Lord Chamberlain was becoming an increasing bone of contention, and in December 1962 a renewed effort was made in the House of Commons to alter the system. The Labour MP for Ipswich, Dingle Foot, requested permission to introduce his 'Censorship of Plays (Abolition) Bill', which sought to make the submission of scripts optional, and although this was denied by 134 votes to 77, it signalled a renewed parliamentary desire to reconsider the issue.

The last censor: Lord Cobbold

In 1963 Scarborough was succeeded by Lord Cobbold as Lord Chamberlain. It is salutary to remember that during his tenure he had actually licensed 10,110 plays, banned only thirty and placed seventy-nine in the 'waiting' tray, where playwrights were asked to reconsider their intentions. Cobbold, a former governor of the Bank of England who was made a life peer in 1960, was from the outset uncomfortable with the aspect of his duties which required him to shape British theatre. Whilst this did not make him a great reformer, he was uneasy at the increasingly contentious rows in which the role of censor involved him. An early difficulty occurred with Harry Tugend's *The Wayward Stork*, which illustrated the 1960s' increasingly open attitude to sex. Heriot's report was gruff. It was a 'nasty sniggering American comedy [about artificial insemination] . . . If all these goings-on are illegal in this country I would be delighted to recommend the withholding of a licence on those grounds since taste is not sufficient. Would it be possible to get a professional opinion? I could ask my own doctor. Otherwise, reluctantly recommended for licence.'[60]

Heriot did consult his doctor and concluded that the play brought doctors into disrepute, since the artificial insemination as described was completely illegal.[61] Sir Charles Dodds of the Courtauld Institute concurred,[62] and a licence was subsequently refused. Similar prevarication occurred with Joe Orton's *Loot*. A new reader, Ifan Kyle Fletcher, the founder of the Society for Theatre Research, had felt that the blasphemy, flagellation, homosexuality and filthy dialogue debarred the work from receiving a licence. 'I find the whole atmosphere of the play repellent',[63] he thundered, but Cobbold, more aware of public tolerance perhaps than his readers, dissented and overruled him 'reluctantly'.

A Patriot for Me

John Osborne's *A Patriot for Me*, submitted on 30 August 1964, had much more serious ramifications for the censorship, however.

Title:	*A Patriot for Me*	
No. of Scenes or Acts:	Three	
Place of Production:	Royal Court Theatre, London	
Date of Production:		
Author:	John Osborne	
Submitted by:	The English Stage Company Ltd.	30.8.64

LORD CHAMBERLAIN'S OFFICE,

ST JAMES'S PALACE, S.W.1

READER'S REPORT

A biographical play about an Austrian Officer, Colonel Redl, who committed suicide in 1913. I have not been able to trace whether Redl was a real person or not – he is not in any of the usual biographical dictionaries or in *Who Was Who*. The play is Schnitzler up to date. Redl is a brilliant young officer first seen as a second in a duel between the aristocratic Kupfer and a Jewish Officer Siczynski. The latter is killed, Redl is promoted, lives a curiously chaste life, becomes the uneasy lover of the Countess Delyanoff (who reports everything to his Commanding Officer) and at the end of Act I we are sure that Redl is homosexual.

In Act II he attends a 'drag' or transvestite ball where he hears of a new Viennese psychologist who specialises in inversion. But his habits are now known and, as a Colonel in Intelligence, he is blackmailed by the Russians to become a spy for them. He takes the money as he is becoming increasingly extravagant. Kupfer, now living in his apartment, does not know that he is to be the scape-goat if anything goes wrong.

After a shrieking match between Redl and the Countess, who has dared to marry one of his favourites, the Rake's progress becomes more precipitant. We see a young man driven mad by his shame at being an invert, there are various vignettes of Redl and his male lovers. Then the news leaks out and Redl, his inversion and his espionage known to the authorities, shoots himself.

This is a serious but not a good play about homosexuality but though we have had plays on the subject which have received a licence, Mr Osborne's overweening conceit and blatant anti-authoritarianism causes him to write in a deliberately provocative way. He almost never misses a chance to be offensive.

I-1-2   Cut from 'His spine . . .' to 'aaa All the way up.'

I-4-24   This scene must not be played with the couple in bed.

I-4-27   Cut the marked passage where Redl spies on the copulating couple next door.

I-5-30   Reference to clap and crabs.

I-7-45   Reference to clap.

I-10-58/59   The whole of this scene where Redl sleeps with a male prostitute and is beaten up by his thugs must come out.

II-1/23   The whole of this scene (the transvestite ball) must come out.

III-1-3   This love passage must be altered

III-1-4   Cut from 'So: you'll turn Stefan . . .' to '. . . ordinary man.'

III-2-6   Cut the marked line.

As it stands this play is
NOT RECOMMENDED FOR LICENCE

If the Company wish to try again then the whole of Acts II and III must be drastically revised with the ball left out and the inverted eroticism toned down. The present text seems to be a perfect example of a piece which might corrupt, since it reveals nearly all the details of the homosexual life usually left blank even in the newspaper reports.

C. Heriot.

The seriousness of refusing a licence to as public a company as the English Stage Company was not lost on the censors. An unsigned memo to the new assistant comptroller, John Johnston, observes that the 'play looks to me like the Pansies Charter of freedom and is bound to be a cause célèbre'. Not much sign of greater tolerance following the secret memorandum here.

Johnston, citing the memorandum, recommended refusal of a licence to Cobbold because the work 'exploits the subject of homosexuality' and includes 'embraces between males and practical demonstrations of love'.[64] And there the matter might have ended if the ESC had not decided, in a singular act of defiance, to copy the precedent of the New Watergate Club and turn the Royal Court into a Theatre Club to stage the unlicenced work.

Alarmed at this overt challenge to his authority, Cobbold sought the advice of the Director of Public Prosecutions as to the advisability of prosecuting the company if it were to go ahead. The response was equivocal. A memo from Mr Barry of the DPP's office, dated 30 June 1965, stated that

to establish a precedent, a case of this kind must be prosecuted in an exemplary way, so that the fines – if we were successful, would be so serious as the defence to require a case to be stated to the Divisional Court [which] alone would be quotable, and would enable the Lord Chamberlain to bring its ruling to the notice of all Theatre Clubs and Managers of Theatres.

Concerned at the situation, Cobbold went to meet the Director of Public Prosecutions himself on 9 July 1965 and recorded the proceedings in a memorandum three days later:

> I explained that we felt in something of a dilemma, felt the 'club' arrangement was a subterfuge, but had no desire to wage war on 'theatre clubs', which, like my predecessors, I consider a valuable contribution to the Theatre if properly managed. Nor had we any desire to appear to be 'taking it out' of the Royal Court out of spite.

Cobbold wanted the DPP to issue 'some form of warning that would put people on notice that any further slide away from genuine theatre clubs was risky and would avoid the dangerous precedent of allowing this performance to go entirely unchallenged'. The DPP, however, felt that this was 'difficult . . . It was of course his responsibility to decide whether to act and what action to take; the Lord Chamberlain was only concerned to report the circumstances . . . He said that it would not be his intention to initiate proceedings unless, as a result of enquiries, he felt reasonably certain that the Courts would uphold his view.'[65]

Johnston had tried to warn off the ESC by writing to the Royal Court on 2 July 1965 about the dangers of turning themselves into a club, but to no avail. The play opened – to great fanfare – in August 1965 and the impotence of the Lord Chamberlain had been exposed for all to see. In many ways, it was the beginning of the end. 'Spying' visits were made, including one on 11 August by the comptroller, who reported that the play was

> well written, well acted, cleverly constructed and produced with great skill . . . it is only the Ball Scene and the dialogue throughout that Scene that is really unpleasant . . . I do not think that the tolerance of homosexuality in this country has yet reached the point where this Play, in its present form, is suitable for public performance.[66]

But they had failed to act and this would only encourage their detractors.

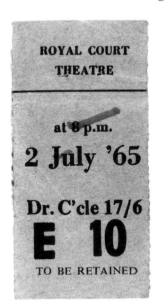

A ticket for *A Patriot for Me*, used by a member of the Lord Chamberlain's Office for an *incognito* visit to the play, July 1965.

ROYAL COURT THEATRE

at 8 p.m.

2 July '65

Dr. C'cle 17/6

E 10

TO BE RETAINED

Saved

If *A Patriot for Me* was the slippery slope for censorship, *Saved* was the nadir. Cobbold had approached the home secretary, Sir Frank Soskice, in February 1965 to inform him of his doubts that censorship could continue much longer, but it was not an issue to which the recently elected Labour government wished to devote much time. With a small majority, it chose to deal with uncontentious issues. The Lord Chamberlain was left to soldier on, and Cobbold's prescience was confirmed when the successor to George Devine at the Royal Court, William Gaskill, emboldened by the success of *A Patriot for Me*, submitted Edward Bond's *Saved* for consideration. All of Heriot's frustration at the changing world and the insubordinate ESC spilled over into his report.

Title:	*Saved*
No. of Scenes or Acts:	Thirteen Scenes
Place of Production:	Royal Court Theatre, London
Date of Production:	October, 1965
Author:	Edward Bond
Submitted by:	

LORD CHAMBERLAIN'S OFFICE,

ST JAMES'S PALACE, S.W.1

READER'S REPORT

30.6.65

A revolting amateur play by one of these dramatists who write as it comes to them out of a heightened image of their experience. It is about a bunch of brainless, ape-like yobs with so little individuality that it is difficult to distinguish between them. They speak a kind of stylised Cockney but behave in an unreal way, not because what they do is false, but that their motivation is not sufficiently indicated.

Pam is a brainless slut of twenty-three living with her sluttish parents who have not spoken to each other for years. Neither of them cares what Pam does, so that she naturally sleeps with whoever she can pick up, though she is 'going steady' with Fred. She picks up and sleeps with Len, who, as far as his moronic intellect goes, is a romantic with vague dreams of marriage and settling down. She has a child, Fred's, and neglects it, so that it cries day and night. Neither she nor her parents pay any attention. Fred has given her up, but she drags after him, whining and nagging. Eventually, later at night in a park, she finds him with The Gang and after an exchange, flounces off, leaving the pram with the baby in it. The gang first kick the pram, pull the baby's hair, punch it, and finally stone it to death and go off, leaving lighted matches in the pram.

Fred is the only one to be charged but even he seems to get off with a short prison-sentence and comes out absolutely unchanged. No one ever expresses a word of regret or a word of criticism. They are all moral imbeciles. Pam still hankers after Fred, but he has been sleeping with her mother while Len watched through the floor-boards. Nobody seems to mind much except Pam's father who has an hysterical outburst which does nobody any good. Pam does mention that life is pretty grim but nobody does anything about it. Len half-heartedly begins to pack but in the end remains in the house as one of the family. The last scene is mostly a mime in which Len mends a chair (as a sort of symbol of domesticity) while Pam and her parents behave as they have always behaved, untidy, feckless, quarrelsome and brutishly stupid.

The writing is vile and the language and conception worse. Whether this could ever be considered a work of art is a matter of opinion; but it does seem that the taste of Messrs. Devine and Richardson has gone rancid – though with all the public money at their disposal, I don't suppose anybody cares.

p .3   Alter 'arse'

p. 4   Warn about position on the couch

p. 5   Cut the reference to waning virility and alter 'Chriss' and warn that Pam must not be unbuttoned too far

p. 6/7   Cut from 'Ow many blokes . . .' to '. . . over sixty' and cut the two jokes about the woman with three tits

p. 8   Cut 'Oo, yer got a lovely soft centre. First time I seen choclit round it!'

p. 9   Pam must not undo Len's belt

p. 19   Cut 'As 'e got 'is rudder stuck?'

p. 20   Cut 'Oo's bin' 'aving a bash on me duckboards?' and cut 'Bashin's extra' and cut 'a bit of a grind'

p. 21   Alter 'bugger'

p. 24   Alter 'bollocks'

p. 26   Cut from 'Sn 'er 'ol' dad . . .' to 'Twisted yer what?'

p. 27   Cut 'She's still got the regulation holes' and cut 'What yer got at the top of yer legs?' and cut from 'Rodger the lodger' on this page

p. 28   to 'An' polished 'is bell' on the next.

p. 40   Alter 'bugger all' and 'for Chrisssake'

p. 41   Alter 'Thank Chriss'

p. 46   Alter 'Crap' and 'sod'

p. 49   Alter 'tight arse' and cut from 'Skip?' to '. . . get that any time'

p. 50   Cut from 'Like the fish that got away' to 'Thass why she's sick'

p. 51   Alter 'Chriss' (twice)

p. 53   Alter 'Cobblers'

p. 58   Alter 'Chriss' (twice)

p. 59   Alter 'Chriss' and 'bin through you' and 'piss off'

p. 60   Alter 'get stuffed'

p. 61   Cut 'Buggered up. Like your arse'

p. 62   Alter 'piss off' and cut 'It'll crap itself t'death'

p. 63   Cut from 'Thought they was pink' to '. . . take after its dad' and warn that there must be no indecent business with the balloon.

Pages 64 to 72   cover the torture and death of the baby

p. 66   Alter 'sod' and cut 'Less case its ol' crutch' and cut the throwing of the napkin in the air

p. 67   Cut from 'gob its crutch' to 'Got it' and warn that there must not be spitting at the baby

p. 68   Cut 'Ere, can I piss on it? Gungy bastard'

p. 69   Cut from 'look! Ugh!' to 'in its eyes' and warn that there must be no business of rubbing the baby's face in its own excrement

p. 70   Alter 'Chriss'

p. 71   Alter 'sod'

p. 72   Alter 'Chriss' and 'sod'

p. 74   Alter 'bugger all'

p. 76   Alter 'Chriss'

p. 82   Alter 'Chriss'

p. 84   Alter 'Chriss'

p. 88   Alter 'thank Chriss'

p. 95   Alter 'bugger' and 'bugger it'

p. 96/98   A scene where Len mends the top of Mary's stocking while she is wearing it. I think this is gratuitously salacious and the scene should come out.

p. 101   Alter 'shag' and 'sod'

p. 107   Cut from 'an I 'as a little slash in 'is tea' to '. . . sugar' (to slash is to urinate)

p. 108   Cut 'We ain' got a crawl up yer arse'

p. 109   Cut the verse about the goalkeeper's daughter and cut 'An try a remember whass up your legs'

p. 110   Cut 'Yer'e as tight as a flea's arse-hole'

p. 111   Cut 'Did yer piss in it?'

p. 113   Alter 'Chriss knows'

p. 117   Alter 'chriss'

p. 125   Cut from 'I juss give 'er a 'and' to '. . . she was late'

p. 127   Cut 'I gad 'er squealing like a pig'

Otherwise reluctantly

RECOMMENDED FOR LICENCE

C. D. Heriot

Following this report, the script was passed like a hot potato from Johnston to Penn to Nugent – the ex-comptroller, called in to advise – and then on to Cobbold. Gaskill met Johnston to inform him that, should a licence for the uncut script be refused (as he surely knew it would be), a club performance was likely. On 6 October 1965 Cobbold asked the DPP whether he would act to uphold the office of the censor, and, while a reply was being formulated, the assistant secretary, Ronald Hill, was sent along to the Royal Court where the play had opened on 3 November 1965 to produce a detailed spy's report. It is one of the most interesting document's in the post-war papers (see Plate 24).

Crisis point had now been reached. On 22 November 1965 Cobbold went to visit the home secretary again to tell him that should they fail to prosecute the ESC for a second time it 'was impossible for him to carry out his duties as theatre censor under the Theatres Act 1843'.[67] The home secretary responded by saying that he was considering setting up an enquiry into the licensing of plays and

Cobbold replied by stating that the enquiry should cover television and film as well.

Shortly after this meeting, a policeman was despatched to a performance and on 6 December 1965 the Attorney General informed the Lord Chamberlain that 'proceedings should be initiated in this case'. On 13 January 1966 a summons was issued against Gaskill, Alfred Esdaile and the ESC for contravening the 1843 Theatres Act, and between 14 February and 1 April 1966 three hearings were held before the magistrate, Leo Gradwell, at Bow Street Magistrates Court, at which star defence witnesses, including Laurence Olivier, appeared on behalf of the ESC.

The defendants were eventually found guilty and discharged for twelve months, with the ESC fined fifty guineas. It was a pyrrhic victory for the Lord Chamberlain, however, since Gradwell had made clear his dissatisfaction with the law – 'I am tied to the rock of the law waiting for some Perseus to rescue me'[68] – and he had crucially failed to rule whether the performance of *Saved* was public or private, denying the setting of a precedent with which the Lord Chamberlain could frighten other errant companies. Norman Skelhorn pointed this out to Cobbold on 3 May 1966, and the Lord Chamberlain conceded that this was the case, but took some comfort in the forthcoming Joint Select Committee that would be investigating censorship.

The Joint Select Committee of 1967

On 17 February 1966, three days after the first magistrate's hearing against the ESC, a debate took place in the House of Lords on the censorship of theatre. Several weighty contributions were made. Lord Annan moved the setting up of a Joint Select Committee to review censorship; Lord Scarborough, the former Lord Chamberlain, claimed that his aim had always been to keep censorship not too far away from the 'centre of public opinion' and favoured the need for censorship, but not by the Lord Chamberlain; Lord Dilhorne wanted a Royal Commission; Lord Goodman, Arts Council Chair, thought that censorship was a bad idea but that the Lord Chamberlain had discharged his duties well; and Cobbold stated that he was in favour of the creation of a Select Committee investigation to provide some clarity. The idea of a Joint Select Committee was enthusiastically received and, once the general election was out of the way and the Labour government re-elected, the Committee met for the first time on 26 July 1966.

Whilst the possibility of an investigation was being discussed, the Lord Chamberlain still needed to discharge his duties. At the beginning of 1966, he lifted the absolute ban on the deity appearing on stage in post-1843 plays following consideration of the following memo by Peter Adamson, with assistance from Johnston and Hill:

Simple Gologtha
The Jesus Revolution
A Man Dies
The Boy Who Carved Birds

(Christ as a Travelling Salesman)
Green Pastures

1. We have only one blanket prohibition today, and that is a refusal to allow the impersonation of Christ or the Deity on the Stage.
2. An uncritical prohibition of this sort is difficult to justify, since it affects all plays reverent or irreverent; and it is in fact a negation of the Lord Chamberlain's general rule of treating each play on its merits.
3. The rule is made additionally difficult to understand by reason of the fact that the Lord Chamberlain does not use powers he possesses to forbid the acting of miracle, mystery and morality plays written before 1843.
4. The reason for the general prohibition so far as I know are that:
    (a) Christ is a supernatural being and any impersonation by a human person is inadequate in greater or lesser degree.
    (b) The personal human characteristics attributed to Christ will vary with the beliefs of the author; they will not necessarily be in accord with Scriptures.
        They may thus greatly disturb beliefs, and may not in principle benefit the cause of religion. Originating in a variety of motives the accumulation of such plays will divert further and further from the Scriptural sources to which authors are largely now confined.
    (c) Where the plays are a source of profit, there is the likelihood of other than religious motives being involved, and a greater possibility of distortion to meet 'popular' requirements. The Christian Religion is after all supposed to be a truth established on revealed facts, and not a subject for fiction.
    (d) In the Commercial Theatre it is quite possible for actors of blemished life to be cast for the role of Christ, again to the distress of the religious. (One actor in the past for instance was prosecuted for living on the immoral earnings of a woman and although he was acquitted, this illustrates the point.)
5. The Medieval Miracle and Mystery plays are folk art of a religiously unsophisticated era, and the touchingly childlike quality of the impersonations of Christ therein convey, in more complicated times, as no currently written play could, the expression of simple faith that is the essence of Christian belief. The essential purity of origin of these plays can overcome even commercial production.

Lord Chamberlains have in the past appreciated these facts by:

6. Accepting that a religious play performed with full clerical supervision in a consecrated building must be regarded as part of the worship therein, and acceptable to a congregation gathered together under the shadow of religion.
7. By assuming that those who write plays about Christ do so from a desire to promote the cause of their religion and not for personal gain. Since the law enables the Lord Chamberlain to ignore performances given not 'for hire', he is

happy to be able to recommend this legal remedy to this class, which if its motives are disinterested is generally pleased to produce on the stated terms.

8. Where Miracle, Mystery or Morality plays are concerned he takes no action provided they are produced in their original dialogue and setting. The Theatres Act enables this dispensation to be made as regards plays written before 1843. He would, however, regard these plays as having lost their immunity from causing offence if they were brought up to date, and he would apply his prohibition.

9. Where plays are produced in a commercial setting he feels that in greater or lesser degree they will be affected by commercial attitudes, and he has to have regard not to the present, but to the fact that the quest for commercial advantage will lead little by little to greater innovation which cannot be based entirely on the disinterested desire to expound the Scriptures which alone ought to actuate the religious playwright.

10. These viewpoints have been put to the leaders of religious bodies from time to time, and although not always endorsed in entirety have generally been agreed to be reasonable and in the best interest of the community.

The Readers also continued to make their recommendations, with significant ones involving *Soldiers*, which the 'Churchill family must agree [to] . . . before any licence is granted';[69] Joe Orton's *What the Butler Saw* – 'best described as a black farce and . . . not unfunny, dealing as it does, with the subject of just how mad are the psychiatrists; but, being Joe Orton, it has, of course, to deviate into tasteless indecencies. . . . [All references to Winston Churchill's 'private parts . . . must come out'];[70] and *Landscape* by Harold Pinter, who still failed to impress Heriot: 'The nearer to Beckett, the more portentous Pinter gets . . . Since there is very little shape, the thing just stops – rather like a contemporary serial musical composition. And, of course, there have to be the ornamental indecencies . . . [with seven small cuts] Licence recommended.'[71]

In September 1966 it looked as if the Lord Chamberlain was going to become embroiled in a controversy with another subsidized company, when Heriot reported on *US*, submitted by the Royal Shakespeare Company. It was, in his view, 'a piece of hysterically subjective anti-Vietnam War propaganda . . . The attitude to America seems to me to be dangerous and insulting to an ally; and since the war in Vietnam is, so to speak, <u>sub judice</u> (would we have permitted a play about the Suez crisis during the crisis?), the piece is not recommended for licence.'[72] On 30 September, Cobbold met the director, Peter Brook, together with the artistic director of the RSC, Peter Hall, and the chairman, Fordham Flower, and told them he was mindful to see cuts imposed, with references to President Johnson and television screens showing interviews with American personalities requiring deletion. However, out of expediency, he decided not to push the matter, explaining in a memo of 11 October that – 'I thought for a time of refusing a licence, but the trouble is that this will cause an enormous hullabaloo and may well do more harm than good'. With the Joint Select Committee investigating his remit, it was important not to upset the applecart at such a sensitive moment.

The Joint Committee on the Censorship of the Theatre was made up of the following mixture of Lords and MPs: the Earl of Scarborough (Con.), the Earl of Kilmuir (Con.), Viscount Norwich (Lab.), Lord Tweedsmuir (Con.), Baroness Gaitskell (Lab.), Lord Lloyd of Hampstead (Lab.), Lord Annan (Ind.), Lord Goodman (Ind.), Andrew Faulds (Lab.), Michael Foot (Lab.), Norman St John-Stevas (Con.), George Strauss, Chairman (Lab.), and William Wilson (Lab.). It held sixteen meetings between July 1966 and June 1967 and called the following nine witnesses: the Lord Chamberlain, Sir Dingle Foot (Solicitor General), John Mortimer (Council of the League of Dramatists), John Osborne, Benn Levy, Peter Hall (Royal Shakespeare Company), Kenneth Tynan (National Theatre), Emile Littler (President, Society of West End Theatre Managers) and Peter Saunders.

The committee established that 'no action was taken to implement the recommendations of the 1909 committee, although successive holders of the office of Lord Chamberlain have, as a matter of practice, made use of the criteria recommended by it as a guidance in the licensing of plays'[73] and that the question they had been asked to pronounce on was 'a question of freedom'.[74] They were faced with essentially four choices – 'a continuation of the present system, the transfer of the present powers of the Lord Chamberlain to another pre-censorship body, with or without a right of appeal, the establishment of some form of voluntary pre-censorship, or the complete abolition of pre-censorship'[75] – and discovered that only the Society of West End Managers were in favour of the present system. They believed that 'the office of the Lord Chamberlain for censoring stage plays works satisfactorily and should be continued' and that 'The Lord Chamberlain to us has been a sort of father confessor . . . We would miss him very much' (Emile Littler). Several reasons were offered by the Society for this view. The Lord Chamberlain by dint of his office possesses 'unique authority which no other censorship body could have'; the licence protects theatre managers; recent Lords Chamberlain had been 'increasingly tolerant'; and 'any change might lead to greater rigidity and restriction'.[76]

This was not a view held by the abolitionist Kenneth Tynan. For him, censorship was simply a lot of hysteria about nothing. 'I really would not take terribly seriously any playwright who wanted to compose a play about the Royal Family', he argued, and 'the so-called orgy of violence in the Royal Court play *Saved* which was widely publicised as an example of sensationalism, did not fill the theatre. There seemed to be no mad rush of sadists into Sloane Square.'[77] Cobbold then added further fuel to the fire with his surprising admission that he did 'at times exercise a political censorship'[78]

The collective view of the investigators was emphatic. 'The Committee are convinced that the case for removing the powers of the Lord Chamberlain over stage plays is compelling and outweighs the administrative convenience of the present arrangements. Accordingly they recommend that these powers should be abolished as soon as possible.'[79] No one man 'should possess unqualified dictatorship over what may or may not be presented in our theatres'[80] and 'a voluntary system would be the worst of both worlds'.[81]

[Consequently, the]Committee are convinced that pre-censorship and licensing of plays should cease. The ending of pre-censorship in its present form will not necessarily mean that henceforth there will be a complete free for all. Censorship in the widest sense of the word will inevitably continue and by various means control will be exercised over what appears on the stage. Managements will continue to refuse to put on plays whenever they think fit. Theatre critics will continue to describe plays as they wish, the public will be free to refuse to attend plays or to walk out if they do not like them. Finally the Courts will have the task of ensuring that those responsible for presenting plays which transgress the law of the land will receive appropriate punishment.[82]

The need for action was urgent – 'The Committee are convinced that the changes they recommend are just and overdue'[83] – but this was dependent on the support of the government, which was initially not forthcoming. The prime minister, Harold Wilson, was concerned that the abolition of stage censorship would permit unmitigated attacks on living persons, something he was nervous about given the submission of a satirical work, *Mrs Wilson's Diary*, in April 1967 for intended production at the Theatre Royal, Stratford East. Therefore, in November 1967, the government dropped its support for new legislation, but George Strauss, the chairman of the Joint Committee and a Labour MP since 1929, took up the cause with a Private Members bill. On 9 February 1968 the government had a further change of heart and decided to support the bill once more, and on 23 February it received its second reading. During its passage through the Commons, the Lord Chamberlain persistently lobbied behind the scenes for a clause to be inserted which would give the royal family, the Archbishop of Canterbury and the Pope the right to sue for slander, as well as preventing reference to living persons 'in a way calculated to offend public feeling', but to no avail. On 19 July the bill was given its third reading and on 26 July 1968 the third Theatres Act (1968) was given royal assent, to come into force two months later on 26 September.

The last gasp

The fag end of the Lord Chamberlain's reign over the British stage was dominated by futile battles against the ESC and the weary acceptance of a production designed to mark the abolition of censorship. Edward Bond's *Early Morning* contravened just about every remaining taboo that the censorship still sought to preclude. T. B. Harward's report made this clear:

> . . . the defamatory treatment of the chief characters (principally royalty) apart, the play appears to this Reader to be the product of a diseased imagination; cannibalism and lesbianism may be legitimate themes for dramatisation, but not in this context. It is not recommended for licence.[84]

Nevertheless, two Sunday club performances (on 31 March and 7 April 1968) took place at the Royal Court. Incredibly, the DPP contemplated prosecution at the urging of Cobbold, but with the Theatres Act nearing royal assent, this was not pursued.

The American musical *Hair* contained much nudity and language formerly not countenanced by the readers, but by the time the first report was written in May 1968, which recommended a licence with cuts,[85] all concerned with censorship knew that the game was up. A new management required a second report, and the indefatigable Heriot pronounced it 'a totally reprehensible affair. Satire is one thing, but the "knocking" at every convention and the tacit glorification of drugs and general intransigence inclines me to agree with Mr Hill that, in effect, this piece is dangerously permissive.'[86] A third report, again by Heriot, commented on the amendments made. 'A curiously half-hearted attempt to vet the script,' Heriot concluded. 'All the drug references seem to be removed and all the 'f . . . s' but there are still a lot of cuts to be made', yet it was nevertheless 'Recommended for licence'.[87]

Johnston wrote to John Barber of James Verner Ltd four days after royal assent had been granted to the bill that would change his job description to inform him of the good news, and to signal the momentous ending of an era. 'Thank you for your letter of July 29th, in which you inform me that the first performance of *Hair* will take place in the Shaftesbury Theatre on Thursday, September 26th. In accordance with the Theatres Act 1968, which has now received the Royal Assent, new plays for production on or after September 26th, 1968, do not require to be allowed by the Lord Chamberlain.'[88]

Looking back and looking forward: the Reading amendment

The report of the Joint Select Committee produced various statistics relating to stage censorship since 1945 (see Tables 1 and 2). Censoring plays had been a vast exercise for an office whose main responsibilities had had nothing to do with the theatre. One unwittingly beneficial aspect of censorship, however, had been the collection of scripts submitted for licence to form a unique record of theatre history. As the possibility of the Theatres Act 1968 began to loom in 1967, Jack Reading, secretary of the Society for Theatre Research (STR), realized that the welcome abolition of censorship would have the unwelcome consequence of ceasing this systematic collection of scripts for the nation. He therefore wrote to Lord Cobbold in September 1967 suggesting that a new provision be put in the legislation which placed the responsibility on theatre managements 'to <u>deposit for record</u> the texts of all material to be placed on stage in place of <u>submitting for licence</u>'.[89] He observed that the receiving body should be the British Museum, thereby resurrecting a clause that the STR had suggested be included in the unsuccessful Censorship of Plays (Repeal) Bill of 1949.

John Johnston replied that Cobbold was 'much in sympathy with your desire to continue in some way the preservation of manuscripts of new stage plays',[90] but felt that this was now a matter for the Home Office. Their response – not delivered until February 1968 – was negative, however. 'We have looked very carefully at the

TABLE I. *Statistics relating to stage plays submitted for the LC's approval 1945–65*

Year	Submitted	Allowed	Banned
1945	765	759	6
1946	966	960	6
1947	1034	1030	4
1948	1190	1185	5
1949	1132	1131	1
1950	1314	1305	9
1951	1286	1278	8
1952	1310	1308	2
1953	1242	1233	9
1954	1215	1210	5
1955	1140	1135	5
1956	1085	1083	2
1957	952	946	6
1958	975	972	3
1959	927	927	0
1960	877	877	0
1961	858	855	3
1962	862	861	1
1963	785	783	2
1964	740	740	0
1965	804	802	2

Source: *Report from the Joint Committee 1967*, p. 186.

proposals that you have put forward', Miss G. M. B. Owen replied, 'and indeed sympathise with your interest in preserving records of theatrical productions. But in our view it is very doubtful if this could properly be made a matter for statutory controls.'[91] The gist of their objection was the difficulty of enforcement and the principle of compelling playwrights to submit unpublished material.

Reading, an assiduous correspondent and indefatigable campaigner, was undeterred, but time was running out. He turned his attentions to the author of the bill, George Strauss, and the director of the British Museum, Sir Frank Francis. Strauss was not very hopeful, fearing in a letter at the end of February that it was too late to amend his bill, but promising to make enquiries.[92] By April, however, his position had hardened, and he told Reading that the difficulties were 'insuperable'. Any amendment at this stage would be ruled out of order and there would be 'a number of technical difficulties such as who should be responsible for sending a copy of the script to the British Museum'.[93] Sir Frank Francis had similar fears. His first response to Reading's call to support had been unambiguous, 'It would be a real loss for posterity if the records of dramatic writing were to be completely lost', and he pledged to give 'any assistance which lies in my power'.[94] Having discussed the

TABLE 2. *Details of plays inspected after licensing*

Year	Warning given after inspection	Prosecutions as a result of inspection	No action required	Total no. inspected
1945	No record	5	No record	23
1946	No record	7	No record	32
1947	5	2	14	21
1948	7	4	19	30
1949	9	2	22	33
1950	13	3	20	35
1951	5	6	22	33
1952	8	2	10	20
1953	14	0	14	28
1954	8	0	14	22
1955	7	0	11	18
1956	11	0	7	18
1957	1	1	6	8
1958	5	0	4	9
1959	10	0	1	11
1960	2	0	3	5
1961	7	0	0	7
1962	3	0	2	5
1963	4	0	5	9
1964	4	0	7	11
1965	2	1	6	9
1966	0	1	0	0

Source: *Report from the Joint Committee 1967*, p. 187.

practicalities of the issue with the keeper of manuscripts at the British Museum, however, he became less sanguine. 'He tells me that such scripts are at present coming into the Lord Chamberlain's Office at the rate of 800 a year or more – an intake which our Manuscripts Department would find very difficult to cope with'.[95]

That would have been it, were it not for a chance meeting with a member of the House of Lords at a dinner party in April, Lord Farringdon, with whom Reading discussed the progress of the Theatres Bill. Farringdon showed himself to be interested, and hinted that he might be willing to move an amendment at the committee stage. Although struck down by flu, Reading, recognizing this as a last opportunity, dragged himself to his typewriter and drew up a possible amendment for the noble lord to consider. Amazingly, Farringdon assented to the wording and he introduced the potential clause on 8 July. George Strauss was incandescent when he found out, believing that the new addition might have a fatal effect on the bill, and this may have influenced the government's initial negative reaction. Lord Stonham, the minister of state at the Home Office, replied to Farringdon that a voluntary system – hopefully administered by the STR! – would be far preferable to a compulsory one, and the government could not, therefore, accept the amendment. However, miraculously and completely unexpectedly, the government returned on 19 July having had a change of mind and, after much debate, in which Lord Goodman, the chairman of the Arts Council, observed that 'if this is legislated it will be the most beneficial piece of bad legislation which has been enacted for centuries', the amendment was approved. Clause 1398, section 11 of the Theatres Act 1968 – the Reading amendment – therefore reads as follows:

> Where . . . there is given in Great Britain a public performance of a new play, being a performance based on a script, a copy of the actual script on which that performance was based shall be delivered to the trustees of the British Museum free of charge within the period of one month beginning with the date of the performance; and the Trustees shall give a written receipt for every script delivered to them pursuant to this section.

In the event of non-compliance, 'any person who presented that performance shall be liable on summary conviction of a fine not exceeding £5'.[96]

From September 1968 scripts began to trickle into the British Museum. In the first year up to August 1969 only fifteen scripts were submitted,[97] and there would be trickles and floods into the British Musuem, and, later, the British Library for the next thirty-five years. For the readers, this represented a sad loss of financial support. 'This will make a big hole in my annual income', the senior examiner, 63-year-old Charles Heriot complained to the newspapers. 'Each of us got two guineas a play. I have been reading them for 21 years now – and it has been my sole job. Getting through them and making notes on my share of the scripts – about 500 a year – is hard work and takes time. Unfortunately as we are only paid a fee instead of a salary, we don't qualify for a pension.'[98]

By 2003 a substantial collection was held in the Department of Manuscripts at the British Library, St Pancras, but although efforts were made by the curators to ensure a comprehensive collection the eroding of the value of the five-pound fine meant that gaps were appearing. This author, therefore, applied to the Arts and Humanities Research Board for a grant to undertake major research development of the British Library theatre archives and was awarded a research grant in June 2003 to undertake a five-year project to – amongst other things – hunt for all the missing scripts since 1968 and to record interviews with as many people as possible associated with the post-1945 theatre collections.

The first interviewee was Jack Reading in July 2003,[99] since his amendment had meant that the most beneficial – and perhaps only positive – legacy of theatre censorship was preserved. On 4 December 2003, at a lecture he and I delivered at the Arts Workers' Guild to the Society of Theatre Research, the 86-year-old Reading fittingly presented the file that contained the correspondence relating to the Reading Amendment to the British Library to reside with the collection of scripts that he had fought so magnificently to create.

Appendix: Licenses refused – 1945–1968[100]

Year	Play	Author	Reader	Reason
1945	*First Thing*		Game	Salacity – 'black-out sketch . . . implying an overindulgence of sexual intercourse'
1945	*Outrageous Fortune*	Franken	Game	Homosexual character – 'pervert theme'
1945	*The Querulous Queens*	Pemberton	Game	Queen Victoria appears in 'non-serious play'
1945	*Surface*	Ambler	Game	Homosexual characters – 'pansies'
1946	*Patricia English*	Pierson	Game	Prostitution – a licence would be granted if the heroine's seven inherited brothels became nightclubs
1946	*God's Punishment*	Ash	Game	Prostitution – 'brothels and the White Slave trade' – and offence to Jews
1946	*Should a Doctor Tell?*	Grade	Game	Salacity – sketch about a man described as suffering from 'too much sexual exercise'
1946	*Oscar Wilde*	Stokes and Stokes	Game	Homosexuality – 'perverts and perversion'
1946	*Getting a Flat*	Norton	Game	Verbal crudity – 'vulgar' misunderstanding over the words 'lavatory and 'laboratory'
1947	*A Ha'porth of Tar*	Jones	Heriot	Salacity, immorality – 'subversion of the Christian attitude to immorality'
1947	*Hinkemann*	Toller, tr. Mendel	Game	Coarseness, embarrassing theme (impotence)
1948	*If He Came*	Raynor	Dearmer	Representation of the deity – second coming of Christ
1948	*Jonathan*	Griffiths	Jones	Salacity – 'silliest and smuttiest Welsh play I have ever read'
1948	*A Pin to See the Peepshow*	Tennyson, Jesse and Harwood	Heriot	Living persons rule – refers to Thompson/Bywaters case
1949	*Modernity*	Morris	Heriot	Incestuous theme of last act – 'a play written from a depraved imagination'

Year	Play	Author	Reader	Reason
1950	*The Baker's Daughter*	Walsh and Walsh	Heriot	Living persons – story of Seretse Khame's marriage
1950	*Birthday Bouquet*	Ginsbury and Maschwitz	Heriot	Queen Victoria
1950	*Hiatus*	McKay	Game	Homosexuality – 'John is an invert'
1950	*House of Shame*	Mabelle	Game	Vice trade
1950	*The House of the Red Lamp*	Mabelle	Game	Vice trade – 'nasty play'
1950	*The Naked Lady*	St John	Heriot	Vice trade – 'sex and sadism'
1950	*Sex for Sale*	Kaplan	Game	Vice trade – 'loathsome'
1950	*Street Girl*	Harris	Heriot	Vice trade – 'pornography . . . salacious and disgusting'
1951	*Ceremony of Innocence*	Huganir	Game	Possibly 'offensive to Christians'
1951	*The Flamingo Screams*	'Chefils' (H. J. Cookson)	Heriot	Vice trade – 'smelly little oeuvre'
1951	*The Happy Time*	Taylor	Heriot	Salacity
1951	*The Lonely Heart*	Warren	Heriot	Lesbianism
1951	*My Good Brown*	Kemp	Heriot	Queen Victoria
1951	*The Ostrich Eggs*	Roussin, trans. Lowe	Heriot	Homosexuality
1951	*Third Person*	Rosenthal	Heriot	Homosexuality
1952	*The Maids*	Genet, trans. Frechtman	St V. Troubridge	Sadism, lesbians – 'definite indication of lesbianism'
1952	*Two Loves I Have*	Baker and Baker	Dearmer	Lesbianism
1952	*White Terror*	Squires	St V. Troubridge	Lesbianism – 'a most definite Lesbian thread'
1953	*Fig Leaf*	Bernard-Kuc, trans. Grew and Ashmore	Heriot	Promiscuity – 'concerned with the impact of the Kinsey report'

179

Year	Play	Author	Reader	Reason
1953	*The House of Death*	Griffith	Heriot	'cash-in on the Christie murders . . . poisonous and degenerate'
1953	*Les Oeufs de l'Autriche*	Roussin	Heriot	Homosexuality
1953	*Old Ladies Meet*		Dearmer	Queen Victoria
1953	*The Rosenberg Story*	Hargreaves	Heriot	Sub-judice
1953	*Strangers in the Land*	Brand	St V. Troubridge	Political objections – deals with Malaya
1954	*The King of Life*	Renaud and de Saix, trans. Adam	Heriot	Homosexuality – Oscar Wilde
1954	*The Trial of Oscar Wilde*	Rostand, trans. Williamson	Heriot	Oscar Wilde – 'General atmosphere of sodomy'
1954	*The Wicked and the Weak*	Chappell	St V. Troubridge	Homosexuality – 'This will not do at all!'
1955	*The Brothel*	Arundel	Heriot	Prostitution – 'pornographic'
1955	*The Golden Mask*	Comstock	St V. Troubridge	Concerned 'entirely with homosexuality'
1955	*Zoe*	Marsan, trans, Frank	St V. Troubridge	Promiscuity – 'sexual perversity'
1956	*The Life of Christ*	Branigan	Dearmer	Representation of deity
1957	*Foolish Attachment*	Wood	St V. Troubridge	Lesbianism
1957	*No Retreat*	Beckwith	Heriot	Homosexuality – 'arguments might encourage rather than deter young persons'
1957	*The Road to Emmaus*	Forsyth	Dearmer	Portrayal of Christ
1957	*Sex*	Saltoun	Heriot	'Pure pornography . . . nauseating mixture of sex, sadism, coprology and sentiment'
1961	*The Boy Who Carved Birds*	Etheridge	Heriot	Representation of deity

Year	Play	Author	Reader	Reason
1961	*Knights of Song*	Allvine	St V. Troubridge	Queen Victoria, Edward VII
1963	*Clap Hands, Here Comes Charlie*	Barnes	Heriot	Bad language and 'scatological'
1963	*The Wayward Stork*	Tugend	Heriot	Promiscuity and artificial insemination
1964	*A Patriot for Me*	Osborne	Heriot	Homosexuality
1965	*Saved*	Bond	Heriot	Language, violence
1965	*Simple Golgotha*	Adamson	Heriot	Representation of Christ
1966	*Leda Had a Little Swan*	Gascoigne	Heriot	'Bestiality'
1966	*Macbird!*	Garson	Heriot	Living person – satire on career of President Johnson
1967	*The Inheritance of the Just*	Watson	Heriot	Portrayal of deity
1967	*White Man, Black Man, Yellow Man, Chief*	Hagopian	Heriot	Sadism, blasphemy, language, race – banned 'for integrational reasons'
1968	*The Car Cemetery*	Arrabel, trans. Wright	Heriot	Blasphemy
1968	*Early Morning*	Bond	Harward	Queen Victoria, lesbianism, cannibalism
1968	*A Fig for Eloquence*	Coppel	Heriot	Salacity – 'one long snigger at the male genitalia'
1968	*Hair*	Ragni and Rado	Harward, Heriot	Nudity, indecent language

NOTES

1 The office of the Lord Chamberlain was not abolished in 1968, simply the duty to censor drama.

2 Reader's report, 14 July 1945. Unless otherwise noted, all archival material is from the Lord Chamberlain's Correspondence Files, Manuscript Room, British Library, London.

3 Place of production stated in correspondence kept in the production file.

4 John Johnston, *The Lord Chamberlain's Blue Pencil*, (London: Hodder and Stoughton, 1990), p. 171.

5　'R.P.M.G.', ' "Oscar Wilde" Revived', 31/8/48, *Daily Telegraph*, 31 August 1948.

6　On 9 September 1948.

7　14 September 1948.

8　25 September 1948.

9　Another disagreement occurred over *House of the Red Lamp*, submitted in 1950 and dealing with 'an innocent young English girl' forced to work in Madame Carmine's brothel. Game recommends a licence in his report because 'it is cheap sensationalism and nothing more' (21 August 1950). Clarendon overruled him, since it was a 'nasty play'. An attempt at revision with a new title, *House of Shame*, failed to change Clarendon's mind on account of its 'brothel theme'.

10　20 May 1947.

11　20 May 1947.

12　28 January 1954.

13　Johnston, *Lord Chamberlain's Blue Pencil*, p. 153.

14　During discussion of the bill in the House of Commons, Herbert observed that 'The Lord Chamberlain is not a horrid ogre. The gentlemen in his department do not simply say, "Out with this line." They sit there and think "How can I help these people?" They are the most kind, considerate, helpful people in the world.' *The Times*, 11 June 1949.

15　25 June 1948.

16　30 June 1948.

17　4 April 1949.

18　William Conway to Tennents, 12 July 1948.

19　6 April 1949.

20　Olivier to Gwatkin, 6 October 1949.

21　11 October 1949.

22　10 February 1951.

23　Handwritten comment on Report, 25 September 1951.

24　5 January 1952.

25　9 January 1952.

26　10 January 1952.

27　I am grateful to Matthew Woodbridge (University of Sheffield, BA in English Literature, 1999) for his research into *Third Person*.

28　1 January 1953.

29　13 January 1953.

30　16 March 1953.

31　Undated handwritten note in the file.

32　17 March 1953.

33　'Versatility', *Observer*, 20 February 1955.

34　'Mixed double', *Observer*, 26 September 1954.

35　24 July 1954.

36　There were, of course, no hard and fast rules, just precedent and whim. That Tynan believed that there *were* rules in existence illustrates the widespread misconception held at the time by many in the theatre profession – unsurprising given the secretive nature of censorship.

37　'In Camera', *Observer*, 7 November 1954.

38　9 September 1954.

39　16 September 1954.

40　28 March 1954.

41 1 March 1956.

42 30 May 1956.

43 21 June 1955.

44 2 May 1956.

45 29 January 1957. Scarborough doubted the play had 'any meaning at all'. The play had already received a club performance at the Arts Theatre in March 1955. This licence was requested by the Oxford Playhouse.

46 16 March 1957.

47 2 November 1955.

48 17 January 1956.

49 'Dodging the ban', *Observer*, 16 September 1956.

50 'The tragic sense', *Observer*, 14 October 1956.

51 'The dismal dilemma', *Observer*, 23 September 1956.

52 'Vice: the storm breaks', *Daily Express*, 5 September 1957.

53 I am deeply indebted to the following web site for the background material to the Wolfenden Report: www.sbu.ac.uk/stafflag/wolfenden.html. This section on the Wolfenden Report first appeared in Dominic Shellard, *Kenneth Tynan: A Life* (New Haven: Yale University Press, 2003), pp. 220–22.

54 5 May 1958.

55 4 January 1961.

56 10 October 1961.

57 17 October 1961.

58 25 October 1961.

59 8 November 1961.

60 19 October 1963.

61 Assistant comptroller to Lord Chamberlain, 23 October 1963.

62 29 October 1963.

63 8 December 1964.

64 7 September 1964.

65 12 July 1965.

66 13 August 1965.

67 22 November 1965.

68 William Gaskill, *A Sense of Direction* (London: Faber, 1988), p. 69.

69 30 August 1967.

70 30 July 1967.

71 15 December 1967.

72 28 September 1966.

73 *Report from the Joint Committee on the Censorship of the Theatre* (London: HMSO, 1967), section vi; see Chapter 2 above, pp. 61–66 for the 1909 enquiry.

74 Ibid., section viii.

75 Ibid., section ix.

76 Ibid.

77 Ibid., p. 80.

78 Ibid., section x.

79 Ibid., p. 23.

80 Ibid., section xii

81 Ibid., section xiv.

82 Ibid., section xv.

83 Ibid., section xix.

84 25 October 1967.

85 18 May 1968.

86 10 June 1968.

87 11 July 1968.

88 30 July 1968.

89 Reading amendment file, British Library, 5 September 1967.

90 Ibid., 12 September 1967.

91 Ibid., 14 February 1968.

92 Ibid., 29 February 1968.

93 Ibid., 8 April 1968.

94 Ibid., 27 February 1968.

95 Ibid., 15 March 1968.

96 *Theatres Act 1968*, in *The Public General Acts 1968* (London: HMSO, 1968), part II.

97 Emile Littler to Society of West End Theatre Managers, 28 September 1969; Reading amendment file.

98 Undated newspaper cutting, ibid.

99 Dominic Shellard, interview with Jack Reading, 7 July 2003.

100 This appendix has been based on a table initially compiled by Kathryn Johnson, Curator of drama at the British Library, the acknowledged curatorial expert on this field.

Bibliography

Manuscripts and archive sources

Daybook, Register of Lord Chamberlain's Plays, vol. 1 1824–1852, ms. 53702 (London: British Library)

Daybook, Register of Lord Chamberlain's Plays, vol. 2 1852–1865, ms. 53703 (London: British Library)

Daybook, Register of Lord Chamberlain's Plays, vol. 3 1866–1873, ms. 53704 (London: British Library)

Daybook, Register of Lord Chamberlain's Plays, vol. 4 1873–1876, ms. 53705 (London: British Library)

Daybook, Register of Lord Chamberlain's Plays, vol. 5 1877–1886, ms. 53706 (London: British Library)

Daybook, Register of Lord Chamberlain's Plays, vol. 6 1887–1897, ms. 53707 (London: British Library)

General Letters (Theatres) (1858–1901) LC 1: 58–752 (London: Public Record Office)

Letters concerning Mary Russell Mitford's *Charles I*, ms. 42873, ff. 402, 405–13 (London: British Library)

The Lord Chamberlain's Collection of Licensed Plays 1900–1968 (London: British Library)

The Lord Chamberlain's Correspondence Files, Manuscript Room, British Library.

The Lord Chamberlain's Daybooks (London: British Library)

Lord Chamberlain's Letter Books (1833–1858), LC 1: 45–51 (London: Public Record Office)

Lord Chamberlain's Office Files to *c.* 1934, transferred from the Royal Archives at Windsor to the British Library, June 2001, not catalogued (London: British Library)

Lord Chamberlain's Office Files *c.* 1934 onwards, Royal Archives, Windsor

Original Letters (1836–1857) LC 1: 19–35 (London: Public Record Office)

Pigott, Edward F. Smyth. Memorandum, 15 March 1883, General Letters (Theatres) for 1890, LC. 1: 546, f. 31, pp. 1–7 (London: Public Record Office)

Lord Chamberlain's plays (British Library)

The Blood Spot; or the Maiden, the miser and the murderer, LCP 52974J, lic. refused 24 May 1858

The Casual Ward; or Workhouse Life, LCP 53048J, lic. 8 February 1866

Eliza Fenning; or the Victim of Circumstance, LCP 52956E, lic. September 1855

Gulliver's Travels; or Harlequin Lilliput, LCP 53081R, lic. December 1869

Harlequin Cock Robin and the Children of the Wood, LCP 53064, lic. 24 December 1866

Harlequin Hop o' My Thumb; or The Sleeping Beauty and the Beast and the Ogre with his seven leagued boots, LCP 53115P, lic. 19 December 1872

Ixion Rewheel'd, LCP 53143N, lic. 20 November 1874

Mathilde and the Mulatto, LCP 53005U, lic. 10 August 1861

Myrrha; en tragedie en cinq actes, LCP 52960D, lic. refused 26 June 1856

Nix the Demon Dwarf; or Harlequin and the seven charmed bullets, LCP 53115O, lic. 20 December 1872

Sleeping Beauty; or Harlequin Peter Wilkins and the Flying Woman of Wonderland, LCP 53143O, lic. 18 December 1874

The Turtle Doves, LCP 53241J, lic. 15 November 1880

The Wrath's Whirlwind; or the Neglected Child, the Vicious Youth and the Degraded Man, LCP 52942U, lic. refused 13 October 1853

Gilbert, W. S., *The Realm of Joy, being a free and easy version of Le Roi Candaule*, LCP 53128E, lic. 1873

——*Rosencrantz and Guildenstern*, LCP 53476B, lic. 30 May 1891

——*Utopia Limited*, LCP 53535B, lic. 29 September 1893

Hodgson, A. H. and Hodgson, A. C., *Doomed*, LCP 53446J, lic. 17 July 1890

[Kenney, James], *Masaniello*, ms. 42895, ff. 100–159, lic. 25 April 1829

Mitford, Mary Russell, *Charles the First*, ms. 42873, vol. 2, ff. 402–99

Muskerry, William, *Lady Godiva; or George and the Dragon and the seven champions of Christendom*, LCP 53443L, lic. 26 December 1889

[Warriner, George A.], *Bob Bretton; the Dead Shot of the Bush*, LCP 53189D, lic. 11 July 1877

Government and parliamentary reports

'An Act for Regulating Theatres', 6 & 7 Vic.c.68, *The Statutes Revised 1836–1844*, vol. 4, 3rd edn (London: HMSO, 1844)

'An Act to Explain and Amend so much of an Act made in the Twelfth Year of the Reign of Queen Anne, intituled, An Act for Reducing the Laws Relating to Rogues, Vagabonds, Sturdy Beggars and Vagrants, into An Act of Parliament; and for the More Effectual Punishing such Rogues, Vagabonds, Sturdy Beggars and Vagrants and Sending them Whither They Ought to be Sent, as Relates to Common Players of Interludes' [The Licensing Act], 10 Geo.II.c.28 (London: HMSO, 1737)

Hansard's Parliamentary Debates, vol. 13, 24 May–3 July 1832 (London: Baldwin & Cradock, 1832)

Hansard's Parliamentary Debates, vol. 16, 1 March–1 April 1833 (London: Baldwin & Cradock, 1833)

Hansard's Parliamentary Debates, vol. 64, 17 June–11 July 1842 (London: Baldwin & Cradock, 1842)

Lord Chesterfield, Speech to the House of Lords, 20 May 1737, in *The Parliamentary* History of England from the Earliest Period to the Year 1803, vol. 10, 1737–1739 (London: T. C. Hansard, 1812). pp. 328–41

Parliamentary Debates (Official Report), 5th ser., vol. 32, House of Commons, 27 November–16 December 1911 (London: HMSO, 1912), col. 582

Parliamentary Debates (Official Report), 5th ser., vol. 51, House of Commons, 31 March 1913–18 April 1913 (London: HMSO, 1913), cols 2036–81

Parliamentary Debates (Official Report), Session 1948–1949, 5th ser., vol. 463, House of Commons, 21 March 1949–14 April 1949 (London: HMSO, 1949), cols 713–95

Parliamentary Debates (Official Report), vol. 64, House of Lords, 4 May 1926–15 July 1926 (London: HMSO, 1926), cols 365–92

Report from the Joint Committee on the Censorship of the Theatre (London: HMSO, 1967)

Report from the Joint Select Committee of the House of Lords and the House of Commons on the Stage Plays (Censorship) together with the Proceedings of the Committee, Minutes and Appendices, British Sessional Papers 8 (London: HMSO, 1909)

Report from the Select Committee on Dramatic Literature with minutes of evidence. Ordered by the House of Commons to be printed 2 August 1832, *Reports from Committees* (London: HMSO), vol. 7, 6 December 1831–16 August 1832

Report from the Select Committee on Theatres and Places of Entertainment, together with the proceedings of the Committee, minutes of evidence, appendix and index, Reports from Committees (London: HMSO), vol. 18, 19 February–28 June 1892

Report from the Select Committee on Theatrical Licenses and Regulations together with the proceedings of the Committee, minutes of evidence and an appendix, Reports from Committees (London: HMSO), vol. 11, 1 February–10 August 1866

Theatres Act 1968, in *The Public General Acts 1968* (London: HMSO, 1968), part II

Newspapers and periodicals

The following have been particularly and frequently valuable sources:

Daily Graphic	*New Statesman*
Daily Mail	*Observer*
The Era	*Referee*
Festival Theatre Review	*Stage*
Imperialist/Vigilante	*Sunday Times*
Morning Post	*The Sketch*
Nation	*The Times*
New Monthly Magazine	

Other sources

Adams, Joseph Quincy (ed.), *The Dramatic Records of Sir Henry Herbert, Master of the Revels 1623–1673* (New Haven: Yale University Press, 1917)

Albright, Evelyn May, *Dramatic Publication in England 1580–1640: a Study of Conditions Affecting Content and Form of Drama* (New York/London: D. C. Heath/Oxford University Press, 1927)

Bagster-Collins, J. F., *George Colman the Younger 1762–1836* (New York: King's Crown Press, 1976)

Barker, Harley Granville, 'The theatre: the next phase', in H. G. Barker, *Offprints of Contributions by Granville-Barker to Various Publications* (London: n.p., 1910)

Brooke, Henry, 'A prefatory dedication to subscribers', in Vincent J. Liesenfeld (ed.), *The Stage and the Licensing Act 1729–1739* (New York/London: Garland, 1981), pp. iii–viii

Brookfield, Charles, 'On plays and playwriting', *National Review* (November 1911), pp. 419–35

Burling, William J., 'A preliminary checklist and finding guide of the correspondence of George Colman Jr', *Bulletin of Bibliography* 54.4 (1997), pp. 339–55

Burt, Richard, *Licensed by Authority: Ben Jonson and the Discourses of Censorship* (Ithaca: Cornell University Press, 1993)

'Chandos, John' [John Lithgow Chandos MacConnell], *To Deprave and Corrupt: Original Studies in the Nature and Definition of Obscenity* (London: Souvenir Press, 1962)

Clare, Janet, 'Censorship and negotiation', in Andrew Hadfield (ed.), *Literature and Censorship in Renaissance England* (Basingstoke: Palgrave, 2001), pp. 17–30

Conolly, L. W., 'The censor's wife at the theatre: the diary of Anna Margaretta Larpent, 1790–1800', *Huntington Library Quarterly* 35.1 (November 1971), pp. 19–28

—— *The Censorship of English Drama 1737–1824* (San Marino, CA: The Huntington Library, 1976)

—— 'Horace Walpole, unofficial play censor', *English Language Notes* 9.1 (September 1971), pp. 42–5

Crean, P. J., 'The Stage Licensing Act of 1737', *Modern Philology* 35 (1937–8), pp. 239–55

Davis, Tracy C., 'The actress in Victorian pornography', *Theatre Journal* 41.3 (October 1989), pp. 294–315

de Jongh, Nicholas, *Not in Front of the Audience: Homosexuality on Stage* (London: Routledge, 1992).

de Jongh, Nicholas, *Politics, Prudery and Perversions: The Censoring of the English Stage 1901–1968* (London: Methuen, 2000)

Deeney, John F., 'Censoring the uncensored: the case of "Children in Uniform"', *New Theatre Quarterly* 16.3 (August 2000), pp. 219–26

Donne, William Bodham, *Essays on the Drama and on Popular Amusements* (London: Tinsley Brothers, 1863)

Dutton, Richard, *Mastering the Revels: the Regulation and Censorship of English Renaissance Drama* (Basingstoke: Macmillan, 1991)

Etienne, Anne, 'Les Coulisses de Lord Chamberlain: la censure théâtrale de 1900 à 1968', Ph.D. dissertation, L'Université d'Orléans, 1999

Findlater, Richard, *Banned!: A Review of Theatrical Censorship in Britain* (London: MacGibbon & Kee, 1967)

Florance, John Allan, 'Theatrical censorship in Britain 1901–1968', Ph.D. dissertation, University of Wales, 1980

Foulkes, Richard, 'Censure and censorship', in Foulkes, *Church and Stage in Victorian England* (Cambridge: Cambridge University Press, 1997), pp. 18–34

Fowell, Frank, and Palmer, Frank, *Censorship in England* (London: Frank Palmer, 1913)

Freehafer, John, 'The formation of the London patent companies in 1660', *Theatre Notebook* 20.1 (October 1965), pp. 6–29

'G.M.G.', *The Stage Censor: An Historical Sketch: 1544–1907* (London: Sampson Low & Co., 1908)

Galsworthy, John, *A Justification of the Censorship of Plays* (London: Heinemann, 1909).

Ganzel, Dewey, 'Patent wrongs and patent theatre: drama and the law in the early nineteenth century', *PMLA* 76.4 (1961), pp. 384–96

Garnett, Edward, *A Censured Play: 'The Breaking Point', with Preface and a Letter to the Censor* (London: Duckworth, 1907)

Gaskill, William, *A Sense of Direction* (London: Faber and Faber, 1988)

Gilbert, Michael, *The Claimant* (London: Constable, 1957)

Gilbert, W. S., *Harlequin Cock Robin and Jenny Wren* (London: The Music Publishing Company, 1867)

—— *Rosencrantz and Guildenstern. Original Plays by W. S. Gilbert*, vol. 3, (London: Chatto & Windus, 1903)

—— *Utopia (Limited); or the Flowers of Progress* (London: Chappell & Co., 1893)

Gildersleeve, Virginia C., *Government Regulation of the Elizabethan Drama* (New York: Columbia University Press, 1908)

Gray, Terence, 'Was that life? Swat it!', *The Gownsman*, 6 June 1931, pp. 14–15

Griffith, Hubert, 'Preface', in Griffith, *Red Sunday: A Play in Three Acts with a Preface on the Censorship* (London: Cayme Press, 1929)

Guest, Ivor, *Ballet in Leicester Square: the Alhambra and the Empire 1860–1915* (London: Dance Books, 1992)

Hadley, Elaine, *Melodramatic Tactics: Theatricalized Dissent in the English Marketplace, 1800–1885* (Stanford: Stanford University Press, 1995)

Handley, Miriam, *Directions in Nineteenth-Century Theatre* (Oxford: Oxford University Press, forthcoming)

——'Performing dramatic marks: stage directions and the revival of *Caste*', in Joe Bray, Miriam Handley and Anne C. Henry (eds), *Ma(r)king the Text: The Presentation of Meaning on the Literary Page* (Aldershot: Ashgate, 2000), pp. 253–70

Harrison, Nicholas, 'Colluding with the censor: theatre censorship in France after the Revolution', *Romance Studies* 25 (Spring 1995), pp. 7–18

Hemmings, F. W. J., *Theatre and State in France 1760–1905* (Cambridge: Cambridge University Press, 1994)

Hicks, William Joynson, *Do We Need a Censor?* (London: Faber and Faber, 1929)

Hook, Theodore, 'Recollections of the late George Colman', *Bentley's Miscellany* 1 (1837), pp. 7–16

Housman, Laurence, 'Sex and the censorship', *World League for Sexual Reform: Proceedings of the Third Congress*, ed. Norman Haine (London: Kegan Paul/Trench, Trubener & Co., 1930), pp. 311–16

——*The Unexpected Years* (London: Jonathan Cape, 1937)

Hume, Robert D., *Henry Fielding and the London Theatre 1728–1737* (Oxford: Clarendon Press, 1985)

Johnson, Catharine (ed.), *William Bodham Donne and his Friends* (London: Methuen, 1905)

[Johnson, Samuel], *A compleat vindication of the Licensers of the stage from the malicious and scandalous aspersions of Mr Brooke, author of Gustavus Vasa, with a proposal for making the office of the Licensers more extensive and effectual* (London: C. Corbett, 1739).

Johnston, John, *The Lord Chamberlain's Blue Pencil* (London: Hodder & Stoughton, 1990)

Jones, Henry Arthur, *The Censorship Muddle and a Way Out of It* (London: Samuel French, 1909)

Kettle, Michael, *Salomé's Last Veil: the Libel Case of the Century* (London: Hart-Davis MacGibbon, 1979)

Kinservik, Matthew J., 'Theatrical regulation during the Restoration period', in Susan J. Owen (ed.), *A Companion to Restoration Drama* (Oxford: Blackwell, 2001), pp. 36–52

Knowles Dorothy, *The Censor, the Drama and the Film* (London: Allen & Unwin, 1934)

Koritz, Amy, 'Moving violations: dance in the London music hall, 1890–1910', *Theatre Journal* 42.4 (December 1990), pp. 419–31

L'Estrange, Revd A. G., *Life of Mary Russell Mitford* (3 vols.), vol. 2., (London: Richard Bentley, 1870)

Lawrence, Elwood P., '*The Happy Land*: W. S. Gilbert as political satirist', *Victorian Studies* 15.2 (1971–2), pp. 161–83

Liesenfeld, Vincent J., 'Introduction', in Vincent J. Liesenfeld (ed.), *The Stage and the Licensing Act 1729–1739* (New York/London: Garland, 1981), pp. ix–xxxiii

Mayer, David, III, *Harlequin in his Element: the English Pantomime 1806–1836* (Cambridge MA: Harvard University Press, 1969)

Mayer, David, III, 'The sexuality of pantomime', *Theatre Quarterly* 4 (February–April 1974), pp. 53–64

Mitford, Mary Russell, 'The original preface to *Charles the First*', in *The Dramatic Works of Mary Russell Mitford* (2 vols), vol. 1, (London: Hurst & Blackett, 1854), pp. 243–9

Moody, Jane, *Illegitimate Theatre in London, 1770–1840* (Cambridge: Cambridge University Press, 2000)

Nicholson, Steve, *British Theatre and the Red Peril: the Portrayal of Communism 1917–1945* (Exeter: University of Exeter press, 1999)

—— 'Censoring revolution: the Lord Chamberlain and the Soviet Union', *New Theatre Quarterly* 8.32 (November 1992), pp. 305–12

—— *The Censorship of British Drama: 1900–1968* (3 vols) (Exeter, University of Exeter Press, 2003)

—— 'Foreign drama and the Lord Chamberlain in the 1950s', in Dominic Shellard (ed.), *British Theatre in the 1950s* (Sheffield: Sheffield Academic Press, 2000), pp. 41–52

—— ' "Nobody was ready for that": the gross impertinence of Terence Gray and the degradation of drama', *Theatre Research International* 11.2 (Summer 1996), pp. 121–31

—— ' "Unnecessary plays": European drama and the British censor', *Theatre Research International* 20.1 (Spring 1995), pp. 30–36

Nicholson, Watson, *The Struggle for a Free Stage in London* (London: Constable, 1906)

O'Higgins, Paul, *Censorship in Britain* (London: Nelson, 1972)

O'Kell, Robert, 'Disraeli's *Coningsby*: political manifesto or psychological romance?' *Victorian Studies* 23.1 (Autumn 1979), pp. 57–78

Palmer, John, *The Censor and the Theatres* (London: T. Fisher & Unwin, 1912)

Patterson, Annabel, *Censorship and Interpretation: the Conditions of Writing and Reading in Early Modern England* (Wisconsin: University of Wisconsin Press, 1984)

Peake, Richard Brinsley, *Memoirs of the Colman Family* (2 vols), vol. 2 (London: Richard Bentley, 1841)

Price, David, *Cancan!* (London: Cygnus Arts, 1998)

Righton, Edward, 'A suppressed burlesque: "The Happy Land" ', *Theatre* 28 (August 1896), pp. 63–6

Shaw, G. B. 'The author's apology', *Mrs Warren's Profession*, in *The Works of Bernard Shaw*, vol. 7 (London: Constable, 1930), pp. 151–80

—— 'The censorship of the stage in England', *North American Review* 169 (August 1899), pp. 251–62, reproduced in E. J. West (ed.), *Shaw on Theatre* (London: MacGibbon & Kee, 1958), pp. 66–88

—— 'Impressions of the Theatre', *Review of Reviews* 32.190 (October 1905), pp. 385–6.

—— 'The late censor', 2 March 1895, from *Our Theatres in the Nineties*, in *The Works of Bernard Shaw*, vol. 23 (London: Constable, 1931), pp. 50–57

—— 'Preface', *Plays Unpleasant*, in *The Works of Bernard Shaw*, vol. 7 (London: Constable, 1930), pp. vii–xxvi

—— 'Preface', *The Shewing up of Blanco Posnet* (1909), in *The Works of Bernard* Shaw, vol. 12 (London: Constable, 1930) pp. 361–433

Shee, Martin Archer, *Alasco. A Tragedy in Five Acts. Excluded from the Stage by the Authority of the Lord Chamberlain* (London: Sherwood, Jones & Co., 1824)

Shellard, Dominic, *British Theatre Since the War* (New Haven: Yale University Press, 2000)

—— *Kenneth Tynan: A Life* (New Haven: Yale University Press, 2003)

Shellard, Dominic (ed.), *British Theatre in the 1950s* (Sheffield, Sheffield Academic Press, 2000)

Shelley, Percy Bysshe, *Poetical Works*, ed. Thomas Hutchinson (Oxford: Oxford University Press, 1971)

Shepherd, Simon, 'Melodrama as avant-garde: enacting a new subjectivity', *Textual Practice* 10.3 (1996), pp. 507–22

Smith, Samuel, *Plays and their Supervision: a Speech Made by Samuel Smith Esq., M.P. in the House of Commons May 15th 1900, and the Reply of the Home Secretary* (London: Chas. J. Thynne, 1900)

Soldene, Emily, 'How the Alhambra was shut', *The Sketch* 9 (30 January 1895), p. 53

Spence, Edward Fordham [E.F.S.], *Our Stage and Its Critics* (London: Methuen, 1910)

Stedman, Jane W., *W. S. Gilbert: a Classic Victorian and his Theatre* (Oxford: Oxford University Press, 1996)

Stephens, John Russell, *The Censorship of English Drama 1824–1901* (Cambridge: Cambridge University Press, 1980)

—— '*Jack Sheppard* and the licensers: the case against Newgate plays', *Nineteenth-Century Theatre Research* 1.1 (1973), pp. 1–13

—— 'The Lord Chamberlain's plays: rescuing the George Colman archive', *Notes and Queries* 34 (March 1987), pp. 30–32

—— 'William Bodham Donne: some aspects of his later career as examiner of plays', *Theatre Notebook* 25.1 (Autumn 1970), pp. 25–32

Stopes, Marie C., *A Banned Play ('Vectia') and a Preface on the Censorship* (London: J. Bale & Co., 1926)

Stottlar, James F., 'A Victorian stage censor: the theory and practice of William Bodham Donne', *Victorian Studies* 13.3 (1970), pp. 253–82

Street, George, *At Home in the War* (London: Heinemann, 1918)

—— 'The censorship of plays', *Fortnightly Review* (September 1925), pp. 348–57

Summerfield, Penelope, 'The Effingham Arms and the Empire: deliberate selection in the evolution of music hall in London', in Eileen Yeo and Stephen Yeo (eds), *Popular Culture and Class Conflict 1590–1914: Explorations in the History of Labour and Leisure* (Brighton: Harvester Press, 1981), pp. 209–40

Swaffer, Hannen, 'If I were the censor', in Swaffer, *Behind the Scenes* (London: George Newnes, 1929), pp. 33–6

Swindells, Julia, *Glorious Causes: the Grand Theatre of Political Change, 1789–1833* (Oxford: Oxford University Press, 2001)

Thomson, Peter, 'The early career of George Colman the Younger', in Kenneth Richards and Peter Thomson (eds), *Nineteenth-Century British Theatre* (London: Methuen, 1971), pp. 67–82

Tickler, T., 'Pike, prose and poetry', *Blackwood's Magazine* 15 (1824), p. 595

Van Druten, John, 'Sex and censorship in the theatre', *World League for Sexual Reform: Proceedings of the Third Congress*, ed. Norman Haine (London: Kegan Paul/Trench, Trubener & Co. 1930), pp. 317–22

Vernon, Mary, '*Mary Stuart*, Queen Victoria and the censor', *Nineteenth-Century Theatre Research* 6.1 (1978), pp. 35–40

Williamson, Jane, *Charles Kemble, Man of the Theatre* (Lincoln: University of Nebraska Press, 1964)

Woodruff, Douglas, *The Tichborne Claimant: a Victorian Mystery* (London: Hollis & Carter, 1957)

Wright, Herbert, 'Henry Brooke's *Gustavus Vasa*', *Modern Languages Review* 14.2 (April 1919), pp. 173–82

Young, Eugene J., *Looking Behind the Censorship* (London: Lovat Dickson, 1938)

Index

Page numbers in *italics* refer to figure captions